Gender in the Classroom

Foundations, Skills, Methods,
and Strategies Across the Curriculum

Gender in the Classroom

Foundations, Skills, Methods,
and Strategies Across the Curriculum

Edited by

David M. Sadker
American University

and

Ellen S. Silber
Marymount College of Fordham University

2007

LAWRENCE ERLBAUM ASSOCIATES, PUBLISHERS
Mahwah, New Jersey   London

Lawrence Erlbaum Associates, Inc., Publishers
10 Industrial Avenue
Mahwah, New Jersey 07430
www.erlbaum.com

Cover design by Tomai Maridou

From the book, *She Had Some Horses* by Joy Harjo. Thunder's Mouth Press © 1983, 1997. Appears by permission of the publisher, Thunder's Mouth Press, a division of Avalon Publishing Group.

From *Literature Circles: Voice and Choice in Book Clubs and Reading Groups,* © 2002, with permission of Stenhouse Publishers.

Thomas Newkirk, Misreading Masculinity: Speculations on the Great Gender Gaps in Writing. *Language Arts, 77*(8). 2002 © by the National Council of Teachers of English. Adapted with permission.

C. O'Donnell-Allen and P. Smagorinsky. Revising Ophelia: Rethinking Questions of Gender and Power in School. *English Journal, 88*(3). 1999 © by the National Council for Teachers of English. Adapted with permission.

Koch, Janice. Science Stories. Third Edition. 2005 © by Houghton Miffin Company. Used with permission.

Library of Congress Cataloging-in-Publication Data

Gender in the classroom : foundations, skills, methods, and strategies across the curriculum / edited by David M. Sadker and Ellen S. Silber.
     p. cm.
Includes index.
ISBN 0-8058-5474-6 (pbk. : alk. paper)
1. Sex differences in education—United States. 2. Sexism in education—United States. 3. Gender identity—United States. 4. Educational equalization—United States. I. Sadker, David Miller, 1942– II. Silber, Ellen S.
LC212.92.G45   2006
371.822—dc22   2006007453
                                                      CIP

Books published by Lawrence Erlbaum Associates are printed on acid-free paper, and their bindings are chosen for strength and durability.

Printed in the United States of America
10   9   8   7   6   5   4   3   2   1

Brief Contents

Contents

3   **Teachers, Students, and Title IX: A Promise for Fairness**   **73**
Karen Zittleman

4   **Citizenship Education for the 21st Century—A Gender**   **109**
    Inclusive Approach to Social Studies
Margaret S. Crocco and Andrea S. Libresco

**8   Practical Strategies for Detecting and Correcting Gender   259
      Bias in Your Classroom**
David M. Sadker and Karen Zittleman

Preface

Teacher education programs have been slow to recognize gender bias and have lacked the resources to respond to its challenge. Few of today's college courses provide insights into the gendered experiences of their students. For both women and men entering teaching, gender remains the invisible issue, the elephant in the classroom. Teacher educators must take the lead in making the invisible visible so that new teachers will not repeat the sexist lessons of their own school days. An inclusive education, one that incorporates information about and concerns of both genders and all races and ethnicities, is every child's right and every teacher's obligation. Such is the rationale for this book: providing perspectives that are absent from the education of new teachers.

When we conceptualized this book, we wanted to avoid the add-on course, the one elective for preservice teachers that addresses gender. That course is too often seen as a sideshow, a diversion, a politically correct course most likely taken by those least likely to need it. Our preferred route would be to ensure that gender equity is a part of all courses and that at the conclusion of a teacher education program student teachers would be rated on the equity of classroom interactions in terms of gender, race, ethnicity, and so on, as well as other effective teaching behaviors. Gender awareness is a gift for teacher educators: In communities where there is little racial or ethnic diversity, there is always the equity challenge of gender. Gender awareness offers a universal tool to teach about equity.

We created this book to be used by professors from a variety of educational fields, professors who share a common commitment to making gender equity a fact of school life. This is a collaborative text, a text that enables diverse professors to teach toward a common goal: gender equity. The book is designed to fit neatly—as neatly as possible, that is—into the core courses of the typical teacher education curriculum, from "Foundations of Education" and "Educational Psychology" to subject area methods, from exploring Title IX to applying new teacher observation techniques. The chapters offered here provide information and skills (about gender and sex differences, curriculum content, and specific teaching skills) that are commonly overlooked. No wonder David Sadker and Ellen Silber often call them the missing chapters. Ideally, a teacher education program would require that students use this book throughout their preparation, in most if not all of their courses. Ideally, all teacher education professors would use the one or sometimes two or three chapters relevant to their courses. But even if only one, two, or three professors at an institution agree to use some of the chapters in the book, it will become part of the students' curriculum, a crucial component for their own professional development, an important addition to their regular textbooks, and a resource for their future teaching and learning. We have tried to assemble a book that is highly readable, to the point, practical, and efficiently organized. We want students and professors to enjoy and profit from the knowledge and insights of the many fine authors who contributed to this volume. We have also created a book that we believe can be useful to students even after they graduate.

Most chapters follow a common format designed to invite student interest and action. Each is built around Essential Equity Questions, EEQs for short. The EEQs focus on pertinent gender-related questions and issues in a specific subject area, such as sex differences in educational psychology, interaction patterns in methods classes, bias identification in social studies texts, and recruitment of girls into the sciences. Each EEQ has two parts: What We Know and Interactions.

What We Know is a brief summary of related gender research. Sometimes this review is illuminated by scenarios, providing a picture of the classroom through the lens of gender. Interactions (INTASC Standards) suggest activities that teacher candidates can do to promote understanding. Interactions connect chapter ideas and concepts with activities, actions that bring these ideas and concepts to life in or beyond class. We want students to move toward effective and equitable instruction, and these practical activities will help achieve that goal. A few of the activities are classroom observations connecting academic research with the real world of school. Sometimes they enable students to sharpen and focus research skills; other times they help students and teachers to evaluate curricular resources or assessment instruments. We believe that accurate data collection and thoughtful reflection may provide many new insights into the teaching–learning process. In addition, each chapter has at least one authentic assessment for evaluation, as well as both print and online resources.

Each Interaction is tied to a specific standard developed by the Interstate New Teacher Assessment and Support Consortium. This consortium, known by the acronym INTASC, is an affiliation of state education agencies and national educational organizations dedicated to the reform of the preparation, licensing, and ongoing professional development of teachers. These INTASC standards are intended to assist state education agencies in their work of licensing teachers and approving teacher education programs. The connection of each Interaction in this text to an INTASC standard is designed to assist teacher education institutions in coordinating their programs with these widely held accreditation standards directed at improving the quality of teacher education across the nation.

The last chapter, "Practical Strategies for Detecting Gender Bias in Your Classroom" differs a bit from the other chapters in that the emphasis is on applying many of the skills learned previously. Using the procedures described in this chapter, student teachers and their supervisors are given several tools for analyzing classroom teaching to detect gender bias, bias in favor of either boys or girls. In fact, these same techniques can also be used to detect race, ethnic, or other forms of biased behaviors. There is also a culminating activity for detecting and correcting curricular bias. This chapter is a capstone piece, focusing on the application of several key skills. It fits well into field experiences and particularly into student teaching because it provides an opportunity to refine some fundamental equity skills. If "the proof of the pudding is in the tasting," assessing teaching behaviors in real classrooms is one way to "taste" and assess whether the lessons from this book are being used.

Because education schools and programs have been slow to recognize and integrate gender issues into their curricula, the preservice experience of most new teachers has created gender blindness, an inability to see the gender bias in the curriculum or in classroom interaction. And even if they saw the problem, their ability to create positive change is limited because preservice teachers graduate learning few if any insights or strategies to address gender bias in the classroom.

How would a preservice teacher react to the words of a 12th-grade Black girl from a New York City high school who said, in 1991, "In all my years of school, I never studied anything about myself" (American Association of University Women. (1992). How schools shortchange girls. Washington, DC: AAUW, p. 61)? Although she managed to graduate, the chances are likely that she will not learn what people like her—female and Black—have done in the world. And she is just one of the many casualties of traditional curricula and college programs that do not prepare teachers to create an inclusive curriculum.

Sadly, most preservice teachers are more likely to reinforce gender bias than to eliminate it. It is no secret that this book is our effort to address this disturbing problem. Our goal is to influence as many teacher educators, teaching as many different courses in as many diverse schools of education as possible.

Bringing this book into existence has been a deeply collaborative venture. Its editors and a number of the authors came together for the first time as presenters at a conference promoting gender equity in teacher education. Our fervent dedication to this project kindled a synergy among us that endured and grew into the writing of the chapters for this book. It connected us with other like-minded educators who helped us complete the volume. What continues to motivate our work is the certainty that gender equity is absent in so many American classrooms and the continuing need to establish a climate of fairness in the nation's schools. We—authors and editors alike—hope you will join us in meeting this critical challenge.

ACKNOWLEDGMENTS

We would like to thank The Ford Foundation for its generous grant to Marymount College of Fordham University that supported the writing of the chapters for this volume and particularly Joseph Aguerrebere, Ellen's program officer at Ford. We would also like to thank Naomi Silverman, our editor at Lawrence Erlbaum Associates, for her support and encouragement. It is always easier to write a book with an editor who shares the vision. We also extend our appreciation to the manuscript reviewers, Nancy Keller-Coffey, State University of New York, New Paltz; Frances Maher, Wheaton College; and Elizabeth M. Penn, Thomas More College, for their comments and insights. And finally, we express our appreciation to you, the teachers and students using this book, for joining us in creating a more humane and equitable world.

—David M.Sadker
Washington, DC
—Ellen S. Silber
New York, NY

1

Strong Women Teachers: Their Struggles and Strategies for Gender Equity

Theresa McCormick
Iowa State University

This chapter provides you with some tools for inquiring into how the history of women in the teaching profession is linked with their increasing political and social activism during the 20th century. It provides a conceptual framework to guide you in the study of teachers as activists and change agents. The chapter contains questions about the exploitation of female teachers and about the struggles and methods they used to overcome this exploitation. You will discover the intersections of the teaching profession, feminism, and the 20th century women's movement and how they interacted to improve female teachers' lives in the classroom and their lives as citizens.

Most educational foundations (and Introduction to Education) courses, and many introductory textbooks used in these classes, offer very little information to the prospective teacher about the role of women in education. This chapter is intended to correct that serious omission. In this chapter, I discuss some of the contributions of female teachers to the field of education, teachers' efforts to expand their rights as workers, the barriers they overcame, and their struggle for agency inside and outside the workplace. This chapter provides preservice teachers an opportunity for an in-depth exploration of the convergence of the teaching profession, feminism, and the exploitation of female teachers in the 20th century.

This chapter has three essential equity questions (EEQs), and each EEQ has a section called What We Know, which briefly discusses relevant research. Also, each EEQ has several Interactions, identified with the INTASC principle(s) they reflect, as well as an Authentic Assessment. At the end of the chapter, you will find resources, including online resources, and references.

Essential Equity Questions

- **Essential Equity Question 1.1:** What are the salient social, cultural, political, and economic factors that affected female teachers in the 20th century?
- **Essential Equity Question 1.2:** What strategies did female teachers use and what roles did they play to respond to social, cultural, political, and economic barriers?
- **Essential Equity Question 1.3:** How did feminist ideology and the contemporary women's movement inform and influence female teachers in their efforts to achieve workplace equity?

ESSENTIAL EQUITY QUESTION 1.1:
WHAT ARE THE SALIENT SOCIAL, CULTURAL, POLITICAL, AND ECONOMIC FACTORS THAT AFFECTED FEMALE TEACHERS IN THE 20TH CENTURY?

WHAT WE KNOW

Sexism and Racism are Structural and Systemic.   That women dominate as classroom teachers—yet gender equity has not received much attention in teacher education programs (Pryor & Mader, 1998)—is testament to the historic devaluation of females in the teaching profession and a blindness to the gender and racial bias in the social, economic, and political structure of schools.

We know that teachers tend to blame themselves when things go wrong in the classroom. "One's inability to see the problem as structural and systemic often leads to worker self-doubt and self-blame," according to Maguire (1993) and Acker (1992) (cited in Carter, 2002, p. 30). Carter (2002) said, "It is to the institution's benefit to orchestrate such individuation of workplace difficulties. If workers see the problem as their own fault, they are less likely to ask the institution to respond to making structural changes" (p. 30).

Schools are patriarchal structures that segregate jobs by sex. The following sections illustrate the structural and systemic gendering of roles in schools according to the "traditional belief that gender differentiation is natural in our culture" (Carter, 2002, p. 30). Teachers are predominantly female (75%), and administrators are still predominantly male. Only 10% of superintendents are women, and about 35% of school principals are women (National Center for Education Statistics, 2000). These figures reflect the gendered history and structure of the teaching profession, one that provides a fertile ground for the exploitation of female teachers.

Low Wages for Female Teachers: Part of HIStory and HERstory.   In a current article, "Teachers Avert Strike, Agree to Work for Free," the problem of teacher pay was made bold (PEN Weekly, 2003). In an effort to stem cuts in education spending and health benefits, Portland teachers agreed to a contract that includes, among other concessions, working free for 10 days. This current problem of inadequate pay for public school teachers is a nationwide epidemic. Although it is indeed troubling, there is much history behind this story. Let's take a look at the historical context of teachers' pay.

Ryan and Cooper (2001) and Sadker and Sadker (2003) skillfully placed the history of low wages for teachers within the context of cultural, social, and economic milieus of the 19th century. During the early 19th century, a common attitude was that teachers were men who could not hold a regular job, were strange or weird, or, on the other hand, were women who had nothing else of importance to do. Men continued to dominate the teaching profession until the middle of the 19th century. As Sadker and Sadker (2003) said, "Teaching was a *gendered career*, and it was gendered 'male.' Although a few women taught at home in *dame schools,* the first women to become teachers in regular school settings, earning a public salary, were viewed as gender trespassers" (p. 313).

In spite of the perception that teachers should be men, a major shift in the gender makeup of the teaching force came about with the establishment of the common school. This coincides with the time when more women than men became elementary school teachers. There were many reasons for this shift, which included the following points about the gendered wage structure for teachers. In the early years of the common school movement, there was a dramatic increase in the number of schools and that naturally increased the demand for more teachers to fill these salaried positions. Because women could be paid much less than men at this time, their hiring was an expedient measure that flaunted then-current sentiments against women in the workforce. As Sadker and Sadker (2003) said, "… the demand for more and inexpensive teachers created by common schools made the hiring of women teachers inevitable" (p. 314).

Webb, Metha, and Jordan (2000) gave us more insight into how teaching came to be seen as primarily a job for women. They tell the fascinating story of Catherine Beecher (1800–1878), founder of the Western Institute for Women and the Hartford Female Seminary. She was a vocal proponent of the common school. Beecher saw her task as focusing the attention of the nation on the need for a corps of female teachers to staff the common schools. Her efforts on behalf of the common school were a force in its acceptance, and her work on behalf of women pointed to a new American consensus concerning female roles (Cremin, 1982, cited in Webb, Metha, & Jordan, 2000, pp. 179–180).

Another source of the exploitation of female teachers is rooted in the ideology of a culture that viewed women as moral mothers. An ideology of strict traditional male and female sex roles in the family became the model for the teaching profession. We know that by the turn of the 20th century, the teaching profession was becoming increasingly feminized. See Redding Sugg's book (1978) on the feminization of American education in which the term *motherteacher* is used to describe teachers.

Spinster was another label pinned on teachers. Sadker and Sadker (2003) indicated that, in the late 19th and early 20th centuries, unmarried women were hired so often "that teaching and spinsterhood became synonymous" (p. 314). Single women were preferred for teaching jobs because they were assumed not to have a struggle of loyalties between "'serving' both husband and employer" (p. 314).

Smith and Vaughn (2000) asserted, "Although women took over the nation's classrooms, males were increasingly in charge of the ever bureaucratized schools, seen as too complex to be run by a woman whose mission was to tend the nation's youth" (p. 8). The commonly accepted conception of male and female roles in schools were those based on the traditional family—"managed by the male patriarch and nurtured by the selfless female" (p. 8). The schoolteacher was expected to do the same things as the homemaker, such as teaching traditional values and morals to children.

Many people saw teaching as a natural vocation for females (Hoffman, 1981). In the early 20th century, the female teacher was particularly valued for her role in socializing immigrants into the White Anglo-Saxon Protestant (WASP) dominant culture. These rigid sex-role expectations and practices in schools laid the foundation for exploitation based on pay inequity. School districts all over the United States established inequitable pay scales for male and female teachers. Even though female teachers' salaries were lower, female teachers usually had more responsibilities, "especially when it came to mothering students. They washed students' hair, cleaned buildings, and sewed" (Smith & Vaughn, 2000, p. 8).

As the pattern of feminization of teaching became entrenched, female teacher's salaries were lower than males' (even though they basically did the same tasks), and the prestige of the teaching profession plummeted. On top of this indignity, women teachers' social and personal lives were more restricted than men's. One teacher remembers that social activities for female teachers, such as dancing, dating, and card playing, were often prohibited (Vaughn-Roberson, 1993, cited in Smith and Vaughn, 2000).

Systemic Control of Female Teachers.   Examples of the administrative control of female teachers' personal lives abound in records of school contracts in the early 20th century. Illustrative of the requirement that female teachers be "controlled" and be paragons of morality for children are these selected parts of a North Carolina contract in the 1920s:

> I promise not to go out with any young man except as it may be necessary to stimulate Sunday School work.
>
> I promise not to fall in love, to become engaged or secretly married.

I promise to remember that I owe a duty to the town people who are paying my wages, that I owe respect to the school board and the superintendent that hired me, and that I shall at all times consider myself the willing servant of the school board and the townspeople. (Knicker & Naylor, 1981, p. 20)

Other areas in female teachers' lives that were "controlled" by patriarchal structures in schools involved work and family life, pregnancy, and child care. All aspects of women's lives linked to their reproductive cycle became fertile ground for exploitation in schools—institutions that were, and still are, set up according to a masculine model of work. The female teacher, but not the male teacher, was expected to carry the double load of mothering and housekeeping, as well as the duties of teaching. Carter (2002) stated, "demands of the workplace, forced women to assimilate to a male work model or drop out of the paid labor force altogether" (p. 2).

Another form of exploitation of female teachers occurred because teaching had become known as "women's work." Women teachers were seen as "careerless" and "semiprofessional," which translated into lower pay than the earnings of "true, elite professionals" (i.e., males in professional careers in medicine and law, who had heavy workloads and huge uninterrupted time commitments). Female teachers were, and still are in many cases, in positions that are "structured without the possibility of promotion. ... Advancement meant becoming an administrator and leaving teaching ... teaching is structured to accommodate the in-and-out patterns of women's employment" (Biklen, 1995, p. 26). Although some people may view this flexible structure of the teaching profession as desirable for balancing work and family, this structure plays a large part in the overall devaluation by society of teaching and its low salaries.

Sari Knopp Biklen (1995) interviewed contemporary female teachers who described the difficulties and some successful methods of balancing their work as teachers and their lives as wives and mothers. These current cases are amazing and inspiring considering the past history of women teachers being barred from marriage. Biklen (1995) explains, "Laws that excluded women from the classroom if they were married or pregnant controlled and regulated teachers' bodies. Teachers sometimes tried to resist this management of their bodies by hiding their marriages or pregnancies for as long as they could. These regulations were also selectively enforced" (p. 105).

INTERACTION 1.1:
Looking in Classrooms

INTASC Principle 6: Effective Communication

With members of your cooperative learning research group (CLRG), interview a classroom teacher and find out about her roles and duties, as well as her perspectives on the cultural context of teaching in her school. Make notes about gender issues that you observe related to what you have been researching and discussing in class.

Write a brief report of your interview and present it to the class later in the semester. In addition, write a creative story about your ideal teacher. What characteristics and behaviors does your ideal teacher model for students? Share these with your CLRG.

INTERACTION 1.2:
Teacher Awareness (Authentic Assessment)

INTASC Principle 8: Assessment

1. Ask the teacher whether she is aware of any gender differences in the roles and expectations of male and female teachers in the school? Are the roles gendered according to traditional stereotypes? Are roles hierarchical or egalitarian?
2. Do you think the teacher has a sense of her own agency in determining classroom time structures and the content and methods of instruction?
3. How does the teacher view the administrators in the school? As helpers, assistants, facilitators, or friends? Or as " the bosses," functionaries, her superiors, or her inferiors?
4. Did you notice any practice that you would classify as a form of structural bias based on gender stereotypes?

ESSENTIAL EQUITY QUESTION 1.2:
WHAT STRATEGIES DID FEMALE TEACHERS USE AND WHAT ROLES DID THEY PLAY TO RESPOND TO SOCIAL, CULTURAL, POLITICAL, AND ECONOMIC BARRIERS?

WHAT WE KNOW

Teachers Collaborated With Other Women's Organization for Workplace Equity.   Women educators made continuous contributions and had a significant impact on education throughout the 20th century (Sadker & Sadker, 2003; Smith & Smith, 1994; Smith & Vaughn, 2000). Their efforts came at a great cost and from heroic attempts by thousands of women, who struggled against the odds for success in an androcentric dominant culture and in a male-as-norm school system. Biklen (1995) affirmed, "The history of women in teaching includes a history of women's struggle for agency both in the workplace and outside it" (p. 93).

One strategy female teachers used to overcome the low odds for success in school was to collaborate with other women's organizations that were working for workplace equity. Patricia A. Carter (2002) elaborated on how female teachers were able to improve their rights in the workplace by forming alliances and networking with other local and national women's organizations. Carter (2002) stated, "Teachers' reading and social groups metamorphosed into organizations that actively campaigned for issues such as equal pay and female principalships" (pp. 11–12). She provided fascinating details on the wide range of organizations that teachers were involved with: the National Women's Party (NWP), the Women's Trade Union League (WTUL), the General Federation of Women's Clubs (GFWC), the National Federation of Business and Professional Women's Clubs (BPWC), the National Association of Colored Women (NACW), and the National Organization for Women (NOW). These memberships helped teachers gain more individual and collective power and influence as well as gather support for their own professional issues. For example, in the NACW, teachers made up about 67% of the largely middle-class, urban affiliates. These women were mostly college graduates and schoolteachers before retiring after marriage (Carter, 2002).

We know that two feminist grade-school teachers, Margaret Haley and Catherine Goggin, were the founders of the Chicago Federation of Teachers (CFT) in 1902. The collaboration of these two teachers came to represent the power of women working together to make changes for better salaries. For instance, their efforts that uncovered tax evasion and other forms of corruption in Chicago resulted in the city finding new tax monies to fund teachers' pay increases.

INTERACTION 1.3:
What About Pay Equity In Your Job?

INTASC Principle 9: Reflective Practice—Professional Development

Interview two groups of teachers: contemporary practicing teachers and retired teachers. Ask the contemporary teachers (male and female) about the policy concerning equal pay for equal work in their school. Is the policy carried out in practice? Or are there still gender differentials in pay in their school system? Do you get the same answers from both sexes? Do the teachers work in unionized school districts or not?

Ask the retired teachers (male and female) what their experiences with equal pay issues were when they taught school. Was pay even discussed? Was there a policy for equal pay for both sexes? If not, was there an effort to obtain such a policy? Did they work in unionized schools or not?

INTERACTION 1.4:
Equal Pay for Female Teachers (Authentic Assessment)

INTASC Principle 8: Assessment

1. Identify two women who struggled for equal pay for female teachers that you found to be most inspiring, strong, and heroic. Write a letter to each of these activists expressing your appreciation for the legacy they left for future generations of teachers.
2. When was the right to equal pay for equal work finally established by federal law? Why did women teachers work for legislation at the federal level to assure equal pay for equal work?
3. In your opinion, which strategy used by women teachers who fought for equal pay could be used today by teachers who want to make a change in the workplace?
4. Visualize yourself as an activist for gender equity in schools today. What images come to mind? Describe the images or draw them on a piece of paper.

Teachers Played Significant Roles in the Suffrage Movement. Many leaders in the suffrage movement had backgrounds as teachers. This included well-known suffragists Lucretia Mott, Ida B. Wells-Barnett, Susan B. Anthony, Margaret Haley, and Carrie Chapman Catt. According to Carter (2002), many of these women said the inequitable treatment they received while teaching prompted them to become activists for women's rights.

Over the years, teachers were welcomed by suffragists to join the movement because teachers had useful public speaking skills, status in their communities, flexible time during breaks and vacations, and the ability to reach audiences that other women could not.

For instance, Lucy Stone spoke to the legislature on May 27, 1853, at the first hearing on female suffrage in the United States (Million, 2004). Because most teachers worked for money to support themselves, their parents, or their siblings, teachers were not able to speak out for suffrage in small school districts, where opposition to suffrage was strong, for fear of losing their jobs. However, many more teachers in larger, more liberal and heterogeneous school districts, notably in the Northeast and in the West, were able to participate actively in the suffrage movement (Carter, 2002).

As discussed earlier in this chapter, one of the strategies female teachers used to improve their working conditions and pay was to form alliances with other women's organizations in the community, including suffragist groups. Carter (2002) described the beneficial results of some of these alliances: As teachers swelled the ranks of suffrage groups, these groups began taking increasingly aggressive positions on teachers' rights. For instance, the Equal Suffrage Association of Covington, Kentucky, passed a resolution condemning the local school board after teachers there were twice passed over for salary increases (see "Teacher's Pay," 1911). Other examples abound: In Birmingham, Alabama, the Equal Suffrage Association investigated complaints that the school board attempted to keep teachers from getting involved in suffrage work (see "Women Teachers Can," 1912). The election of the first woman president of the Nebraska State Teachers Association came about with the help of local suffragists who lobbied for her candidacy (see "Teachers Choose," 1913).

The teacher-suffragist alliance strategy proved to be beneficial for teachers' achievement of their own goals and provided crucial strength for coalitions of other women's groups that promoted the female vote on school issues, then on city matters, and eventually on state and national matters (Carter, 2002).

Racism and the Suffrage Movement. It is an interesting quest to look at women teachers' involvement in suffrage in different regions and states. For example, Ida B. Wells-Barnett, born to slave parents, became a teacher at the age of 16, then a lecturer, and later a journalist. A strong suffragist, she established what is considered to be the first Black female suffrage organization, the Alpha Suffrage Club of Chicago. She also was an organizer and leader of women in the fight against lynching (McCormick, 1994). The Alpha Suffrage Club was founded in 1913 so Black women could set their own agenda in the suffrage movement. Many of the Chicago group members were teachers or former teachers. They worked to counter the racism embedded in many White-led suffrage groups, and they raised awareness about the unique problems Black women faced when they sought the vote (see Hendricks, 1993, cited in Carter, 2002, p. 87).

Carrie Chapman Catt, suffragist and educator, received the Iowa Award in 1992, which recognizes Iowans who make a significant national contribution. However, during the early 1990s, there was a reexamination of her life and work in connection with people of color and immigrants. Unfortunately, Catt, the well-educated and strong woman who led the suffrage movement to success in 1920, had some blind spots. First, she believed that equality with men would be a result of having the vote. Second, she and other suffragists fell into the trap of xenophobia and racism that spread across the United States in the last years of the 19th century and the early part of the 20th century (McCormick, 1994).

Historian of the Iowa women's suffrage movement, Louise Noun, wrote extensively about Carrie Chapman Catt in her book *Strong-Minded Women—The Emergence of the Woman-Suffrage Movement in Iowa* (1969). In the early 1990s, when the charge was made by Black students and others at Iowa State University that Catt, an alumna, was a bigot and should not have a campus building named in her honor, Noun decided to take a closer look at her work:

Catt and other suffragists compromised their principles ... as the possibility of winning the vote increased. This compromise was made as a matter of political expediency to win allies and eliminate perceived opponents to their cause. ... During this time in the United States, powerful nativistic influences engendered fear of anyone who was not a "native" [defined as a middle-class WASP]. (Noun, 1993, p. 1-C, cited in McCormick, 1994, p. 6)

According to Noun (1993), to obtain crucial White-Southerner support for women's suffrage, Catt, and the whole suffrage movement, ignored efforts to withhold voting rights to Blacks in the South. However, Catt was not racist concerning individual Blacks, according to Noun. Catt was friends with many Blacks, including Mary Church Terrell, president of the National Association of Colored Women, who described Catt as "completely free of racial prejudice" (Noun, 1993, p. 1-C).

Teachers as Activists.   We know that in addition to racism as a pitfall along the rocky road to enfranchisement for women, there was also the opposition of the Catholic Church to contend with. Carter (2002, p. 89) gives a pertinent example that occurred in 1912:

Teacher Aimee Hutchinson's Catholic school dismissed her for participating in a suffrage parade ... the parish priest, Father Taylor, called her into his office several days after the parade and expressed his distress: "You know how much I like you and your work, but since you have marched in the parade of suffragists I cannot have you any longer in the school. The suffragist movement is the next thing to socialism and I cannot countenance it." ("Suffrage Parader," 1912, p. 24)

Several times in this chapter I mention the work of teacher and suffragist Margaret Haley, a Catholic. She strongly objected to the interference of the Church in the issue of women's suffrage. According to Carter (2002), one time during Haley's travels for suffrage, she wrote her Chicago friends asking them to send funds to help with her rebuttal to a blitz of antisuffrage material put out by Catholic media. She wrote, "I enclose you a copy of 6 columns of 'stuff' that appeared in most of the Catholic papers throughout Ohio last week. ... We are trying to offset it but it takes money and the women are exhausted. ... I am giving my time free and paying my own expenses up to the limit of my ability (Haley, 1912, cited in Carter, 2002, p. 89).

INTERACTION 1.5:
Women Suffragists in Our State or City

INTASC Principle 10: School and Community Involvement

To grasp completely the history of the U.S. women's suffrage movement, Louise Noun (1969), woman suffragist historian, recommended that we study how it developed in different states and examine the lives and actions of the recognized leaders in the then-new state organizations. News articles and reports from the early 1900s give ample details about the National American Woman Suffrage Association (NAWSA) activities in each state. After the vote was won, NAWSA disbanded and reorganized as the League of Women Voters, which is still active (McCormick, 1994).

Invite a panel of women from the League of Women Voters and the historical society in your town or city to make a presentation on the history of the local suffrage movement. Ask them to include a discussion of the teacher-leaders in the local or state suffrage movement.

INTERACTION 1.6:
Graffiti Murals—The Role Women Teachers Played in the Suffrage Movement (Authentic Assessment)

INTASC Principle 8: Assessment

This is a good closure activity for summing up what you learned about the role women teachers played in the suffrage movement. In your CLRG, create a wall mural on a large piece of butcher paper with a variety of colored felt pens. Write words, phrases, or graphics on the theme "The Role Women Teachers Played in the Suffrage Movement." Write ideas that answer the four Ws: Who, What, When, Where? With what results, reactions, rewards, losses, gains, and so on?

Pass the graffiti sheet to a different CLRG in the room and ask them to respond to the topic and pass the graffiti sheet on to another group. When the murals have been to every group, return them to the original CLRG.

Original members then read, discuss, summarize, and share the results of their finished murals (adapted from Bennett, Rolheiser, & Stevahn, 1991).

ESSENTIAL EQUITY QUESTION 1.3:
HOW DID FEMINIST IDEOLOGY AND THE CONTEMPORARY WOMEN'S MOVEMENT INFORM AND INFLUENCE FEMALE TEACHERS IN THEIR EFFORTS TO ACHIEVE WORKPLACE EQUITY?

Motivation: Surf the Internet for Feminist Teachers' Stories

Conduct a search for Web sites that link activist teachers with feminism and the contemporary women's movement (for starters, see the Web site section in the resources at the end of this chapter).

In 1952 the United States Office of Education initiated the National Teacher of the Year program, in cooperation with the Council of Chief State School Officers, to give public recognition to the nation's finest teachers. The Teacher of the Year award, which emphasizes teaching excellence as an achievement and an inspiration, is the oldest ongoing award program honoring classroom teachers on the local, state, and national levels. Search for National Teacher of the Year program winners. Determine whether any of the honored teachers were also feminists or activists for teachers' rights.

INTERACTION 1.7:
Think, Pair, Share

INTASC Principle 6: Communication and Technology

After conducting your individual Internet searches, meet in the classroom for a Think, Pair, Share activity. Spend some time organizing and thinking about the Web sites and the pages you printed about feminist teachers and Teachers of the Year whom you deem to be feminists and activists for female teachers' rights. Then, pair with a member of your CLRG and share your results. See where there are overlaps, duplicates, and gaps. Then, finish your search on the Internet. Finally, compile your finished work in a printed booklet of resources and in an electronic version to share with the rest of your class.

WHAT WE KNOW

About Feminism—Different Strokes for Different Folks.   Just as varied as the lives of female teachers in the 20th century, so are the definitions, understandings, and uses of feminism and feminist ideology. It is more accurate to use the plural term *feminisms* when discussing the ideologies of female teachers and women in other occupations working for social, political, and economic change during the 20th century—for example, liberal feminism, radical feminism, socialist feminism, cultural feminism, reformist feminism, material feminism, and more. There's the womanist ideology adopted by many Black women to bind race and gender. The dynamic nature of the women's movement is evident in all of these terms used to describe feminism in various cultural and political contexts and in different places and times (Carter, 2002).

Although many teachers who worked for improved workplace conditions and pay never used the term *feminist* to describe themselves, nor had, in today's terms, "a feminist consciousness," they were doing what we now think of as feminist acts. The work of teachers in the progressive reform era gave them unusual opportunities to engage in political and personal change (Carter, 2002). For example, Carter (2002) stated, "Women teachers quickly discovered that their professional skills were a valuable asset in assuming leadership" (p. 22). Some scholars, such as Biklen (1978) argued that leaders of the progressive education movement "failed to make women's equality a goal" ... and that "feminism was not a concern of the progressive education movement" (p. 316). Carter (2002) challenged Biklen's description of progressive education reform as primarily a male domain and her tendency to define feminism narrowly as related to suffrage, reproductive rights, and economic independence. Carter argued that Biklen did not explore fully the importance of women's clubs and their influence on the progressive education movement. Carter contended that these women were engaging in feminist acts by participating in women-identified groups led by women to demonstrate confidence in women's capabilities to effect change.

Historians often use the terms *domestic* or *social feminism* to describe the work of women in the progressive era. Such descriptions are rooted in the notion that these women believed they had a moral duty to bring the unique perspectives of women, as mothers or potential mothers, into the public sphere. This position was later challenged by so-called hard-core or radical feminists whose tendency was to deny that women had any special insights related to their roles as mothers or potential mothers; rather, women's insights were attributed to their position in a male-dominated society. Hard-core feminists held women's rights as most important, whereas, domestic feminists placed other social reforms ahead of individual women's rights (Carter, 2002).

Some people wonder whether female teachers' reactions to gender bias in the profession are considered to be feminist actions. Vaughn-Roberson's study (1984) of women teachers in Oklahoma suggested that even though they worked for economic parity with men, they still perceived their work as teachers as an extension of their domestic role. In another study, Vaughn-Roberson (1985) compared traditional domestic ideology with feminist ideology and found that, in 1970, it was still common among female teachers in Oklahoma, Texas, and Colorado to hold anti-feminist attitudes (cited in Carter, 2002, p. 28).

Catherine A. MacKinnon (1987), a noted legal scholar and feminist—most scholars would say she's a hard-core radical feminist—contended, "Feminism seeks to empower women on our own terms. To value what women have always done, as well as to allow us to do everything else. We seek not only to be valued as who we are, but to have access to the process of the definition of value itself. In this way, our demand for access becomes also a demand for change" (p. 22). MacKinnon believes that regarding gender as a matter of sameness and difference, as most of existing law and theory have in the past, hides the reality that gender is a system of social hierarchy, based on an imposed inequality of power. Her ideology of feminism demands this system of inequality be changed and transformed. In her book *Feminism Unmodified—Discourses on Life and Law*, feminism, for MacKinnon, is unconstrained by the barriers of past traditions.

Florence Howe, a self-declared feminist, was a teacher in the Mississippi Freedom Schools in the 1960s and later became a professor of American studies and president and publisher of The Feminist Press. She wrote about "the woman question" in her book *Myths of Coeducation* (1984). The following statement helps us understand that her position on feminism in education is aligned with transformational equity, not status quo equality:

> One of the central ideas of coeducation provides a central myth: that if women are admitted to men's education and treated exactly as men are, then all problems of sexual equity will be solved. The myth assumes that the major problem for women is "access" to what men have, and it continues to ignore the content and quality of what it is women may gain access to. Education that teaches girls and women to accept their subordinate position in a male-centered world does not offer education equity to them. (p. x)

After all of these complex iterations of feminism we have just explored, here is an author, bell hooks, who brings some simplicity and clarification to the topic. In her book, *Feminism Is for Everybody*, bell hooks (pen name of Gloria Watkins, Black writer, teacher, theorist, and cultural critic) explained in a clear, concise way what a feminist stands for and answered the question, "What is feminism?"

> Feminism is a movement to end sexism, sexist exploitation, and oppression. ... I love it [this definition] because it so clearly states that the movement is not about being anti-male. It makes it clear that the problem is sexism. And that clarity helps us remember that all of us, female and male, have been socialized from birth on to accept sexist thought and action. As a consequence, females can be just as sexist as men. And while that does not excuse or justify male domination, it does mean that it would be naive and wrong minded for feminist thinkers to see the movement as simplistically being for women against men. To end patriarchy (another way of naming institutionalized sexism) we need to be clear that we are all participants in perpetuating sexism until we change our minds and hearts, until we let go of sexist thought and action and replace it with feminist thought and action. (pp. viii–ix)

INTERACTION 1.8:
A Feminist Is One Who ...

INTASC Principle 3: Diverse Learners

Think about the diversity of perspectives on feminism in the readings you just completed and think of your own understanding of what it means to be a feminist. In your CLRG, brainstorm ideas to finish the following statement: "A feminist is one who ..." For example:

"A Feminist Is One Who ...

... believes in equal pay for equal work."

... believes in the empowerment of women on their own terms."

... thinks women and men should have equal opportunities for education."

... seeks to put an end to sexism and sexist exploitation."

... believes men and women must have equal political and social rights."

... can be a male as well as a female."

INTERACTION 1.9:
Create a Collage

INTASC Principle 2: Student Development

Now, create a large wall-sized poster, using the collage technique of cutting and pasting overlapping images—including letters, words, symbols, and logos cut from magazines—to make an artistic visual that portrays what feminism represents to you. Use old magazines, colored construction paper, scraps of cloth, found objects (e.g., gum and candy foil wrappers, twigs, leaves) to make your visual statement about feminism today. Display your collage in the classroom.

WHAT WE KNOW

Feminist Alliances Helped Teachers.   Having a feminist consciousness helped teachers working for their rights in society and in schools to keep focused on the problem of sexism. Feminism helped them identify sexism and then work toward ending sexist exploitation and its institutionalization in schools that were modeled after the patriarchal family. bell hooks (2000) says, "Before women's studies classes, before feminist literature, individual women learned about feminism in groups. The women in those groups were the first to begin to create feminist theory which included both an analysis of sexism, strategies for challenging patriarchy, and new models of social interaction" (p. 19).

Teachers' involvement in the women's movement became more pronounced and meaningful as the acceptance of feminist theory and practice took hold in the 20th century. By 1920, when women won the right to vote, nearly 5 million women, including teachers, belonged to some kind of women's organization. More than half of women teachers or former teachers in urban areas were in a club associated in some way with the women's movement (Carter, 2002). Having a feminist ideology and forming alliances with women in other organizations strengthened teachers' efforts to work for their rights, including, among others, salary equity and the right to marry and take maternity leave (Carter, 2002).

We know that two feminist elementary school teachers, Catherine Goggin and Margaret Haley, led the Chicago Teachers' Federation from the 1890s to the 1920s. Their feminist ideology guided them in securing an impressive array of improvements for grade school teachers: salary raises, pension plans, tenure laws, and tax money for school maintenance (see women's history Web sites at the end of this chapter).

INTERACTION 1.10:
Join a National Dialogue With the Feminist Leadership Alliance (FMLA) on the *Choices* E-Zine

INTASC Principle 5: Motivation and Management

INTASC Principle 6: Communication and Technology

Find out what today's feminists on campuses are thinking and doing. Being a part of the current feminist movement on campuses will help you appreciate the courage, creativity, and persistence of the strong feminist educators from past years who paved the way for us today.

It's easy to join the discussion and start receiving the *Choices* e-zine (electronic magazine) by signing on at campusteam@feminist.org. Feminist college students and professors across the United States are engaging in dialogue (chatting) about what's happening on campuses related to feminism, gender equity, and social justice. Highlights of the March 19, 2003, edition of *Choices* e-zine include sections on campus news (West Coast Team hosts first Leadership Institute), online news (Special N.O.W. vs. Scheidler Chat), feminist news (ERA Reintroduced in House of Representatives), global news (Feminist Majority Foundation Hosts Global HIV/AIDS Chat), and feminist community news (Women's Soccer Movie Sneak Preview Screenings Nationwide).

WHAT WE KNOW

Roots of Women's Movements Run Deep. To understand the influence that feminism and the contemporary women's movement have had on the efforts of teachers to achieve workplace equity, we need to examine the historical background of the women's movement of the 1960s and 1970s, which has roots in earlier movements for women's equality. These roots go back before suffrage, to the time in the 1800s when women were involved in the antislavery movement. In this chapter, I do not go into detail about that history, but it is important to understand that the suffrage movement—which resulted in the 19th Amendment's ratification in 1920, giving women the vote—was not an isolated reform effort. Both suffrage and feminism were parts of a larger independent social movement for women's liberation. Using the framework of an independent social movement, researchers (e.g., Banner, 1974; DuBois, 1978; Marilley, 1989; Taylor, 1989), assessed the continuities among the many efforts for women's rights and liberation over different time periods (McCormick, 1994).

As we know, getting the vote did not solve all problems of gender inequality. Though this is true, the suffrage movement should not be minimized nor its importance to contemporary women devalued. DuBois (1978) argued that when viewed as a part of a larger social movement, women's suffrage is highly relevant to women today. It models for women how participation in an independent social movement of women, by and for women, can actually change one's life. McCormick (1994) explained the significance of the suffrage movement for today's women: It illustrates that we cannot rely on other social reform movements (e.g., abolition) to make changes that specifically benefit women.

Other interesting roots of the contemporary women's movement that bear inspection are the years between suffrage (1920) and World War II (1945). What happened to the social movement for women's rights during those 25 years? This was a time of transition and transformation for the women's movement and for feminism in the United States. It was a time of factionalism, with women breaking into new groups with specific concerns, such as pay equity, employment, or peace making. From 1920 to 1945, the earlier unity that had held people together during the women's suffrage movement vanished. In spite of the lack of a single focus or unifying goal, feminism and the women's movement did not die. Women continued working in peace groups, in social welfare programs, and on legislation for improvement of education and health care for women and children (McCormick, 1994). All these efforts included women teachers.

Earlier in this chapter, I explained how female teachers affiliated themselves with and became leaders of numerous organizations that promoted their own advancement in the workplace and in the community. Banner (1974) believes that, during these years of transition, from 1920 to 1945, if there were any common unifying purpose for women's efforts, it should be characterized as social feminism. Social feminism is exemplified by Eleanor Roosevelt's leadership for a variety of social welfare, health, and education programs that benefitted women and children.

Many writers have said that the women's movement was on hold after the conclusion of World War II (1945) to the mid-1960s. Among the numerous reasons for this chilly political and social climate for the women's movement was a return of the "feminine mystique," emphasizing the importance of domesticity and femininity as the proper attributes of women. Of course, this return to emphasis on the home meant that many women who had been working in factories (e.g., Rosie the Riveter) and in other important jobs while the men were off fighting the war had to give up their work so the men could be employed after their return. Another reason for the abeyance of feminism and the women's movement after 1945, according to Banner (1974), was a severe outbreak of antifeminism in the country that blamed women for all of society's problems because they had worked outside the home during the war years. (Note the discussion of the current backlash against feminism later in this chapter.)

In spite of women having to give up jobs that men wanted after the war and of the renewed emphasis on women's place being in the home, many women continued to pursue higher education and to work outside the home. This further inflamed virulent antifeminists, including welfare workers, educators, law officers, and others, who were fueled by Freudian ideas, and led them to blame working mothers for the problems of 1950s youth.

The social movement for women's liberation responded to these attacks, not by fading away, but by becoming somewhat dormant. Taylor's (1989) research illustrated how social movements maintain continuity during dormant periods between cycles of peak activity. She argued that there were many carry-overs and carry-ons between earlier social movements for women's rights and the resurgence of feminism and the contemporary women's movement in the mid-1960s. Taylor stated that most researchers trace the roots of the contemporary women's movement to the civil rights movement, but she posited that it "can also be viewed as a resurgent challenge with roots in an earlier cycle of feminist activism that presumably ended when suffrage was won" (p. 761).

The resurgence of feminism in the mid-1960s pushed the contemporary women's movement into the foreground of U.S. debate and challenged society to make women's equality a reality. The emergence of the contemporary women's movement was prompted by several significant pieces of writing that supported gender equity, among them Betty Freidan's *The Feminine Mystique* and Alice Rossi's *Equality Between the Sexes: An Immodest Proposal.* Some key executive actions and federal laws for gender equity included Executive Order 10980, which established the President's Commission on the Status of Women, which, among other things, investigated discrimination against women in the workplace; the Equal Pay Act of 1963; and Title VII of the Civil Rights Act of 1964, which prohibited discrimination in employment based on sex, race, color, religion, or national origin (see McCormick, 1994). June of 1966 is considered to be the official beginning of the contemporary women's movement. That is when the National Organization of Women (NOW) was founded to protest the lack of enforcement of Title VII of the Civil Rights Act of 1964, concerning gender fairness in employment (McCormick, 1994).

Feminist groups began doing consciousness raising, a method to help women in supportive small groups explore their common problems and formulate ways to take individual and group action to make changes in their own lives and in their communities. Consciousness-raising groups appealed to many women, among them homemakers who did not call themselves feminists. Participating in consciousness-raising groups helped women (including teachers) explore their identities outside of their roles as wife and mother (or "motherteacher") and enabled them to develop ways to challenge oppressive patriarchal practices at home or in schools.

Florence Howe (1984) described her growth as a person and as a teacher through consciousness-raising after her return from teaching in the Mississippi Freedom Schools in 1964:

I began very tentatively and timidly to learn to teach what people now call "consciousness-raising" and of course my own consciousness was growing at the same time ... let me emphasize that political consciousness about my own life and the lives of black people preceded my efforts to change my classroom. We all know women (and some men, too) today who are changing their classrooms because of the women's movement. (p. 52)

By the late 1960s, the resurgent women's movement had gained a permanent foothold in public consciousness. Activities of the women's movement frequently made front-page news, as in 1967, when a group of hard-core feminists picketed the Miss America beauty pageant to protest the images and stereotypes it promoted about women. In addition to NOW, other women's groups, such as the Women's Equity Action League (WEAL), organized to address specific issues. WEAL's mission was to eradicate sex discrimination in higher education, taxation, and employment.

Another outgrowth of the women's movement was increased awareness of the lack of women in the college curriculum. Both women's studies programs and feminist pedagogy gained tremendous momentum as a result of the women's movement. During the early 1970s, there was a major expansion of courses on women's history, psychology, and sociology in higher education, and by 1975 there were at least 900 colleges and universities offering women's studies programs (McCormick, 1994, p. 15). With the institutionalization of women's studies programs in higher education, the traditional Western male-centered curriculum was disrupted and significant curriculum transformation was underway (McCormick, 2005). This chapter, as well as the whole book, reflects this approach. It brings forgotten, but crucial, feminist voices and perspectives to teacher education. In this way, the book significantly benefits from more than 30 years of women's studies scholarship.

The important gains for women's rights made during the 1960s and 1970s were due in part to several key pieces of legislation:

1. In 1963, the Equal Pay Act was passed by the U.S. Congress after a coalition of women's organizations, teachers' groups, and unions formed to support it. The act prohibited discrimination on the basis of sex in wages and fringe benefits by any employer in the United States.
2. In 1972, the Equal Rights Amendment was passed by the U.S. Congress (the requirement that it be ratified by 38 states was never met).
3. Title IX of the Education Amendments of 1972 was passed. This legislation prohibited discrimination on the basis of sex against students and employees

of a school receiving federal assistance. Title IX has influenced education for women and girls (see McCormick, 1994, p. 19). In 2002–2003, Title IX was challenged in court as discriminatory toward males in certain sports. The Bush administration created a commission to review Title IX in the summer of 2002. According to Casta (2003), "The commission was stacked with opponents of Title IX—its real purpose apparently to provide cover for the dismantling of Title IX and the opportunities that it ensures for women and girls" (p. 1). The commission made some recommendations that many gender equity and feminist groups are deeply concerned about. Nicole Casta, NOW Foundation Government Relations Associate, said, "Now the Commission has recommended a series of complicated but deadly changes to the Title IX standards ..." (Casta, 2003, p. 1).

4. In 1973, the U.S. Supreme Court ruled in the now famous case *Roe V. Wade* that the decision to have an abortion, during the first trimester of pregnancy, is to be one made solely by the woman and her doctor. (Currently, this basic right of women to control their bodies and reproduction is also being eroded by the Bush administration and the courts.)

5. In 1974, The Women's Educational Equity Act (WEEA) was passed. This act authorizes support for educational equity for women and targets a variety of activities that challenge gender bias in education. Representative Patsy Mink from Hawaii was a major force in getting the WEEA legislation through Congress. Currently, WEEA is not being funded and can no longer provide the services initiated in 1974. An e-mail message sent to me via the Multicultural Education discussion list announced that, because the federal contract was not renewed for the WEEA Resource Center, their office would no longer be able to provide the usual services to equity educators (WEEA Equity Resource Center, 2003).

Far-reaching social changes for women's rights had been initiated by the women's movement, which had, by the late1970s, taken hold as a mainstream social movement. Following these years of amazing growth for women's liberation (1965–1979), a major change in national political power occurred, and an ultraconservative backlash (see Faludi, 1991) against civil rights in general and women's rights in particular took hold (McCormick, 1994). Since the presidency of Ronald Reagan began in 1980, continuing with the first Bush administration and now the second Bush administration, there has been a steady erosion of the 1960s and 1970s advancements made for women of all ethnicities and men of color. Setbacks have occurred through lack of support and funding for existing legislation, such as WEEA, and by overt actions to undermine others, such as affirmative action, Title IX, and *Roe v. Wade*.

As is evident on talk radio, late night TV, popular media, and some academic discourse, we are in a time of intense backlash against feminism and women's rights. For example, Rush Limbaugh coined the term *feminazi,* which has caused many people to shun associations with feminism even though they believe women should have educational, economic, social, and political equality with men. Rowe-Finkbeiner's (2004) book, *The F-Word: Feminism in Jeopardy— Women, Politics and the Future,* revealed that 68% of the young, college-age women (18–24 years old) interviewed by the author reject being identified as a feminist, as well as by the identifiers of ethnicity, race, religion, and sexual orientation. In her review of the book, Hartnett (2004) stated that Rowe-Finkbeiner "wisely takes the high road in describing the disenfranchised young women who reject much of the rhetoric of their feminist foremothers" (p. 9-H). The last part of the book includes practical tips on voter registration and how to get involved in the political process. Unfortunately, other popular culture writers, including many women, are riding this wave of antifeminism all the way to the bank with the sales of their books, which warn young women about the perils of feminism for marriage and child rearing. Katha Pollit (2002) stated that the author of *Creating a Life: Professional Women and the Quest for Children,* Sylvia Ann Hewlett, "calls herself a feminist, but *Creating a Life* belongs on the backlash bookshelf with ... all those books warning women that feminism—too much confidence, too much optimism, too many choices, too much 'pickiness' about men—leads to lonely nights and empty bassinets" (p. 2).

INTERACTION 1.11:
Quiz-Bowl—Test Your Women's History IQ

INTASC Principle 1: Content Pedagogy

INTASC Principle 8: Assessment

Play a friendly quiz game fashioned after the National Women's History Projects (NWHP) quiz and contest to help "write women back into history." After looking at the NWHP Web site, which is listed at the end of this chapter, develop your own questions to "write female teachers back into the history of education."

Just for starters, here are a few questions, some from the NWHP Web site quiz and some focused specifically on teachers. *(See answers at the end of this chapter.)*

1. Who was the educator and political leader of the early 20th century who worked for racial and gender equality and founded the Daytona Educational and Industrial School for Negro Girls in Florida?
   a. Fannie Lou Hamer
   b. Mary McLeod Bethune
   c. Mary Church Terrell
   d. Mahalia Jackson
2. In what year did the Equal Credit Opportunity Act make discriminating against women illegal?

    a. 1920
    b. 1950
    c. 1974
    d. 1985

3. In 1920 the 19th Amendment became part of the Constitution and expanded democracy by guaranteeing women's right to vote. How long did it take for women to win the right to vote?
    a. 22 years
    b. 12 years
    c. 52 years
    d. 72 years

4. August 26th is celebrated as Women's Equality Day to commemorate
    a. the work of women during World War II
    b. women teachers achieving the right to marry and keep their jobs
    c. the anniversary of women in the USA winning the right to vote

5. Who was the first woman teacher to be appointed as superintendent of a major metropolitan school system in the United States?
    a. Georgia Lee Witt Lusk
    b. Susan Dorsey
    c. Ella Flagg Young
    d. Carrie Chapman Catt

6. Teacher, Mary Murphy, was fired for misconduct in 1901 because
    a. she had an affair with a male teacher
    b. she got married
    c. she stole the fire wood for the school stove
    d. she petitioned for equal pay with male teachers

7. In what year was the Equal Pay Act passed by the U.S. Congress?
    a. 1972
    b. 1980
    c. 1963

INTERACTION 1.12:
Looking in Classrooms

INTASC Principle 9: Reflective Practice—Professional Development

INTASC Principle 10: School and Community Involvement

Observe a classroom of a professor who teaches women's studies courses. Given what you have learned about feminist teachers and the contemporary women's movement, assess the professor on his or her use of feminist ideas, theory, inclusiveness of multicultural perspectives, and use of inclusive and unbiased language

	WOMEN'S STUDIES	**GENERAL EDUCATION**

1. Uses unbiased, inclusive language

Yes _____   _____

No _____   _____

Give Examples

Comments

2. Uses feminist ideas, theories

Yes _____   _____

No _____   _____

Give Examples

Comments

3. Includes women's contributions

Yes _____   _____

No _____   _____

Give Examples

Comments

4. Includes multicultural perspectives

Yes _____   _____

No _____   _____

Give Examples

Comments

(based on race, sex, ability/disability, social class, language, religion, or affectional/sexual orientation). Notice the particular terminologies used by the professor to describe diverse groups. For example, the term, *affectional* orientation is preferred by some gays over *sexual* orientation because affectional orientation more accurately identifies their understanding of themselves by indicating a broader basis for their relationship than simply a sexual one.

For comparison, observe a general class (not in women's studies or a required diversity class) and make similar observations about the use of inclusive and unbiased language, inclusion of information about women's contributions to the subject being studied, and inclusion of multicultural perspectives. Write your findings in a comparative chart (see p. 23) and make comments and give examples below your checkmarks.

INTERACTION 1.13:
Brainwriting (Authentic Assessment)

INTASC Principle 8: Assessment

Brainwriting is similar to brainstorming, but it serves to encourage every group member to contribute and prevents outgoing personalities from dominating the discussion. With brainstorming, the goal is the generation of the greatest quantity of ideas on a question or solution to a problem. With brainwriting, the emphasis is on generating of ideas of quality from every person in the group.

In your CLRG, do the following brainwriting activity to answer this question: "What have I/we learned about the influences of feminist ideology and the contemporary women's movement on teachers' efforts to achieve workplace equity?"

1. Begin with a silent time of 5 to 10 minutes in which each member of the group writes as many ideas as possible in answer to the question.
2. Next, members take turns reading ideas from their lists, one idea at a time. Continue this rotation until every idea from each person has been read aloud. You may pass at any time and join in again at your next turn.
3. During this process, feel free to add to your list and build on each other's ideas.
4. A recorder writes the idea down exactly as the person said it on a large chart that everyone can see.
5. After every idea has been written down, the group discussion begins.
6. The group clarifies ideas and, if the contributor agrees, combines similar ones.
7. Next, the group can prioritize the ideas by having each member write the five most important ones and ranking them.
8. Sum the rankings of each member and then attain group totals to arrive at the top five ideas generated by the group.

9. Your final group report represents the ideas of the whole group, but each member's ideas have been incorporated in the process of brainwriting.

Another Way to Do Brainwriting:

1. Form small groups (5–10) people around a table or on the floor.
2. Provide each person with a sheet of 9" × 12" paper.
3. Put an extra piece of paper in the middle of the circle or table. This is done in silence.
4. Write one idea on your paper in response to the question and put your paper in the center of the table.
5. Take a new sheet from the center of the table and write another idea.
6. This process continues in silence until all the papers are filled with ideas (or the allotted time has expired). Repetition is fine; just keep the papers moving and the ideas flowing.
7. Build on other members' ideas.
8. Discuss your filled papers, noting how your first idea was expanded by the input of your group.

INTERACTION 1.14:
Final Concept Assessment

INTASC Principle 8: Assessment

1. Identify three key concepts from each EEQ in the chapter to work with for your concept assessment.
2. Define each concept according to your understanding and drawing from your reading and engagement with the ideas and activities in the chapter.
3. Write several paragraphs about each concept, going beyond definition to its context and meaning for you.
4. Create an imaginary scenario, a situation, a case, or a role play where the concept is applied.

Answers to Quiz

1. B   2. C   3. D   4. C   5. C   6. B   7. C

RESOURCES

Media

Those Who Can ... Teach.   This video/DVD program traces the evolution of teaching as a profession, honoring educators who risked everything to stand up for teachers' rights. Stanford University's Linda Darling-Hammond, Lorraine Monroe of the School Leadership Academy, and others talk about issues such as training, unionization, standards, bureaucracy, and professional growth, and four intern teachers share the lessons of their first teaching experiences. (56 minutes, color). Available from Films for the Humanities & Sciences at www.films.com; phone: 1-800-257-5126; e-mail: custserv@films.com; fax: 609-275-3767. #GUU11504-A: Video: $149.95; #GUU11504-KS: DVD-R: $174.95.

Web Sites

American Schoolteachers. http://www.ialhi.org/news/i0207_1.html. This site provides a review by Susan B. Carter of the book *Women's Work? American Schoolteachers, 1650–1920,* written by Joel Perlmann and Robert Margo. Of particular interest is chapter 5, in which the authors examine gender differences in the structure and rewards to teachers in bureaucratic urban schools. They make use of detailed personnel records to document discrimination against women in both pay and promotion.

Women in Education. http://womenshistory.about.com/library/prm/bleducation1.htm. This Web site gives a history of women in education, from the 19th to the early 20th centuries. It includes the historical context of how female teachers came to be paid less than males. It highlights some of the outstanding women teachers (Ella Flagg Young, Margaret Haley, and Catherine Goggin) who fought for equal pay and other rights. The contributions of two Black women teachers, Mary McLeod Bethune and Mary Louise Baldwin, are detailed. This article was written by Madelyn Holmes and was originally published in *Women's History Magazine* (Summer 1996).

Women's History Month: Internet Resources. http://cimc.education.wisc.edu/ref/resources/webliographies/women'shistory.html.

Women's History Resource Center. An excellent place to start your Internet search. The Women's History Resource Center offers lesson plans, biographies, a virtual art gallery, online magazines, and a place to submit poetry.

American Maid: Growing Up Female in Life and Literature. From the Yale-New Haven Teachers' Institute, American Maid presents a series of 10 lesson plans on women's history. Plans include "The Struggle of Black Women," "The Lives of Western Women," "American Women in the Civil Rights Movement," and "American Girls through Time and Trial." Each lesson plan indicates the targeted grade level.

Internet Resources About Women's History. Developed and maintained by the Madison Metropolitan School District, this annotated list of Internet sites is not full of superfluous links but is instead a concise, quality list related to K–12 education.

ProTeacher! Women in History. This site lists 25 Internet resources for lesson plans on women's history, including topics such as Eleanor Roosevelt, Florence Nightingale, Jane Addams, and others.

Distinguished Women of Past and Present. This site offers a searchable database of women's biographies, covering a wide range of careers: writers, scientists, teachers, politicians, artists, and activists. Searching by subject yields both well-known women and those who have been left out of history books.

Suffragists Oral History Project. Seven prominent figures in the 20th century suffrage movement are portrayed with full-length oral histories that are each a discrete unit. Transcripts of extensive interviews along with background information make this a wonderful source for discovering the stories of the strong women who fought for suffrage.

Teach Women's History. Part of the Feminist Majority Foundation, Teach Women's History focuses on the modern day women's rights movement. The site includes the text *The Feminist Chronicles: 1953–1993.* Lesson plans are linked to this text.

Women Pioneers in American Memory. From the Library of Congress's American Memory project, Women Pioneers covers not only women of the West but also suffragettes, social activists, and working women. On each topic page within descriptive text, there are many links that lead to primary source documents, such as digital recordings of pioneer folk songs and excerpts from diaries.

Women's Rights. http://usinfo.state.gov/usa/women/rights/rightslinks.htm. This site is produced and maintained by the U.S. Department of State's Office of International Information Programs (usinfo.state.gov). It provides examples of public and private organizations interested in promoting the rights and interests of American women, and it examines the history of women's rights in the United States.

Carrie Chapman Catt Childhood Home. Her efforts ensured equal voting rights for women in America. In addition to providing information about Catt, the women's suffrage movement, and efforts to restore her 1866 rural Iowa home, the site includes links to academic programs, other museums and historic sites, and related organizations.

Women's Suffrage. This page takes you back to 1912 when the public debate over women's suffrage was contested in editorial pages, in political cartoons, in the streets, and in the home. The prosuffrage arguments, the antisuffrage arguments, and information about the political process are portrayed using cartoons, essays, and photographs.

Women's Suffrage and the 19th Amendment.   The National Archives's salute to women's suffrage, including primary sources, activities, and links to related sites for educators and students.

Women's Suffrage From About.com.   These links from About.com focus on woman suffrage in the United States. They include articles and biographies for in-depth information on the long struggle to win the vote for women and include information on Susan B. Anthony, Elizabeth Cady Stanton, the Pankhursts, Mathilda Jocelyn Gage, and others.

Women's Suffrage—Online Resources.   http://home.columbus.rr.com/ bradshaw/women/suffrage.html

Women and Social Movements in the United States, 1830–1930.   This site is intended to introduce students, teachers, and scholars to a rich collection of primary documents related to women and social movements in the United States between 1830 and 1930. It is organized around editorial projects completed by undergraduate and graduate students at the State University of New York at Binghamton. Each project poses a question and provides 15–20 documents that address the question.

Documents From the Women's Liberation Movement, an Online Archival Collection.   http://scriptorium.lib.duke.edu/wlm. These items are scanned and transcribed from original documents held in Duke University Special Collections Library. The materials in this collection document the various aspects of the Women's Liberation Movement in the United States and focus on the radical origins of this movement during the late 1960s and early 1970s. Items range from theoretical writings to humorous plays to the minutes of an actual grassroots group.

The Women's Liberation Movement: An Insider's View.   http:// www.fathom.com/feature/35638. This speech by Susan Brownmiller, given at Barnard College to a group of young women, provides an insider's view of the workings of the women's liberation movement in the 1960s and 1970s. She is famous for her controversial and seminal book *Against Our Will: Men, Women and Rape.*

Women Who Made History—A Guide to Women's History Sites in Washington, DC.   http://www.gsa.gov/staff/pa/whc.htm. This site is prepared by The President's (Clinton) Commission on the Celebration of Women in American History. It describes the historic sites, monuments, memorials, and exhibits that pay tribute to American women who helped shape American history. If you are in the nation's capital, be sure to go on a guided tour of these inspiring places. Following are some specific sites for women teachers, activists, and suffragists that are included in the Guide to Women's History Sites in Washington, DC

Mary McLeod Bethune Council House National Historic Site. http:// www.stamponhistory.com/people/bethune.html. This house was the first national headquarters for the National Council of Negro Women and then served as the home of Bethune, a famous educator, from 1943 to 1955. Today, the house holds both the Mary McLeod Bethune Memorial Museum and the National Archives for Black Women's History.

Sewall-Belmont House National Historic Site. http://www.national parks.org/ guide/parks/sewall-belmo-1727.htm. Another important place to explore this house was the home of suffragist and Equal Rights Amendment activist Alice Paul who moved into it in 1929 and turned it into the headquarters for the National Woman's Party. A large collection of portraits and memorabilia of the women who led the fight for suffrage, including the desk Susan B. Anthony used to draft the 19th Amendment, is displayed, as well as flags used by suffragists who picketed the White House.

National Women's History Project (NWHP). http://www.nwhp.org. The NWHP is an excellent resource for finding books, gifts, and curriculum materials, including posters and videos on multicultural women's history. This is the non-profit educational organization that has helped write women back into history and established the National Women's History Month in 1980. Good sections to check out are the "History Quiz" and the "Program Ideas."

Feminist Majority Leadership Alliance (FMLA) and Feminist Majority Foundation (FMF). http://www.feministcampus.org/launchprocess.asp. The FMLA and FMF are organizations that support feminist activities, leadership institutes, an electronic magazine, and other activities for students and others on campuses across the country.

Choices E-Zine. campusteam@feminist.org. This e-mail address will connect you with the FMLA electronic magazine, which has online chats on current topics, information, campus news, feminist news, global news, and feminist community news features.

REFERENCES

Acker, S. (1992). Creating careers: Women teachers at work. *Curriculum Inquiry, 22,* 141–163.

Banner, L. W. (1974). *Women in modern America—A brief history.* New York: Harcourt Brace Jovanovich.

Bennett, B., Rolheiser, C., & Stevahn, L. (1991). *Cooperative learning: Where heart meets mind.* Toronto, Canada: Educational Connections.

Biklen, S. K. (1978). The progressive education movement and the question of women. *Teachers' College Record, 80,* 316.

Biklen, S. K. (1995). *School work—Gender and the cultural construction of teaching.* New York: Teachers College Press.

Carter, P. A. (2002). *Everybody's paid but the teacher—The teaching profession and the women's movement.* New York: Teachers College Press.

Casta, N. (2003, Spring). Bush administration trying to bench female athletes. *National NOW Times, 35*(1), p. 1.

DuBois, E. C. (1978). *Feminism and suffrage—The emergence of an independent women's movement in America 1848–1869.* Ithaca, NY: Cornell University.

Faludi, S. (1991). *Backlash—The undeclared war against women.* New York: Crown.

Freidan, B. (1963). *The feminine mystique.* New York: Norton.

Haley, M. (1912, August 12). Letter to Miss Kendall on Cincinnati Woman's Suffrage Party letterhead. Located in Chicago Teachers' Federation Collection, file box 18, Chicago Historical Society.

Hartnett, K. M. (2004, September 24). For young women today, feminism and politics are dirty words. *The Seattle Times,* p. 9-H.

Hendricks, W. (1993). The Alpha Suffrage Club. In D. C. Hine (Ed.), *Black women in America: An historical encyclopedia* (pp. 25–26). Bloomington: Indiana University.

Hoffman, N. (1981). *Women's true profession: Voices from the history of teaching.* Old Westbury, NY: The Feminist Press.

hooks, bell. (2000). *Feminism is for everybody—Passionate politics.* Cambridge, MA: South End.

Howe, F. (1984). *Myths of coeducation—Selected essays, 1964–1983.* Bloomington: Indiana University Press.

Knicker, C. R., & Naylor, N. A. (1981). *Teaching today and tomorrow.* Columbus, OH: Merrill.

MacKinnon, C. A. (1987). *Feminism unmodified—Discourses on life and law.* Cambridge, MA: Harvard University.

Maguire, M. (1993). Women who teach. *Gender and Education 5,* 269.

Marilley, S. (1989). Towards a new strategy for the ERA—Some lessons from the American woman suffrage movement. *Women and Politics 9*(4), 23–42.

McCormick, T. M. (1994). *Creating the nonsexist classroom: A multicultural approach.* New York: Teachers College Press.

McCormick, T. M. (2005, May). History and theory of feminist pedagogy. Paper presented at Kharkiv National University, Gender Studies Program, Kharkiv, Ukraine.

Million, J. (2004, March/April). Lucy Stone, Woman's rights champion. *UU World,* p. 64.

National Center for Education Statistics. (2000). *Digest of education statistics, 2000.* Washington, DC: U.S. Department of Education.

Noun, L. (1969). *Strong-minded women—The emergence of the woman-suffrage movement in Iowa.* Ames: Iowa State University.

Noun, L. (1993, July 7). Carrie Chapman Catt, a bigot? It's a conclusion that's hard to avoid. *The Des Moines Sunday Register,* p. 1C.

PEN Weekly Newsblast. (2003, March 6). Teachers avert strike, agree to work for free. *Public Education Network*. (E-mail message to theresmc@iastate.edu from PEN@Publiceducation.org)

Pollitt, K. (2002, April 25). Subject to debate—Backlash babies. *The Nation*. Retrieved March 25, 2006, from http://www.thenation.com/doc.mhtml?l=200205138s=pollitt

Pryor, S. E., & Mader, C. E. (1998, April 16). *Gender equity instruction in teacher education: What do students learn? What do faculty teach? What are the influences?* Paper presented at the annual meeting of the American Educational Research Association, San Diego, CA.

Rossi, A. (1964). Equality between the sexes: An immodest proposal. In R. J. Lifton (Ed.), *The woman in America* (pp. 98–143). Boston: Beacon.

Rowe-Finkbeiner, K. (2004). *The f-word: Feminism in jeopardy—Women, politics and the future*. Washington, DC: Seal Press.

Ryan, K., &. Cooper, J. M. (2001). *Those who can, teach*. Boston: Houghton Mifflin.

Sadker, M. P., & Sadker, D. M. (2003). *Teachers, schools, and society*. Boston: McGraw-Hill.

Smith, L. G., & Smith, J. K. (1994). *Lives in education—A narrative of people and ideas*. New York: St. Martin's.

Smith, J. K., & Vaughn, C. A. (2000). A conundrum: Perceptions of gender and professional educators during the nineteenth and early twentieth centuries. *Educational Foundations, 14*(3), 5–20.

Suffrage parader loses teaching job. (1912, May 22). *New York Times*, p. 24.

Sugg, R. (1978). *Motherteacher: The feminization of American education*. Charlottesville, VA: University Press of Virginia.

Taylor, V. (1989). Social movement continuity: The women's movement in abeyance. *American Sociological Review, 54*(5), 761–776.

Teachers' pay. (1911, July 11). *Woman's Journal, 42*, 20.

Teachers choose woman president. (1913). *Woman's Journal, 44*, 369.

Vaughn-Roberson, C. A. (1984). Sometimes independent but never equal—Women teachers, 1900–1950: The Oklahoma example. *Pacific Historical Review, 53*, 39–58.

Vaughn-Roberson, C. A. (1985, Spring). Having a purpose in life: Western women teachers in the twentieth century. *Great Plains Quarterly, 5*, 107–124.

Vaughn-Roberson, C. A. (1993). Independent but not equal: Oklahoma women teachers, 1900–1950. In N. Cott (Ed.), *History of women in the United States: Professional and white collar employments* (pp. 396–415). Munich, Germany: K.G. Saur.

Webb, L.D., Metha, A., & Jordan, K.F. (2000). *Foundations of American education*. Upper Saddle River, NJ: Merrill.

WEEA Equity Resource Center. (2003, May 8). WEEA Equity Resource Center is No Longer Available. (E-Mail Message to NAME-MCE@LISTSERVE.UMD.EDU from WEEAPUB@EDC.ORG).

Women teachers can participate, Birmingham board of education will not prohibit them from suffrage work. (1912). *Woman's Journal, 43*, p. 408.

2

Gender Differences in Cognitive Ability, Attitudes, and Behavior

Kimberly Wright Cassidy
Bryn Mawr College

The typical educational psychology text tries to do many things but often glosses over gender issues, usually assigning them a few pages in a chapter that includes socioeconomic and cultural diversity. An essential ingredient in making good choices about teaching practices is having knowledge about the similarities and differences among your students. This chapter highlights what is known in psychology about gender similarities and differences to help you understand why certain kinds of educational practices have been shown to be more effective, particularly as they pertain to issues of equity. The information in this chapter will also help you make better choices about the issues that arise in your own classroom situation. This chapter supplements the educational psychology textbook in several ways. First, it considers gender issues that typically are not covered in educational psychology texts. Second, this chapter provides more in-depth coverage of research on gender differences from the field of psychology. The depth is provided both by giving more detailed accounts of the research literature and by raising some of the more complex issues in interpreting this research. Third, the chapter attempts to examine the practical applications of psychological research to actual classroom settings and to real issues for teachers.

This chapter discusses the following essential equity questions (EEQs):

- **Essential Equity Question 2.1:** Are there gender differences in cognitive ability?
- **Essential Equity Question 2.2:** What are some of the psychological and social differences between boys and girls?
- **Essential Equity Question 2.3:** Are there gender differences in learning styles?
- **Essential Equity Question 2.4:** How might classrooms be organized to improve academic achievement for boys and girls?

Each EEQ includes two components: What We Know and Interactions. The What We Know component is a brief summary of relevant gender research. Interactions are based on the research and suggest an activity that you can do to ensure learning. These interactions stretch you to *inter*sect what you have read with *actions* you can do, in or beyond class. We want you to think about what you know and don't know (metacognition) and then move toward effective and equitable instruction. A few of these activities are classroom observations connecting academic research with the real world of school. Sometimes these will help you sharpen and focus your action research skills; other times they will help you to assess curricular resources. Accurate data collection and thoughtful reflection provide new insights into the ways in which teaching and research intersect. The final interaction is an authentic assessment task—a real-world evaluation giving you the opportunity to put your psychological knowledge to work.

ESSENTIAL EQUITY QUESTION 2.1:
ARE THERE GENDER DIFFERENCES IN COGNITIVE ABILITY?

There are several issues to keep in mind when thinking about gender differences in cognitive ability. First, although this EEQ talks about gender differences in cognition that have been found, it is important to keep in mind that there are far more areas where no such cognitive differences are found. Second, this chapter presents data on the differences between the average male and female performances. One must remember that even though there may be a statistically significant difference between the mean scores of males and females in a particular area, there is considerable overlap in the distributions of male and female scores. Third, though the gender differences discussed are statistically significant, often the size of this difference is quite small (small effect size) or has little practical significance. Fourth, for most areas of cognition, there is far more variability within a gender than there is between genders. Finally, it is important to keep in mind that while males or females in general may perform differently on average, in a particular cognitive task, this tells us little about how any individual will perform.

So then why even review this literature? Of what relevance is this to teachers? First, it is important to be knowledgeable about where gender differences actually exist. This avoids the problem of making inaccurate generalizations or assumptions about our students. Once we are aware of these differences, we can then use them to help guide good classroom instruction. To illustrate, if some students (girls) have difficulty mentally rotating objects in space, but others (boys) do this well, then it might be helpful to adapt instruction accordingly. For example, in chemistry, it may be useful to physically demonstrate how molecules orient themselves during chemical processes (or describe this phenomenon verbally) rather than leaving the spatial alignment to the imaginations of the students. Learning about gender patterns can be useful, but we need to avoid ascribing characteristics to all group members (e.g., "all girls are good at writing"). When we assume all members of a group share the same trait, we are stereotyping; however, valid generalization may be useful. So what is the difference between potentially helpful generalizations and potentially destructive stereotypes? Cortés (2000) draws three fundamental distinctions between the two:

1. Flexibility: Generalizations are open to change, especially as new information develops. On the other hand, stereotypes are inflexible, rigid, and impervious to new information.

2. Intragroup heterogeneity: Generalizations recognize that within a group there are amazing differences and diversity; not all members of a group are the same. Stereotypes make the assumption that all group members are homogeneous. When an individual does not easily fit the group definition, a stereotypic perception would conclude that the individual is atypical, an anomaly, the exception that proves the rule.

3. Clues: Generalizations give teachers a start, an insight about group members. Because we know that groups have different characteristics, when we learn that an individual belongs to a particular group, we then have a clue about that individual. Stereotypes replace clues with assumptions. Because an individual belongs to a group, a stereotype assumes that certain characteristics must apply to that individual. Whereas generalizations are subtle, stereotypes are blatant.

Everyone is both a unique individual and a member of various groups. Both of those realities offer insights into people's abilities. Understanding the power of group membership helps teachers to understand students better and therefore design more effective teaching strategies. Although generalizations can be beneficial in creating such strategies, it is important to use them cautiously. As Cortés (2000) warned, careless generalizations can lead to unintended bias and damaging stereotyping. With this important caution in mind, I turn to my review.

WHAT WE KNOW

Gender Difference in Perceptual and Motor Skills.   Gender differences can be found at the lowest levels of sensation. Thus, even at the point where information enters the brain, males and females may receive this information slightly differently. In hearing, for example, females are better at detecting pure tones (tones of one frequency) than are males (Halpern, 2000). In terms of olfaction, females are also better than males in their ability to categorize, identify, and remember odors (e.g., Lehrner, 1993). Vision is a critically important mode of gaining information. In general, males are better able to detect small movements in the visual field. Age-related loss of far vision also occurs earlier for women than for men (Halpern, 2000). These examples of gender differences in sensory processes are interesting because there are likely few gender role stereotypes regarding these abilities. People generally have little conscious awareness of the way in which their sensory systems function. Thus, differences are less likely to be the result of differential socialization (Halpern, 2000).

Gender differences favoring females have been found on speeded perceptual tasks. These tasks require participants to perform such skills as matching stimuli, scanning visual arrays for certain targets, and copying forms (Gouchie & Kimura, 1991). Numerous studies have also shown that females are better at tasks that require fine motor manipulations (Nicholson & Kimura, 1996; O'Boyle, Hoff, & Gill, 1995). In contrast, motor tasks that involve throwing a projectile or aiming at a moving or stationary target show large advantages for males (Hall & Kimura, 1995; Watson & Kimura, 1991).

Gender Difference in Memory.   In an examination of gender differences in memory, Stumpf and Jackson (1994) analyzed a battery of tasks that measured different aspects of memory. They found that women perormed significantly better on these tasks than were men. Jensen (1998) conducted an extensive review of multiple tests and found that females have better short-term memories (memory that is tested 1–2 minutes after presentation) than do men. Females have also been shown to have larger working memories (Huang, 1993). It is important to note that the size of these differences is modest. Females have also been reported to have better memory for words from a word list (Geffen, Moar, O'Hanlon, Clark, & Geffen, 1990), better memory for spatial locations (Eals & Silverman, 1994), and better recognition memory (McGivern et al., 1997). Thus across a variety of tasks tapping many different varieties of memory, females have been shown to perform better than males.

Gender Difference in Verbal Ability.   Although, in general, females are found to perform better than males for most verbal tests, it is important to keep in mind that the term *verbal abilities* covers a wide range of skills. The size and reliability of gender differences in verbal ability depend in part on which aspect of verbal ability is being measured (Halpern, 2000). For example, Martin and Hoover (1987) conducted a large-scale longitudinal study of children's performance on the Iowa Test of Basic Skills. They reported that girls scored better than boys on tests of capitalization, punctuation, language usage, reference materials, and reading comprehension. Hines (1990) found large differences favoring females on a test that required the generation of synonyms. However, Hyde and Linn (1988), in their meta-analytic review of the literature on gender differences, reported inconsistent differences in verbal ability, including some ages and tasks where there was a male advantage. Most of the differences that were found were small or modest in size. Thus, for some aspects of verbal ability, females show a modest advantage. However, larger female advantages have been found in the area of writing proficiency (Halpern, 2004). In fact, a writing test was added to the standardized tests for college admissions and females have outperformed males on this measure (Halpern, 2004).

Gender Differences in Visual-Spatial Abilities.   Halpern (2000) divided visual-spatial abilities into five types which prove to be useful in thinking about gender differences:

1. Spatial perception: These tasks require participants to locate the horizontal or vertical in a display, while ignoring distracting information. The classic test in this area is the Rod and Frame task, where participants position a rod in the vertical position within a frame that is tilted.

2. Mental rotation: This task requires participants to imagine how objects will look when they are rotated in space. For example, participants might be asked to mentally rotate a figure in a certain way (e.g., 180 degrees) and then choose the resulting image from a display.

3. Spatial visualization: These tasks require participants to perform complex, analytic processing of spatial information. For example, participants might be asked to look at a two-dimensional representation of a figure and choose from a display what that figure would look like when it is folded into a three-dimensional form.

4. Spatiotemporal ability: These tasks ask participants to make judgments about a moving display and frequently involve judgments of time. For example, participants might be asked to judge when a moving object will arrive a particular point.

5. Generation and maintenance of a spatial image: These tasks ask subjects to generate a mental image from memory and then use this image to perform a task. For example, participants might be asked to generate an image of a letter and then are asked if this letter would cover a particular portion of a rectangular frame.

Gender differences favoring males are found for spatial rotation tasks and mental rotation tasks but not for spatial visualization tasks (Linn & Peterson, 1986). Males also perform better than females on spatiotemporal tasks (Schiff & Oldlak, 1990; Smith & McPhee, 1987). Tasks that require the generation and maintenance of a visual image favor males in terms of speed but not accuracy (Loring-Meier & Halpern, 1999). Males are also more likely to use imagery when solving problems (Richardson, 1991). The size of the gender difference in visual-spatial tasks varies among types of tasks, with the largest differences found for mental rotation tasks (Halpern, 2000).

Studies involving more ecologically valid tests of visual-spatial knowledge also show a male advantage. Males are more accurate in their estimation of traveled distances (Holding & Holding, 1989), are faster and more accurate at learning a route from a two-dimensional map (Galea & Kimura, 1993), and are more accurate and quicker at negotiating computer-simulated mazes (Astur, Ortiz, & Sutherland, 1998). Data also suggest that women and men may use different strategies to solve certain spatial tasks. For example, Lawton (1996) found that in navigating through space, women tend to use a route strategy (room number and signs), whereas men tend to use an orientation strategy (knowledge of direction).

Gender Differences in Quantitative Abilities.   Hyde, Fennema, and Lamon (1990) performed a meta-analysis of more than 100 studies of quantitative abilities. They found that females performed slightly better than males in elementary and middle school, that males performed better in high school, and that male superiority becomes bigger in college and later adulthood. Hyde et al. did find that these differences varied depending on the type of task, with the largest male advantages occurring in mathematical problem solving. Examination of testing trends indicates that males consistently outperform females on the SAT-M by an average of 40 points.

Gender differences in quantitative ability seem to be greater at the highest end of the ability distribution. For example, Johns Hopkins University has been identifying mathematically precocious seventh and eighth graders nationwide for many years using the College Board's SAT-M. The male to female ratio in mathematical ability using these scores is as follows: 2:1 at a score of greater than 500, 5:1 at a score greater than 600, and 17:1 at a score greater than 700 (Stanley & Benbow, 1982).

There are two important issues to keep in mind when thinking about gender differences in quantitative ability. The first is that reported gender differences in cognitive ability usually fail to take into account that females are underrepresented in advanced math courses. Given that the best predictor of scores on mathematical tests is the number of math courses taken, this puts the data on poorer female performance in a different light. When the number of math courses taken is considered, gender differences in quantitative ability do get smaller but are not eliminated (e.g., Gallagher, 1998; Willingham & Cole, 1997).

The second issue is that many quantitative skills depend to some extent on visual-spatial ability, particularly in the more advanced areas of geometry, trigonometry, and calculus (Halpern, 2000). Data from a variety of sources suggest a relationship between visual-spatial skill and mathematical skill (Casey et al., 1995; Hunt, 1985; Luchins, 1979; Robinson, Abbott, Berninger, & Busse, 1996). To the extent that spatial abilities are involved in some math tests, females' poorer performance on quantitative tests may be reflective of their underlying visual-spatial abilities.

Recently Halpern (2004) argued that, rather than thinking of male and female differences in terms of topics in a typical school curriculum (e.g., verbal, quantitative), people should conceive of these differences in terms of the cognitive processes that they involve, such as acquisition of information, storage of information, selection of information, retrieval of information, and use of information. Halpern argued that gender differences can be better understood by thinking about these differences as occurring as the result of differences in underlying cognitive processes. For example, the slight female advantage in quantitative tasks in early elementary school may derive from the fact that the early math curriculum involves learning math facts and arithmetic calculations. These math skills may require rapid retrieval from memory, which is an area where females have been shown to have an advantage. To take another example, Gallagher, Levin, and Cahalan (2002) examined gender differences in performance on particular problems of the Graduate Record Examination (GRE). They found that males performed better on problems where there was an advantage to using a strategy that involved spatial representation but not on problems where solution strategies were more verbal.

The advantage for teachers of an approach that thinks of gender differences in terms of cognitive processes is that it may enable teachers to better understand where and why girls and boys may struggle with or excel at particular tasks. Further, such an analysis suggests specific areas or processes where teachers may intervene. It is important to note that cognitive differences between males and females show little change in their direction and magnitude in more recent times (see Hedges & Nowell, 1995; Stumpf & Stanley, 1998; Voyer, Voyer, & Bryden, 1995). Thus, unlike other areas where gender differences have disappeared (e.g., the number of women attending college), cognitive differences remain largely unchanged.

Biological Bases of the Gender Differences in Cognitive Ability. Recent advantages in technology have enabled researchers to examine biological differences in the brains of males and females. For example, Johnson et al. (1994) found that women have a larger corpus collosum relative to cranial capacity than do men. (The corpus collosum is a structure composed of nerve fibers that transfer information from one hemisphere of the brain to the other.) Male brains may also be more lateralized than females' brains for both the visual and auditory modalities (Voyer, 1996). That is, females have more involvement of both halves of the brain when performing cognitive tasks, compared with males, who tend to rely more on one half of the brain (which half depends on the cognitive task). Male and female brains also appear to differ in the way in which they are organized within a given brain hemisphere. Females tend to have their cognitive functions more focally organized (contained in one small area of a hemisphere), whereas men have their cognitive functions more diffusely organized (spread more throughout a given hemisphere; Kimura, 1999).

Psychologists and educators frequently have mixed reactions to data regarding male–female brain differences. Here is one potential response that teachers might have to the idea that there may be a biological explanation for gender differences in cognitive ability: Teacher A: "I find that girls in my upper level calculus class have more trouble grasping the concepts that I teach than do the boys. Scientists seem to be discovering that male and female brains are different. For me, that explains everything. Now I understand why my girls struggle, but I also know that there is little I can do about it. Biology has created this difficulty, and there is nothing that I can do to change that. You just can't argue with nature."

Although these discoveries of brain differences are exciting and important, they should not be used as a justification for avoiding equity issues in the classroom, as Teacher A has done, for several reasons. First, although there are gender differences in both cognitive abilities and brain structure/function, the direct links between a particular cognitive difference and a particular brain difference are weak (Halpern, 2000). So we do not know for sure whether these brain differences have anything to do with gender differences in cognitive ability. As a related point, that the female brain is organized differently regarding a particular ability such as language does not mean that this organization is better or worse. We are a long way from being able to say which organization is better, and the answer will most likely depend on the particular brain that we are talking about. So what might be a good organization for language in one brain might not work nearly as well in another. Furthermore, even where a brain–cognitive ability link may appear, the direction of the effect is not clear. For example, a difference in the degree of lateralization of the brain may cause better spatial ability, but it is also possible that greater participation in spatial activities causes greater lateralization. So differences in the behaviors of boys and girls may cause their brains to develop differently. Perhaps most important, even if it turns out that brain differences cause differences in cognitive ability, this does not mean that experience is not important. Even biology is influenced by environment, and, more important, gender differences are likely the product of an interaction between biology and psychosocial influences.

INTERACTION 2.1:
Working With Student Strengths and Weaknesses

INTASC Principle 2: Human Development and Learning

INTASC Principle 3: Diversity in Learning

Imagine that you are a teacher of Student A (you can assign the subject and grade level of Student A depending on your own interests). Imagine that Student A has good verbal abilities and weak spatial and quantitative skills. List several kinds of activities and areas of content that will come more easily to Student A. List several kinds of activities and areas of content that will prove to be more challenging for Student A. For each challenge, list one instructional strategy that you can use to help Student A. Now imagine that you also have Student B in your class. Student B has strong spatial and quantitative skills but weak verbal abilities. Perform the same analysis of activities and content area for Student B. What you might notice when you are finished is that many of the strategies that you proposed are beneficial to all students, not just those who have weaknesses in a particular area. Your students may also have a fuller experience as your teaching becomes richer and more inclusive.

Student A	Student B
Easy Activities/Content Areas:	Easy Activities/Content Areas:
Challenging Activities/ Content Areas:	Challenging Activities/ Content Areas:
Strategies to Improve Weakness:	Strategies to Improve Weakness:

ESSENTIAL EQUITY QUESTION 2.2:
WHAT ARE SOME OF THE PSYCHOLOGICAL AND SOCIAL DIFFERENCES BETWEEN BOYS AND GIRLS?

If you open up a developmental psychology textbook, don't bother looking for one chapter describing development in boys and another describing development in girls. Generally, boys and girls are described as developing in the same way. For example, the text might describe the typical way that children learn language instead of describing how boys develop language and how girls develop language. In a few notable cases, texts may make distinctions—for example, when talking about physical development. Although for many aspects of development this collapsing across genders may be appropriate, there are at least some areas where it may be useful to think about typical development separately for each gender. The areas discussed in the following sections are not meant to represent a complete list but rather provide a sampling of some relevant areas of gender differences in development for classroom teachers to consider. These examples will be useful to you in their own right but will also help you to think about other areas where gender differences might be important.

WHAT WE KNOW

Gender Differences in Aggression.   *Aggression* has been broadly defined as behaviors that are intended to harm others. Studies have found that males tend to be more aggressive than females (see Eagly & Steffen, 1986; Hyde, 1984; Knight, Fabes, & Higgins, 1996, for meta-analytic reviews). Recently, researchers have begun to consider the possibility that males are more aggressive than females because most studies of aggression have only looked at physical aggression, defined as harm through damage (or the threat of damage) to another's physical well-being (Crick & Grotpeter, 1995). Physical aggression may be more characteristic of males than females, and this is what leads to the apparent gender difference. It has been proposed that there may be other forms of aggression that may be more characteristic of females (e.g., Crick & Grotpeter, 1995; Galen & Underwood, 1997; Ostov, Woods, Jansen, Casas, & Crick, 2004). One such type of aggression is relational aggression. Relational aggression is behavior that harms others through damage (or threat of damage) to relationships (Crick et al., 1999). Examples of this type of behavior include giving someone the silent treatment to get one's way, using social exclusion as a way to retaliate against a wrong (e.g., not allowing someone to sit at a table or come to a birthday party because they did something to you), or threatening to end a friendship unless a request is granted (e.g., "if you don't give me that, I won't be your friend anymore").

Relational aggression appears to be as harmful to children as physical aggression. For example, school-aged children listed relational aggression as the most common form of mean behavior that occurs within their peer groups. In addition, studies of children who are frequent targets of relationally aggressive behavior have shown that this victimization is associated with problems such as depression, peer rejection, and low self-esteem (Crick & Grotpeter, 1995; Crick, 1996).

Research suggests that relational aggression is more often used by girls. In the preschool years (e.g., Casas & Crick, 1997; Ostov et al., 2004), in the middle childhood years (e.g., Crick & Grotpeter, 1995), and in adolescence (e.g., MacDonald &

O'Laughlin, 1997) girls show more relationally aggressive behavior than do boys. In fact, when studies of aggression count both physical aggression and relational aggression as instances of aggression, boys and girls are almost equally aggressive (Crick & Grotpeter, 1995). Thus, it may not be the case that boys are more aggressive but rather that girls and boys may express their aggression in different ways.

There are many ways in which teachers can benefit from considering gender differences in aggression in their classrooms and schools. First, relational aggression may be harder to see because it can be delivered in a whisper and can look like (from far away) a normal conversational turn. A failure to see these acts can color teachers' views about who is aggressive in classrooms. Second, relational aggression may be viewed by some teachers as less harmful, so they may punish more severely the student who hit another child than the child who spitefully excluded another from her game of tag. Yet the research suggests that children find this second form of aggression as painful as the physical type, so teachers may need to work just as hard to keep it from happening in their classrooms.

Gender Differences in Friendships.   One of the most important aspects of peer relationships is the establishment of intimacy. *Intimacy* has been defined as an emotional connection between two persons that arises as a result of interpersonal behaviors, such as sharing, play, self-disclosure, and so forth (Selman, 1989; Sullivan, 1953). The positive feelings resulting from the connection to another person (affective connection) that define intimacy may be quite similar across different ages, but the behaviors that lead to intimacy may change as children mature (Selman, 1989). For example, in childhood, children typically create intimacy by sharing in play, in common activities, or even by imitating actions. In late childhood and adolescence, intimacy may be also be obtained by engaging in alliances, shared discussion, and self-disclosure. Finally, in adolescence, disclosure of inner psychological states also may contribute to intimacy (Sharbany, Gershoni, & Hoffman, 1981).

In the past it was believed that girls' friendships were more intimate than those of boys (e.g., Burmester & Furman, 1987; Jones & Bembo, 1989; Sharbany et al., 1981). More recently, Camarena, Sarigiani and Petersen (1990) suggested that this gender difference results from the female-biased perspective that intimacy is synonymous with self-disclosure. Thus, because females engage more in the behavior of self-disclosure, it is assumed that they achieve greater intimacy (have a greater affective experience of connection). In contrast, society may discourage boys from self-disclosure because it is regarded as not masculine; thus, it may appear as if boys are not achieving intimacy. However, boys may achieve intimacy through alternative behaviors. Thus, boys and girls may differ in their preferred pathway to intimacy, although their affective experience of intimacy may not be different (McNelles & Connolly, 1999).

Consistent with this idea, Camerena et al. (1990) found that the gender differences in the degree of intimacy in friendships were significantly reduced when intimacy was defined affectively as emotional closeness rather than behaviorally as self-disclosure. That is, boys reported that they felt emotionally close to their friends, even though they did not engage in much self-disclosure. More recently, McNelles and Connolly (1999) examined the social interactions of girls and boys. These researchers found that girls and boys do not differ in their ability to sustain shared intimate affect during their interactions with friends. However, girls and boys differ in the behaviors that appear to lead to feelings of intimacy. Girls are more likely to establish intimacy through discussion and self-disclosure, and boys are more likely to establish intimacy through shared activities. Richards, Crowe, Larson, and Swarr (1998) found that adolescent boys and girls spend roughly the same amount of time with peers and that they experience the same level of positive feelings while with their friends. Richards et al. found that when not with their peers boys spend little time thinking about them, whereas girls spend more time thinking about their peers when not with them.

Thus, in thinking about the social relationships of students, it may be important to consider that there are many different ways for students to meaningfully connect with one another. The act of sharing an activity with a peer may have a different significance for one student as compared to another. Similarly, in making connections with students it may be important for some students to be able to feel as if they can share their thoughts and feelings. For others, simply engaging in a mutual activity may be enough to establish an affective connection.

Gender Differences in Attention Deficit and Hyperactivity Disorder.   In the most recent version of the manual frequently used by psychologists to make diagnoses (*Diagnostic and Statistical Manual of Mental Disorders;* DSM-IV), attention deficit hyperactivity disorder (ADHD) is defined as having three subtypes. Individuals can have ADHD primarily hyperactive type. These individuals manifest their ADHD primarily as symptoms of abnormally high activity levels and a decreased ability to control their impulses. Individuals can have ADHD primarily inattentive type. These individuals manifest their ADHD primarily with symptoms of distractibility and difficulty focusing and sustaining attention. Individuals with ADHD combined type have both inattentive and hyperactive/impulsive symptoms.

At least at the current time, the DSM does not define ADHD differently for males and females, yet recent research points to a variety of differences in males and females with ADHD. There are differences in the prevalence rates of ADHD in boys and girls; however, the magnitude of this difference depends on the source of the data. Some studies have studied prevalence rates by measuring the number of males and females that come to clinics for psychological evaluation or treatment (clinic-referred sample). The male-to-female prevalence ratio in clinic referred samples ranges from 9:1 to 6:1 (American Psychiatric Association, 1994). Other studies have sampled the general population (most of whom do not have psychological difficulties) to see how many males and females report significant ADHD symptoms (population-based sample). The male to female ratio for population-based studies is approximately 3:1. This discrepancy suggests that clinical settings treat far fewer ADHD females than males and that females with ADHD are less likely to be referred to clinics than males with ADHD. Because research on ADHD uses primarily clinic samples, much less is known about females with ADHD, but recent studies comparing boys and girls with ADHD suggest that there might be at least some important differences.

First, the way in which ADHD manifests in girls and boys may be different. Although ADHD combined type is the most common type of ADHD for both genders, more girls than boys have the predominantly inattentive subtype (e.g., Biederman et al., 2002). In addition, ADHD often co-occurs with other psychological disorders. However, girls are at a lower risk than boys for other co-occurring disorders, such as major depression, conduct disorder, and oppositional defiant disorder (e.g., Biederman et al., 2002; Gaub & Carlson, 1997). Girls are also less likely to manifest problems in school (e.g., Biederman et al., 2002). However, girls and boys with ADHD have a similar degree of social impairment relative to their peers (Greene et al., 2001). Given the way that ADHD manifests in girls, it seems likely that girls with ADHD are less likely to be referred to clinics because they display fewer disruptive behaviors within structured settings than do boys (Gaub & Carlson, 1997). Interestingly, gender differences in reported ADHD symptoms are found to be greatest when teachers are the ones providing the ratings of the children (e.g., Gaub & Carlson, 1997; McGee & Feehan, 1991).

Second, in the normal population, girls enact fewer hyperactive/impulsive behaviors. Thus, the base rate of hyperactive/impulsive behaviors is lower for girls, in general. Given that the number of hyperactive/impulsive behaviors required to receive an ADHD diagnosis is the same for boys and girls, girls who actually meet the diagnosis (have the requisite number of ADHD behaviors) have to be more extreme in their behaviors relative to other girls than do boys who get the same diagnosis. In addition, if girls with ADHD are less likely to be referred to clinics, then the girls who are seen in treatment clinics may be the most severely affected.

These findings have several implications for teachers. Girls with ADHD may go undetected in school because they do not display many of the disruptive behaviors that boys with ADHD display. This inattentiveness, though easier to deal with from a classroom management perspective, may be equally damaging to a student's academic progress. Further, teachers may be less inclined to think of ADHD as a potential explanation for underachievement in girls because teachers' idea of the disorder may reflect the large body of literature from clinic-referred samples where boys are more highly represented. Finally, girls who have ADHD combined type or ADHD primarily hyperactive type are further from the norm in terms of their behavior than are boys. Thus, their peers, teachers, and parents may find their behavior more aberrant, and this may affect the ways in which they are treated.

INTERACTION 2.2:
Conceptions of Typical Development

INTASC Principle 2: Human Development and Learning

A good way to begin considering the ways that gender may be relevant to the way teachers think about their students is to examine one's own beliefs about "normal" development. To begin, think about the general age group (within a span of 2 years) that you will be teaching. Write for several minutes about what a typical student in that age group would be like. Do not describe a particular child but rather children of this age (on average). Your descriptions can include classroom behaviors but should be broader to get a whole picture. What are children of this age like socially, cognitively, motivationally? Describe the child's general activity level and how the child might be inclined to reason about moral, social, and cognitive problems. It would be helpful to write using a double-spaced format so that you can add in notes later.

When you have completed this generic description, read it over and think about girls. How might this generic description change if you were describing girls of this age? What kinds of behaviors are you used to seeing in girls of this age and what kinds of behaviors do you not see? You can note these differences in the appropriate space within your generic description using one color of ink. Next, read the generic description in the same way but this time think of boys. Note the differences in a different color. Now reflect on what you have written. In what ways might the differences that you have identified affect the ways you view the students in your classroom? Think of at least one thing you might do differently as a result of thinking about boys and girls as developing differently.

INTERACTION 2.3:
Investigating Differences in Typical Development

INTASC Principle 2: Human Development and Learning

One way that you might "observe" gender differences in typical development is by looking at the personal web sites of girls and boys to compare them. To begin this activity, brainstorm a list of ways in which typical development may be different for boys and girls. Some examples might be interests, level of comfort with self-disclosure, degree of concern with relationships, and level of confidence in abilities. Choose a small subset of these dimensions and try to operationalize the dimension. That is, try to define the dimension in terms of an observable event. So, for example, if you think that girls and boys differ in how much emotion they express, you could operationalize this idea by counting the number of times they use feeling words (e.g., love, hate, happy, sad) in the text of their web site. The examples in Box 2.2 below may help you.

Dimension of Difference	Operational Definition
Girls express more emotion	Number of feeling words on Web page
Girls more interested in personal relationships	Number of links to other Web pages
Your Turn … .	

ESSENTIAL EQUITY QUESTION 2.3:
ARE THERE GENDER DIFFERENCES IN LEARNING STYLES?

For purposes of this chapter, *learning style* is defined as an individual's characteristic or preferred way of receiving, processing, and responding to information in a learning situation. Learning style is an indicator of preference and ease in a particular manner of learning. For example, some people like to figure out how to put together a piece of furniture by looking at a diagram, and other people like to put it together from a list of written instructions. A learning style is not an indicator of ability to perform a task; however, people tend to be stronger in their performance in their preferred modes, if for no other reason than they practice them more (Pearson, 1992). Unfortunately, the literature on learning styles suffers from little agreement on the dimensions of learning that are relevant to learning styles, with many proposed theories of learning styles making little contact with other psychological literature. Thus, there is no common conceptual framework that structures and unites the field (Sternberg & Grigorenko, 2001). Given that there are countless definitions of learning styles, descriptions of the various learning styles, and measures to assess them, this chapter selects a subset of these approaches, all of which have documented gender differences.

WHAT WE KNOW

Researchers and theorists have designed several ways to characterize people's learning styles, using different dimensions to divide the learning approach or focusing on different aspects of the learning task. What follows is a selection of these various approaches and the potential gender differences that have been proposed to exist along these dimensions.

Kolb's Learning Styles.   Smith and Kolb (1986) divided people by how they prefer to perceive new information and how they process new information. According to Kolb, people can prefer to perceive new information either by direct apprehension of concrete experience or by indirect comprehension of symbolic representation of experiences. The resulting information can then be processed either by an internal system of observation and reflection or by active experimentation (Pearson, 1992). Characterizing individuals by their preference for each process creates four major learning styles:

- Accomodators (concrete experience, active experimentation): People with this learning style like new experiences, are efficient at planning and executing plans, and prefer hands-on learning.
- Convergers (abstract conceptualization, active experimentation): People with this learning style are good at problem solving, decision making, and the practical application of ideas.
- Divergers (concrete experience, reflective observation): People with this learning style like to use their imagination and are aware of the meaning and value of their learning.
- Assimilators (abstract conceptualization, reflective observation): People with this learning style like to logically organize and analyze information, build and test theories, and design experiments.

Research on Smith and Kolb's (1986) theory seems to suggest that males' and females' preferences for processing information are equally distributed. That is, an approximately equal number of males and females like to process information by active experimentation compared with reflective abstraction. Females seem to prefer perceiving new information from concrete experience more so than men (Philbin, Meier, Huffman, & Boverie, 1995; Severiens & Ten-Dam, 1994; Smith & Kolb, 1986). For example, Philbin et al. found that 51% of females in their sample preferred to process information by active experimentation (were either accomodators or convergers). Similarly, 44% of males showed the same pattern. In contrast, 51% of females preferred to perceive new information by concrete experience (were either accomodators or divergers), whereas only 28% of males preferred to get knowledge in this way. In fact only 8% of males were divergers (concrete experience, reflective observation) compared with 29% of the females. Although Philbin et al. interpreted these findings as evidence for gender differences in learning style, there might be alternative ways to view this information. First, females were evenly distributed across the four learning styles with at least 20% categorized as each type. Although males were not as evenly distributed across learning styles, there were a substantial number in three of the four types (48% assimilators, 24% convergers, 20% accomodators). Second, males and females showed the same preferences for processing information (were evenly split in their preference between active experimentation and reflective observation). So one might argue that males and females show few differences in their learning style preferences and that at least females as a group (given their dispersion across the learning types) do not have a "characteristic" learning style.

Belenky's Ways of Knowing. Belenky, Clinchy, Goldberger, and Tarule (1986) examined women's ways of knowing and modes of learning by interviewing women about their experiences as learners and knowers. From these interviews they developed educational dialectics, which are descriptions of modes of thought or ways of knowing. Each dialectic represents opposite modes, such as rational versus intuitive, objective versus consciously subjective, and concern for self versus concern for others. Belenky et al. found that women prefer connected knowing, characterized by being consciously subjective, involved, integrative, and empathic. This is compared to separate knowing, which is objective, impersonal, and abstract. Although this preference may be true of females, it is not necessarily untrue of men. For example, Philbin et al. administered 12 questions (based on Belenky et al.'s dialectics) about learning styles to a sample of women and men. They found a gender difference on only one question ("Is 'concern for self' vs. 'concern for others' an issue in your educational decision making?"). Although Philbin et al. take this as evidence for gender difference in learning styles, one might focus instead on the fact that males and females did not differ on any other dialectic.

Field Independence Versus Field Dependence. Adopting a more cognitive approach, Witkin (1973) suggested that people could be categorized in terms of the degree to which they are dependent on the structure or context of the current environment or visual field. Field dependent or field sensitive learners have difficulty viewing information independently from its context. These learners think holistically and prefer to make connections among fact, theory, and personal experience. Field independent learners find it easier to segregate information from its context. These learners prefer learning isolated information in a more impersonal environment, prefer to think about information in an abstract way, and are more interested in concepts for their own sake.

One way Witkin (1973) measured field dependence/independence was by using the Rod and Frame test (discussed earlier). In this test, an individual must ignore the visual context of a rectangular frame (which is set at an angle) and move a rod within that frame so that it is vertical. Field sensitive people have difficulty placing the rod at true vertical because they are influenced by the tilt of the frame, which they cannot ignore. A majority of females (as well as Blacks and Hispanics of both sexes) tend toward field sensitivity (e.g., Howard, 1987; Witkin, Moore, Goodenough, & Cox, 1977). For example, in the Rod and Frame test, they have difficulty separating the rod from the context of the frame and thus misplace the rod based on the positioning of the frame.

More recently, the idea of field sensitivity has come under some criticism for two reasons. First, for a construct to be labeled as a style, it needs to be separable from ability. Yet one of the supposedly complementary styles (field independence) seems to be better than the other. That is, in many situations it appears to be better to be field independent (Sternberg & Grigorenko, 2001). Perhaps even more important, field independence has been shown to be indistinguishable from spatial ability (Macleod, Jackson, & Palmer, 1986). Thus, it appears that this dimension may be more accurately thought of as an ability rather than as a learning style. Second, there seems to be large extrapolation from one's ability to orient a rod in a frame to one's preferences for personal interactions in learning and teaching or to one's preferences for facts over personal experiences.

Mental Self-Government. In yet another approach to learning styles, Sternberg (e.g., Sternberg, 1997) proposed a theory of mental self-government to describe people's thinking styles. People are categorized according to the mental functions that they like to perform (e.g., creating plans vs. choosing from established options vs. evaluating others' rules, procedures, or products), by how they like to work through tasks (e.g., pay attention to one task at a time vs. work toward multiple products at the same time), by the level they like to focus on (e.g., details vs. the big picture), by who they like to work with (e.g., independently vs. situations that afford the opportunity to forge relationships), and by the type of tasks they like (e.g., working on tasks where there is novelty and ambiguity vs. working on tasks with established procedures). Research has suggested some gender difference in mental self-government. For example, males tend to score higher on global thinking style than do females (Zhang & Sachs, 1997). That is, males like to focus more on the big picture than do females. Males also seem to enjoy evaluating rules, procedures, or products more than females do (Zhang, 1999).

Critique of Learning Styles.   If one assembled a group of cognitive psychologists in a room, there would likely be a lot of eye-rolling if the discussion turned to learning styles. This section briefly reviews some of cognitive psychology's criticisms of learning styles and then turns to a discussion of why learning styles may be important despite these critiques.

One criticism of learning styles is that it is not clear when learning styles are measured if they are truly tapping some underlying construct. Thus, most findings in the field appear to be instrument bound. That is, whatever is measured by a particular learning styles instrument is labeled a style of _____, but it is not clear if there really is such a thing as _____ (Sternberg, 2001). Therefore, the field has generated as many styles as there are instruments to measure them. It is rare to find a case in which the same type of learning style (latent construct) has been measured in different ways. So, though a particular incarnation of a learning style theory may appear intuitively appealing, it often does not emerge from a strong theoretical framework with appropriate validity (Sternberg, 2001).

Another criticism of learning styles is that there is considerable weakness in the reliability and validity of many of the measurement instruments. So many measures have only moderate test-retest reliability (particularly problematic when measuring an allegedly stable trait). Construct validity, face validity, and convergent and divergent validity have also been shown to be lacking (see Curry, 1990, and Reynolds, 1997, for reviews). So learning style researchers have been criticized for failing to pursue the iterative process of research investigation followed by modification of measure/theory but rather have gone prematurely to print based on one data set (Curry, 1990). Some more recent learning styles theories/approaches have responded to this criticism. For example, Sternberg collected considerable validity and reliability data on his theory of mental self-government (see earlier discussion), including some cross-cultural data (see Zhang & Sternberg, 2001, for a review).

Others have likened the assessment of learning style to fortune telling. Frequently, the statements found on learning style inventories are designed to sound predictive but are ambiguous enough so that they could apply to a number of situations (Stahl, 1999). Thus, at first glance, these statements on a learning style inventory seem specific enough to capture real differences among people; however, oftentimes people make the same choices, so the statements ring true but rarely differentiate meaningfully among people.

In addition to these criticisms, there are certain other realities that make categorizing someone's learning style problematic. People are rarely dichotomous and categorical in their preferences, and frequently it is more accurate to think of people on a continuum. So, for example, one person may be somewhat field sensitive and another more so. In addition, people's learning styles may vary somewhat depending on the particular thing to be learned. So one person might be an auditory learner for ancient history and a visual learner for organic chemistry.

Finally, there is little evidence that suggests that assessing an individual's learning style and then matching a particular type of instruction to that style produces superior learning. Certain proponents of learning styles have argued that matching one's teaching style to the type of learner will maximize learning because students will perform best under these circumstances. The greatest amount of research on the effectiveness of learning styles matching is in the area of reading instruction. Critiques of this approach have been particularly harsh, arguing that there is no evidence that matching facilitates learning to read. In fact, many argue that certain kinds of matching may actually be detrimental to children's development of reading skills (Snider, 1992; Stahl, 1999). Thus, the idea of matching learning styles to instructional methods does not appear to be supported by research.

Given the severity and number of these critiques, why continue to discuss learning styles? Perhaps most simply the consideration of learning styles might be the impetus to be reflective about the diversity that is present in the classroom. So, rather than focusing on typing students' learning styles, particularly as they relate to gender, and then individually matching instruction to these styles (which is probably completely unrealistic), it may make more sense to teach in a more inclusive manner, using multiple and varied approaches. Thus, talking about learning styles may raise to conscious awareness and reflection the multiple ways that people may differ (or perceive themselves to differ) in how they take in, process, and create information. Consideration of learning styles may make it easier to think about concrete ways to change our pedagogy to make our teaching more effective for more people, even if we never are able to adequately define or measure a learning style. Learning style inventories may also provide a vehicle for students to be more reflective about their own learning.

In addition, taking a more varied approach to teaching (one that is informed by learning styles) may be beneficial to all students. A variety of teaching styles may allow more students to operate within their preferred mode. In addition, there may be advantages to having to use alternative modes of learning. For example, a student who prefers lectures may benefit by having to engage in a group discussion, even if this experience may feel less comfortable. It may be beneficial for all students to increase their ability to perform in other modes because, in real life, their preferred mode may not always be possible (Pearson, 1992).

Finally, though data do not at the current time support the idea of matching as an effective teaching approach, research does point to other ways in which learning styles might be important. Drysdale, Ross, and Schulz (2001) found that learners who think sequentially are better suited to science- and math-related fields, whereas random learners (nonlinear thinkers) excel in fine arts courses. These researchers found that all learners perform equally well in the liberal arts and social sciences. In a similar vein, Zhang and Sternberg (2001) reported that thinking styles contributed to the prediction of academic achievement (beyond ability). In addition, research shows that teachers tend to give better evaluations to students whose styles more closely match their own (Sternberg & Grigorenko, 1997). Thus, learning styles are relevant to thinking about effective instruction for all learners. Given that more recent theory and research have begun to respond to its critics, learning styles may become even more important in the future.

Gender Differences in Approaches to Science.   An appreciation of differences in learning styles can also have an effect on the way teachers practice and teach a particular field. One such discipline is science, where feminist critiques have begun to change the way teachers think about how people learn, how people practice, and how people teach science. In Belenky et al.'s (1986) work on women's ways of knowing, the authors talk about the idea that the scientific method (with its emphasis on objectivity and distance between observer and the object) may be at odds with women's preference for connection to the things that they are learning. Science, as it is typically taught and practiced, emphasizes critical thinking skills, logical reasoning, and abstract analysis, a type of thinking that may be more synonymous with a male worldview. Rosser (1991) suggested that this may be one reason that women are not attracted to and have less of an interest in higher level math and science. From her study of the characteristics and practices of women scientists, Rosser identified some practices that would make science more female-friendly and would provide ways for women to make connections as they use objective methods to obtain knowledge. These practices also allow women to see themselves as creators of knowledge, to value and use both objective and subjective strategies for knowing, and to embed this knowledge in a deeper context.

These practices identified by Rosser include (see Rosser, 1991, 2000, for a complete list) the following components:

- Expansion of the kinds of observation traditionally used in science, which may include observations of alternative types of relationships or may involve the expansion of methods to include qualitative kinds of data collection; these methods may also be more interactive and thus shorten the distance between observer and the object of study
- Acceptance of personal experience as a valid piece of experimental observation
- Exploration of problems that are relevant to social concerns
- Exploration of problems that are more holistic, more global in scope, and more "messy" because of interwoven issues, compared with the focused and limited-scale problems typically tackled by science

Current Way	Alternative Way
How is information gathered?	
What counts as legitimate arguments/evidence?	
How is information exchanged among people in the field?	
How is this field generally taught?	
What is the role of personal experience/personal opinion in this field?	

- Consideration of biases such as race, class, and sexual preference that may permeate theories and data interpretation
- Development of theories that are more relational, interdependent, and multicausal as compared to hierarchical, reductionist, and dualistic
- Use of a less competitive and more cooperative model for practicing science
- Emphasis on communicating with nonscientists to decrease the gap between science and the layperson
- Responsible applications of science to its appropriate place in society and in its application to real-world problems

The use of such strategies may make the teaching of science more female friendly because it allows for ways of knowing that are more consonant with female learning styles. However, it may also have numerous other benefits. First, these more connected ways of knowing are not limited to females and thus may be beneficial to many male learners as well. Second, women do not hold a monopoly on being disenfranchised by science. Many men view themselves as either having a poor basic understanding of science, accept the findings of science without question, or distrusting and rejecting the findings of science (Rosser, 1991). Finally, science may benefit from such a revision of its practice. Practitioners of science who do such things as use a more cooperative model, think about the social and practical applications of science, adopt multiple methods, and consider more forms of bias in the end must "do" better science.

INTERACTION 2.4:
What Is Your Learning Style?

INTASC Principle 9: Reflection and Responsibility

To better evaluate the usefulness of considering learning styles, it may be helpful to learn about your own. As discussed earlier, there are probably at least 100 different learning style inventories out there. One interesting inventory is available online and provides you with immediate feedback about your learning style and effective strategies for each type of learner. This inventory was created by Barbara Solomon and Richard Felder of North Carolina State University and is located at http://www.engr.ncsu.edu/learningstyles/ilsweb.html. For another interesting learning style inventory see http://www.usd.edu/trio/tut/ts/stylest.html. When you are finished, it may be useful to reflect on the following questions: Was it easy to answer the questions? Did you feel the inventory was biased in any way? What kinds of things were not asked that you wish had been asked? Is this type of information useful to teachers and in what ways? How does your learning style fit with the way that most of your courses are currently taught? How might your learning style influence the way that you structure your classroom?

INTERACTION 2.5:
"Opening Up" Other Disciplines

INTASC Principle 1: Subject Matter Knowledge

INTASC Principle 9: Reflection and Responsibility

I discussed earlier how science might benefit from opening up to different approaches or learning styles. How might other fields be opened in the same way? For this exercise, choose one field. First, describe that field in terms of how it currently operates. For each of these modes of typical operation, devise a different way of doing it. When you are finished, reflect on these changes. How has the field improved or benefited from being opened up in this way?

ESSENTIAL EQUITY QUESTION 2.4:
HOW MIGHT CLASSROOMS BE ORGANIZED TO IMPROVE ACADEMIC ACHIEVEMENT FOR BOYS AND GIRLS?

When teachers begin to design their classrooms, they must consider many factors, and they try to make good choices. This section reviews some recent data from psychology about people's performance in different situations. The results of these studies could be used to make adjustments in the classroom environment that might facilitate students' performance. This section is not meant to be a complete presentation of all of the relevant research but samples from some recent and important work that you might not encounter in other education courses.

WHAT WE KNOW

The Influence of Sociocultural Stereotypes on Performance.   Although gender differences in mathematics performance have declined considerably over time, they have not disappeared. The explanation of these remaining differences likely involves many factors. Recent research in the area of social psychology suggests that one of these factors may be peoples' susceptibility to prevailing sociocultural stereotypes associated with gender. That is, making people think about a particular stereotype that applies to a group to which they are a member (e.g., "girls are bad at math") influences the way people perform on a given task. Although many studies have been conducted with adults, researchers are only beginning to see whether these same stereotype effects appear with children. Given the importance of the conditions that create stereotype effects for the construction of classroom environments, I describe a study involving children with more detail.

Ambady, Shih, Kim, and Pittinsky (2001) chose an interesting sample for study: female Asian American schoolchildren. Their presumption was that, as a group, these girls would have two kinds of relevant stereotypes regarding mathematics performance, a positive stereotype associated with their cultural identity and a negative stereotype associated with their gender identity. These researchers implicitly activated either gender stereotypes, cultural stereotypes, or no stereotype in groups of Asian American, lower elementary, upper elementary and middle school girls to see whether it had an effect on their performance on a standardized mathematics achievement test. Lower elementary school girls and middle school girls who had gender stereotypes activated by answering some questions that involved gender (e.g., whether most of their friends were boys or girls, whether they resembled their mother or father, whether girls and boys were treated differently in school) before the math test performed more poorly than the comparison group who received neutral questions (e.g., what their favorite season was, what their favorite animal was). Lower elementary school girls and middle school girls who had their cultural stereotypes implicitly activated did better than the group who received the neutral questions. Contrary to expectations, upper elementary school girls (Grades 3–5) showed the opposite effect: Girls did better when their gender stereotypes were activated and worse when their cultural stereotype was activated. This is likely due to the fact that at this age (8–10 years old) children have been shown to be extremely chauvinistic about their gender identity. They seem to feel that their own gender is superior to the other and hence perhaps their enhanced performance is due to the activation of this belief (Kaminski & Sheridan, 1984; Powlishta, 1995; Yee & Brown, 1994). On the other hand, it is in these late elementary school years that self–race identity becomes accurate (Aboud, 1988). Children may want to distance themselves from their minority ethnic identity in an attempt to fit in with the majority.

In a separate study, Ambady et al. (2001) repeated this experiment using Asian American boys. They found that boys at all ages did better on a math test when their male gender stereotype was activated as compared to a group of boys who did not have their male stereotype activated. Lower elementary school boys and middle school boys also did better than the no-stereotype-activation group when their cultural stereotype was activated. However, similar to the girls, middle elementary school boys did worse than the no-stereotype-activation group when their cultural stereotype was activated.

For these same groups of boys and girls, both their implicit and explicit stereotypes were measured. Explicit stereotypes were measured by asking the children (at the end of the study) who was better at math, boys or girls. The majority of both boys and girls said that they were the same. Implicit stereotypes were measured by telling the students a story about a character who performed very well in mathematics. No information about the gender of the student was given. The students were then asked to retell the story. Pronoun use in the retelling was used to determine what gender the students had assigned to the character. Overall, students were more likely to assume that the character was a boy. The results of these stereotype awareness tests suggest that implicit stereotypes affected the behavior of these children, even when the stereotypes were not explicitly endorsed.

These results suggest that both positive and negative self-relevant stereotypes can improve or impair children's academic performance. Social psychologists call this effect *stereotype threat*. They propose that these effects occur when targets of stereotypes alleging inferiority are reminded of the possibility of confirming these stereotypes. The experience of stereotype threat may, in turn, interfere with intellectual performance. Overall, it appears that the activation of gender stereotypes has a negative effect on girls' performance and a positive effect on boys' performance. The one exception to this pattern was for upper elementary school girls, who appeared to do better when their gender stereotype was activated. Activation of a cultural stereotype for Asian American children appears to be beneficial to lower elementary and middle school children (boys and girls) and detrimental to upper elementary school children.

Recently, several studies have suggested that the detrimental effects of stereotype threat may be eliminated by particular interventions. One study showed that teaching college-aged women about the effects of stereotype threat eliminated the negative effects of stereotype priming. Two groups of women in this study were told that they were going to take a standardized math test for a study of gender differences in mathematics performance. One group was also told about stereotype threat and was told to keep in mind that any anxiety that they may feel while taking the math test could be the result of these negative stereotypes. Women instructed about stereotype threat in this way did better on the math test than women without such instruction and also did as well as women and men who were told that the test was a measure of problem-solving ability, with no mention of gender (Johns, Schmader, & Martens, 2005). Another study showed that having college-aged women think about individuating information (answer questions about their favorite books, movies, and special interests) after the activation of gender stereotypes caused them to perform as well as women who did not have their gender stereotypes activated (Ambady, Paik, Steele, Owen-Smith, & Mitchell, 2004). Further research is needed to investigate these kinds of interventions with younger students, but these studies suggest the possibility of counteracting the negative effects of stereotype threat.

There are several important things to notice about studies of stereotype threat when thinking about structuring classrooms. First, activation of stereotypes can be both positive and negative. It may therefore be equally important to avoid raising negative stereotypes and to try to find positive beliefs about an individual's group membership that might enhance performance. It is also important to note the subtle way that the stereotype was activated. The experimenters did not have to ask the students, "Are girls good at math?" or even, "Are you a girl?" They hinted at gender in more subtle ways: "Are more of your friends boys or girls?" or "Do you look more like your mom or dad?" Second, most of the children did not explicitly endorse the negative stereotypes. That is, most of them said that girls and boys are equally good at math. Yet implicitly most appeared to believe that boys were better. This suggests that if we want to change the effects of stereotypes, we need to do it at the implicit level. We cannot be satisfied when students say that the genders are equal; they need to believe it implicitly as well.

The Effect of Group Composition on Performance. Recent research in social psychology has also demonstrated that the gender composition of groups can affect students' performance. Inzlicht and Ben-Zeev (2000) examined college student's performance on both a verbal and a math test when in groups that varied in gender composition. Half of the females were assigned to a same-sex group (completed the tests in the presence of two other females who also took the tests). The other women were assigned to the minority condition and completed the tests in the presence of two men, who also took the tests. Females in the minority condition did more poorly on the math test than females in the same-sex condition. Both groups did equally well on the verbal test. In a follow-up experiment, Inzlicht and Ben-Zeev repeated the study, but with two changes. They added a mixed-sex majority group where males were present in the group but females constituted the majority. They also tested males in the same kinds of conditions (same-sex and minority conditions). In this study, participants completed a math test only. Females in the minority condition (one female in a group where the rest of the members were male) performed more poorly on the math test than females in the same-sex group. The data also suggested that as the number of males in the group increased, female performance decreased. That is, females in the mixed-sex majority group did better than those in the minority group but not as well as those in the same-sex group. Male participants did equally well in same-sex groups as in groups that were composed completely of females. Interestingly, these researchers did not test male participants in an area where females are sometimes assumed to perform better than males, such as on a test of verbal fluency. Do you think that the effects of group composition would be the same for males in areas of relative weakness for males? Why or why not?

One potential explanation of these effects is that they are caused by stereotype threat. That is, for a female, being in the presence of only males increases the saliency of group stereotypes, which, in turn, leads to poorer performance in the area where the negative stereotype is held. That women's performance was only affected by group composition for math (and not on a verbal test where women are assumed to excel) is consistent with this explanation of negative stereotype activation.

These effects certainly are relevant to considerations of single-sex schools and to the recent movement in some public schools to segregate girls and boys for math and science classes. The data discussed here suggest that single-sex groupings (at least in subjects where stereotypes hold that women do poorly) may be beneficial for women. For men, at least in the area of math, the type of grouping seems to have no effect. The effect of an all-male group on verbal performance remains to be tested.

The Potential Influence of Attributions.   Some motivation theorists assign an important role to the causal attributions that students make to themselves regarding their achievements and failures (e.g., Weiner, 1992). In fact, these attributions have been linked to students' reactions to academic successes and failures. For example, children who attribute their achievements to internal factors, such as effort and ability (e.g., "I did well because I worked hard" or "I did well because I am good at math"), have higher rates of actual academic achievement than children who attribute their successes to external factors, such as luck (e.g., Georgiou, 1999). Children who believe that their achievement outcomes are caused by controllable factors, such as effort, also tend to persist longer in the face of failure. In contrast, children who assign their failures to uncontrollable factors, such as task difficulty ("I did not do well because the teacher assigned problems that were too hard") or lack of ability, tend to give up under failure conditions (e.g., Diener & Dweck, 1978; Dweck & Repucci, 1973; Licht & Dweck, 1984). Diener and Dweck (1980) demonstrated that beliefs about the cause of achievement outcomes also affect children's reactions to success. Children who tend to attribute success to uncontrollable causes underestimated the number of their successes, overestimated their number of failures, tended to not view their successes as indicative of ability, and tended not to expect success in the future.

Some studies have found gender differences in attributions that may contribute to gender differences in cognitive ability or gender discrepancies in math and science achievement. Many studies have found that females are less likely than males to attribute success to their own ability and more likely to attribute failure to low ability (e.g., Cramer & Ashima, 1992; Stipek, 1984). Gender differences are more prominent in stereotypical domains such as math and science (Ryckman & Peckhan, 1987; Stipek, 1984; Stipek & Gralinski, 1991). Research also suggests that science, in particular, is less valued by girls than by boys and that this difference increases with age (Kahle & Meece, 1994).

INTERACTION 2.6:
Activation of Stereotypes in the Classroom

INTASC Principle 2: Human Development and Learning

INTASC Principle 5: Motivation and Management

The research discussed earlier is only relevant if students' gender stereotypes are activated in the classroom. Think about the various ways gender stereotype activation might occur in the classroom. Be sure to consider the full range of possibilities (e.g., physical aspects of the classroom, such as seating arrangement, classroom management procedures, teacher behaviors, student behaviors). It may be something as simple as coloring the gender bubble on the demographic portion of a standardized test or the gender of the teacher. Now, try to think about some ways that these stereotype activators might be avoided.

INTERACTION 2.7:
Looking for Potential Activators of Sociocultural Stereotypes

INTASC Principle 2: Human Development and Learning

INTASC Principle 5: Motivation and Management

In Interaction 2.4, you generated several possible ways in which gender stereotypes may be activated in classrooms. Now, visit a classroom and try to document occurrences of these kinds of situations. Of course, you will be unable to tell if, in fact, stereotype activation has occurred. Use the observation chart in Box 2.4 to record your observations. For the first 10 minutes of the observation, you should focus on the physical environment (what is on the walls, how the chairs are arranged, what is on the cover or pages of their text). For the next 10 minutes you should focus on the teacher's behavior (e.g., how does the teacher address students, seat students, organize them to hand in work, line up, or divide into groups). For the last 10 minutes, focus on the students' behavior (e.g., how do they refer to one another, what is the content of what they say to each other, how do they dress). Stereotypes can also be activated by the content of what students are doing (e.g., reading about technological discoveries or reading about women in history). If possible, observations should occur during stereotypical male subjects (science and math) and stereotypical female subjects (English/language arts, foreign languages). It is important not to overgeneralize from one observation. What goes on in a classroom on the day that you observe may be very different from what goes on during a different day. In addition, what happens in one teacher's social studies class may be different from what goes on in another teacher's social studies class. Although single observations can be quite useful in sparking ideas, you should avoid making generalizations on such limited information.

INTERACTION 2.8:
Weighing the Benefits of Single-Sex Schools

INTASC Principle 2: Human Development and Learning

Imagine that you are the parent of a school-age girl and you need to decide whether to send your child to a single-sex school. Construct a list of the advantages and disadvantages of single-sex schooling for girls. You should draw on the research dis-

Activators of stereotypes in the physical environment:

Activators of stereotypes in teacher behavior:

Activators of stereotypes in student behavior:

cussed in this chapter and you can also use data from other sources and your own feelings about the potential strengths and weaknesses of this type of environment. Ultimately, if the choice were yours, what would you decide?

INTERACTION 2.9:
Making Helpful Attributions

INTASC Principle 2: Human Development and Learning

The ways that we explain our successes and failures to ourselves have important effects on our later performance. Teachers also make attributions about students' successes and failures. Presumably, these attributions affect students both because of what they directly communicate to students and because students may internalize them as models for how they make their own attributions in the future. For successes, attributions are best if they are about internal or controllable factors. Failures are best attributed to controllable factors. To gain some practice in making helpful attributions, respond to the scenarios in Box 2.5.

Situation	Your Response
Tina fails a spelling test:	"I think the reason that you had trouble was that you didn't study hard enough."
Derek hands in a terrific social studies portfolio:	
Towanda remembers her homework for an entire week:	
Lewis gets out of his seat way too many times in math:	

Marcus can't understand
the steps in long division:

Julie wins first prize at
the district science fair:

INTERACTION 2.10:
Putting It All Together (Authentic Assessment)

INTASC Principle 9: Reflection and Responsibility

It is hoped that you are now more aware of gender differences and similarities as well as ways that classrooms and other educational environments may promote the achievement and development of boys and girls. For this assignment, you need to observe a classroom (or you may observe yourself in a learning or teaching environment). For one class period, subject or academic assignment, you need to try to observe all of the areas where gender differences may have an impact. Later you should consider how these situations can be improved to better accommodate differences and enhance the performance of all students. Keep in mind that many aspects of the situations you are observing may already be at their optimal state. Finally, share your findings and recommendations with others in your class to see if you can generate more suggestions for improvement.

RESOURCES

NPR: Gender Difference and Cognitive Abilities: Talk of the Nation
(Dec. 2, 2005)

Remote broadcast from the American Psychological Associations' Science Leadership Conference. This program discusses what science has to say about the gender differences in male and female brains as they relate to cognitive ability and academic achievement. http://www.npr.org/templates/story/story.php?storyId=5036084

Current Way	Alternative Way
Physical space:	
Type of curriculum:	
Teacher's way of relating to students:	
Activator of stereotypes:	
Composition of groups:	
Behavior of students:	
Attributions of success/ failure:	
Other:	

NPR: The Gender Gap in Math and Science Careers: Day to Day
(Jan. 2, 2005)

Program on the potential reasons behind the gender gap in careers in math and science. Guest: Nicole Weekes. http://www.npr.org/templates/story/story.php?storyId=4458519

Gender and Aggression Project

This is a web site created by a team of researchers studying aggression in girlhood. The research and site are supported by a grant from the Institute on Gender and Health and the Institute of Human Development. The site includes conference presentations, publications, and information about ongoing research projects and research sites. http://www.sfu.ca/gap/

ResearchWorks: Aggression and Bullying in Girls

This web site provides an accessible summary of Nicki Crick's groundbreaking research on bullying behavior in girls. http://education.umn.edu/research/ResearchWorks/Crick.html

All Kinds of Minds

Based on the work of Mel Levine, this Web site is devoted to understanding and educating teachers, parents, and children about learning differences. It includes research articles, video clips, case studies, and educational programs. http://www.allkindsofminds.org

Index of Learning Styles Questionnaire

Prepared by Barbara Soloman and Richard Felder, of North Carolina State University, this is a brief inventory that can be taken to evaluate one's learning style. http://www.engr.ncsu.edu/learningstyles/ilsweb.html

VARK – A Guide to Learning Styles

This site contains a brief learning style inventory as well as information about learning styles and strategies to capitalize on learning preferences. http://www.vark-learn.com/english/index.asp

"Thin Ice: Stereotype Threat and Black College Students"

This is an *Atlantic Monthly* article by Claude Steele that explains the theory and research behind stereotype threat. http://www2.newton.mec.edu/~gary_shiffman/Thin%20Ice

Ethnic and Gender Issues in Science, Technology, Engineering and Math Courses: An Annotated Bibliography

This Web site contains articles on stereotype threat as well as other topics related to gender and education. It is sponsored by the New York University Center for Teacher Excellence. http://www.nyu.edu/ctc/ethnicgenderbib.html

REFERENCES

Aboud, F. E. (1988). *Children and prejudice.* Oxford, UK: Blackwell.

Ambady, N., Paik, S. K., Steele, J., Owen-Smith, A., & Mitchell, J. P. (2004). Deflecting negative self-relevant stereotype activation: The effects of individuation. *Journal of Experimental Social Psychology, 40,* 401–408.

Ambady, N., Shih, M., Kim, A., & Pittinsky, T. L. (2001). Stereotype susceptibility in children: Effects of identity activation on quantitative performances. *Psychological Science, 12*(5), 385–390.

American Psychiatric Association. (1994). *Diagnostic and statistical manual of mental disorders* (4th ed.). Washington, DC: Author.

Astur, R. S., Ortiz, M. L., & Sutherland, R. J. (1998). A characterization of performance by men and women in a virtual Morris water maze: A large and reliable sex difference. *Behavioral Brain Research, 93,* 185–190.

Belenky, M. F., Clinchy, B. M., Goldberger, N. R., & Tarule J. M. (1986). *Women's ways of knowing.* New York: Basic Books.

Biederman, J., Mick, E., Faraone, S. V., Braaten, E., Doyle, A., Spencer, T., et al. (2002). Influence of gender on Attention Deficit Hyperactivity Disorder in children referred to a psychiatric clinic. *The American Journal of Psychiatry, 159,* 36–42.

Burmester, D., & Furman, W. (1987). The development of companionship and intimacy. *Developmental Psychology, 58,* 1101–1113.

Camarena, P. M., Sarigiani, P. A., & Petersen, A. C. (1990). Gender-specific pathways to intimacy in early adolescence. *Journal of Youth and Adolescence, 19,* 19–32.

Casas, J. F., & Crick, N. R. (1997). Social information processing and relational aggression in preschool.

Casey, M. B., Nuttal, R., Pezaris, E., & Benbow, C. (1995). The influence of spatial ability on gender differences in mathematics college entrance test scores across diverse samples. *Developmental Psychology, 31,* 679–705.

Cortés, C. E. (2000). *The children are watching: How the media teach about diversity.* New York: Teacher College Press.

Cramer, J., & Oshima, T. (1992). Do gifted females attribute their math performance differently than other students? *Journal for the Education of the Gifted, 16,* 18–35.

Crick, N. R. (1996). The role of overt aggression, relational aggression, and prosocial behavior in the prediction of children's future social adjustment. *Child Development,, 67,* 2317–2327.

Crick, N. R., & Grotpeter, J. K. (1995). Relational aggression, gender, and social-psychological adjustment. *Child Development, 66,* 710–722.

Crick, N. R., Werner, N. E., Casas, J. F., O'Brien, K. M., Nelson, D. A., Grotpeter, J. K., et al. (1999). Childhood aggression and gender: A new look at an old problem. In D. Bernstein (Ed.), *Gender and motivation* (pp. 75–141). Lincoln, NE: University of Nebraska Press.

Curry, L. (1990). A critique of the research on learning styles. *Educational Leadership*, *48*(2), 50–52, 54–56.

Diener, C., & Dweck, C. (1978). An analyses of learned helplessness: Continuous changes in performance, strategy, and achievement cognitions following failure. *Journal of Personality and Social Psychology, 36,* 451–462.

Diener, C., & Dweck, C. (1980). An analysis of learned helplessness II: The processing of success. *Journal of Personality and Social Psychology, 39,* 940–952.

Drysdale, M. T. B., Ross, J. L., & Schulz, R. A. (2001). Cognitive learning styles and academic performance in 19 first-year university courses: Successful students versus students at risk. *Journal of Education for Students Placed at Risk, 6*(3), 271–289.

Dweck, C., & Repucci, N. (1973). Learned helplessness and reinforcement responsibility in children. *Journal of Personality and Social Psychology, 25,* 109–116.

Eagly, A. H., & Steffen, V. J. (1986). Gender and aggressive behavior: A meta-analytic review of the social psychological literature. *Psychological Bulletin, 100,* 309–330.

Eals, M., & Silverman, I. (1994). The hunter-gatherer theory of spatial sex differences: Proximate factors mediating the female advantage in recall of object arrays. *Ethology and Sociobiology, 15,* 95–105.

Galea, L. A. M., & Kimura, D. (1993). Sex differences in route learning. *Personality and Individual Differences, 14,* 53–65.

Galen, B. R., & Underwood, M. (1997). A developmental investigation of social aggression among girls. *Developmental Psychology, 33,* 589–599.

Gallagher, A. M. (1998). Gender and antecedents of performance in mathematics testing. *Teachers College Record, 100,* 297–314.

Gallagher, A. M., Levin, J., & Cahalan, C. (2002). GRE research: Cognitive patterns of gender differences on mathematics admissions tests (ETS Report No. 02–19). Princeton, NJ: Educational Testing Service.

Gaub, M., & Carlson, C. L. (1997). Gender differences in ADHD: A meta-analysis and critical review. *Journal of the American Academy of Child and Adolescent Psychiatry, 36*(8), 1036–1045.

Geffen, G., Moar, K. J., O'Hanlon, A. P., Clark, C. R., & Geffen, L. B. (1990). Performance measures of 16- to 86-year-old males and females on the Auditory Verbal Learning Test. *The Clinical Neuropsychologist, 4,* 45–63.

Georgiou, S. N. (1999). Achievement attributions of sixth-grade children and their parents. *Educational Psychology, 19,* 399–412.

Gouchie, C., & Kimura, D. (1991). The relationship between testosterone levels and cognitive ability patterns. *Psychoneuroendocrinology, 16,* 323–334.

Greene, R. W., Biederman, J., Faraone, S. V., Monuteaux, M. C., Mick, E., & DuPre, E. P. (2001). Social impairment in girls with ADHD: Patterns, gender comparisons, and correlates. *Journal of the American Academy of Child and Adolescent Psychiatry, 40*(6), 704–710.

Hall, J., & Kimura, D. (1995). Performance by homosexual males and females on sexually-dimorphic motor tasks. *Archives of Sexual Behavior, 24,* 395–407.

Hapern, D. F. (2000). *Sex differences in cognitive abilities* (3rd ed.). Mahwah, NJ: Lawrence Erlbaum Associates.

Halpern, D. F. (2004). A cognitive-process taxonomy for sex differences in cognitive abilities. *Current Directions in Psychological Science, 13,* 135–139.

Hedges, L. V., & Nowell, A. (1995). Sex differences in mental test scores, variability, and numbers of high-scoring individuals. *Science, 269*(5220), 41–45.

Hines, M. (1990). Gonadal hormones and human cognitive development. In J. Balthazart (Ed.), *Brain and behaviour in vertibrates 1: Sexual differentiation, neuroanatomical aspects, neurotransmitters, and neuropeptides* (pp. 51–63). Basel, Switzerland: Karger.

Holding, C. S., & Holding, D. H. (1989). Acquisition of route network knowledge by males and females. *Journal of General Psychology, 116,* 29–41.

Howard, B. C. (1987). *Learning to persist/persisting to learn.* Washington, DC: Mid-Atlantic Center for Race Equity, American University.

Huang, J. (1993). An investigation of gender differences in cognitive abilities among high school students. *Personality and Individual Differences, 15,* 717–719.

Hunt, E. (1985). Verbal ability. In R. J. Sternberg (Ed.), *Human abilities: An information processing approach* (pp. 31–58). San Francisco: Freeman.

Hyde, J. S. (1984). How large are gender differences in aggression: A developmental meta-analysis. *Developmental Psychology, 20,* 722–736.

Hyde, J. S., Fennema, E., & Lamon S. J. (1990). Gender differences in mathematics performance: A meta-analysis. *Psychological Bulletin, 107,* 139–153.

Hyde, J. S., & Linn, M. C. (1988). Gender differences in verbal ability: A meta-analysis. *Psychological Bulletin, 104*(1), 53–69.

Inzlicht, M., & Ben-Zeev, T. (2000). A threatening intellectual environment: Why females are susceptible to experiencing problem-solving deficits in the presence of males. *Psychological Science, 11*(5), 365–371.

Jensen, A. R. (1998). *The g factor: The science of mental ability.* New York: Praeger.

Johns, M., Schmader, T., & Martens, A. (2005). Knowing is half the battle: Teaching stereotype threat as a means of improving women's math performance. *Psychological Science, 16,* 175–179.

Johnson, S. C., Farnworth, T., Pinkston, J. B., Bigler, E. D., & Blatter, D. D. (1994). Corpus callosum surface area across the human adult life span: Effect of age and gender. *Brain Research Bulletin, 35,* 373–377.

Jones, G. P., & Bembo, M. H. (1989). Age and sex role differences in intimate friendships during childhood and adolescence. *Merrill Palmer Quarterly, 35,* 445–462.

Kahle, J. B., & Meece, J. (1994). Research on gender issues in the classroom. In D. L. Gabel (Ed.), *Handbook of research on science teaching and learning* (pp. 542–557). New York: Macmillan Publishing Company.

Kaminski, D., & Sheridan, M. E. (1984). Children's perception of sex stereotyping: A five-year study. *International Journal of Women's Studies, 7,* 24–36.

Kimura, D. (1999). *Sex and Cognition.* Cambridge, MA: MIT Press.

Knight, G. P., Fabes, R. A., & Higgins, D. A. (1996). Concerns about drawing causal inferences from meta-analyses: An example in the study of gender differences in aggression. *Psychological Bulletin, 119*(3), 410–421.

Lawton, C. A. (1996). Strategies for indoor wayfinding: The role of orientation. *Journal of Environmental Psychology, 16*(2), 137–145.

Lehrner, J. P. (1993). Gender differences in long-term odor recognition memory: Verbal versus sensory influences and the consistency of label use. *Chemical Sciences, 18,* 17–26.

Licht, B., & Dweck, C. (1984). Determinants of academic achievement: The interaction of children's achievement orientations with skill area. *Developmental Psychology, 20,* 628–636.

Linn, M. C., & Petersen, A. C. (1986). A meta-analysis of gender differences in spatial ability: Implications for mathematics and science achievement. In J. S. Hyde & M. C. Linn (Eds.), *The psychology of gender: Advances through meta-analysis* (pp. 67–101). Baltimore: Johns Hopkins University Press.

Loring-Meier, S., & Halpern, D. F. (1999). Sex differences in visual-spatial working memory: Components of cognitive processing. *Psychonomic Bulletin and Review, 6,* 464–471.

Luchins, E. H. (1979). Women and mathematics: Fact and fiction. *American Mathematical Monthly, 88,* 413–419.

MacDonald, C. D., & O'Laughlin, E. M. (1997, April). Relational aggression and risk behaviors in middle school students. Poster presented at the biennial meeting of the Society for research in Child Development, Washington, DC.

MacLeod, C. M., Jackson, R. A., & Palmer, J. (1986). On the relation between spatial ability and field dependence. *Intelligence, 10,* 141–151.

Martin, D. J., & Hoover, H. D. (1987). Sex differences in educational achievement: A longitudinal study. *Journal of Early Adolescence, 7,* 65–83.

McGee, R., & Feehan, M. (1991). Are girls with problems of attention underrecognized? *Journal of Psychopathological Behavior Assessment, 13,* 187–198.

McGivern, R. F., Huston, J. P., Byrd, D., King, T., Siegle, G. J., & Reilly, J. (1997). Sex differences in visual recognition memory: Support for a sex-related difference in attention in adults and children. *Brain and Cognition, 34,* 323–336.

McNelles, L. R., & Connolly, J. A. (1999). Intimacy between adolescent friends: Age and gender differences in intimate affect and intimate behaviors. *Journal of Research on Adolescence, 9*(2), 143–159.

Nicholson, K., & Kimura, D. (1996). Sex differences for speech and manual skill. *Perceptual and Motor Skills, 82,* 3–13.

O'Boyle, M. W., Hoff, E. J., & Gill, H. S. (1995). The influence of mirror reversals on male and female performance in spatial tasks: A componential look. *Personality and Individual Differences, 18,* 693–699.

Ostov, J., Woods, K., Jansen, E., Casas, J., & Crick, N. (2004). An observational study of delivered and received aggression, gender and social-psychological adjustment in preschool. *Early Childhood Research Quarterly, 19,* 355–371.

Pearson, C. S. (1992). Women as learners: Diversity and educational quality. *Journal of Developmental Education, 16*(2), 2–4, 6, 8, 10, 38–39.

Philbin, M., Meier, E., Huffman, S., & Boverie, P. (1995). A survey of gender and learning styles. *Sex Roles, 32*(7–8), 485–494.

Powlishta, K. K. (1995). Intergroup processes in childhood: Social categorization and sex role development. *Developmental Psychology, 31,* 781–788.

Reynolds, M. (1997). Learning styles: A critique. *Management Learning, 28*(2), 115–133.

Richards, M. H., Crowe, P. A., Larson, R., & Swarr, A. (1998). Developmental patterns and gender differences in the experience of peer companionship during adolescence. *Child Development, 69*(1), 154–163.

Richardson, J. T. E. (1991). Gender differences in imagery, cognition, and memory. In R. H. Logie & M. Denis (Eds.), *Mental images in human cognition* (pp. 271–303). New York: Elsevier.

Robinson, N. M., Abbott, R. D., Berninger, V. W., & Busse, J. (1996). The structure of abilities in math-precocious young children: Gender similarities and differences. *Journal of Educational Psychology, 88,* 341–352.

Rosser, S. V. (1991). *Female friendly science: Applying women's studies methods and theories to attract students.* New York: Teachers College Press.

Rosser, S. V. (2000). *Women, science, and society.* New York: Teachers College Press.

Ryckman, D. B., & Peckham, P. (1987). Gender differences in attributions for success and failure situations across subject areas. *Journal of Educational Research, 81*(2), 120–125.

Schiff, W., & Oldak, R. (1990). Accuracy of judging time to arrival: Effects of modality, trajectory, and gender. *Journal of Experimental Psychology: Human Perception and Performance, 16,* 303–316.

Selman, R. L. (1989). Fostering intimacy and autonomy. In W. Damon (Ed.), *Child development today and tomorrow* (pp. 409–435). Cambridge, UK: Cambridge University Press.

Severiens, S. E., & Ten-Dam, G. T. M.(1994). Gender differences in learning styles: A narrative review and quantitative meta-analysis. *Higher Education, 27,* 487–501.

Sharbany, R., Gershoni, R., & Hoffman, J. E. (1981). Girlfriend, boyfriend: Age and sex differences in intimate friendship. *Developmental Psychology, 17,* 800–808.

Smith, D. M., & Kolb, D. A. (1986). *User's Guide for Learning Style Inventory.* Boston: McBer.

Smith, G. A., & McPhee, K. A. (1987). Performance on a coincidence timing task correlates with intelligence. *Intelligence, 11,* 161–167.

Snider, V. E. (1992). Learning styles and learning to read: A critique. *Remedial and Special Education, 13*(1), 6–18.

Stahl, S. A. (1999). Different strokes for different folks? A critique of learning styles. *American Educator, 23*(3), 27–31.

Stanley, J. C., & Benbow, C. P. (1982). Huge sex ratios at upper end. *American Psychologist, 37,* 972.

Sternberg, R. J. (1997). *Thinking styles.* New York: Cambridge University Press.

Sternberg, R. J., & Grigorenko, E. L. (1997). Are cognitive styles still in style? *American Psychologist, 52*(7), 700–712.

Sternberg, R. J., & Grigorenko, E. L. (2001). A capsule history of theory and research on styles. In R. J. Sternberg & L. F. Zhang (Eds.), *Perspectives on thinking, learning and cognitive styles* (pp. 1–21). Mahwah, NJ: Lawrence Erlbaum Associates.

Sternberg, R. J., & Zhang, L. F. (2001). *Perspectives on thinking, learning, and cognitive styles.* Mahwah, NJ: Lawrence Erlbaum Associates.

Stipek, D. J. (1984). Sex differences in children's attributions for success and failure on math and spelling tests. *Sex Roles, 11,* 969–981.

Stipek, D. J., & Gralinski, J. H. (1991). Gender differences in children's achievement-related beliefs and emotional responses to success and failure in mathematics. *Journal of Educational Psychology, 83*(3), 361–371.

Stumpf, H., & Jackson, D. N. (1994). Gender-related differences in cognitive abilities: Evidence from a medical school admissions testing program. *Personality and Individual Differences, 17*(3), 335–344.

Stumpf, H., & Stanley, J. C. (1998). Standardized tests: Still gender biased? *Current Directions in Psychological Science, 7,* 192–196.

Sullivan, H. S. (1953). *The interpersonal theory of psychiatry.* New York: Horton.

Voyer, D. (1996). On the magnitude of laterality effects and sex differences in functional lateralities. *Laterality, 1,* 51–83.

Voyer, D., Voyer, S., & Bryden, M. P. (1995). Magnitude of sex differences in spatial abilities: A meta-analysis and consideration of critical variables. *Psychological Bulletin, 117*(2), 250–270.

Watson, N. V., & Kimura, D. (1991). Nontrivial sex differences in throwing and intercepting: Relation to psychometrically-defined spatial functions. *Personality and Individual Differences, 12*(5), 375–385.

Weiner, B. (1992). *Human motivation: Metaphors, theories, and research.* Beverly Hills, CA: Sage.

Willingham, W. W., & Cole, N. S. (1997). *Gender and fair assessment.* Mahwah, NJ: Lawrence Erlbaum Associates.

Witkin, H. A. (1973). *The role of cognitive style in academic performance and in teacher-student relations.* Unpublished report, Educational Testing Service, Princeton, NJ.

Witkin, H. A., Moore, C. A., Goodenough, D. R., & Cox, P. W. (1977). Field-dependent and filed-independent cognitive styles and their educational implications. *Review of Educational Research, 47*(1), 1–64.

Yee, M., & Brown, R. (1994). The development of gender differentiation in young children. *British Journal of Social Psychology, 33,* 183–196.

Zhang, L. F. (1999). Further cross-cultural validation of the theory of mental self-government. *Journal of Psychology, 133*(2), 165–181.

Zhang, L. F., & Sachs, J. (1997). Assessing thinking styles in the theory of mental self-government: A Hong Kong validity study. *Psychological Reports, 81,* 915–928.

Zhang, L. F., & Sternberg, J. (2001). Thinking styles across cultures: Their relationships with student learning. In R. J. Sternberg & L. F. Zhang (Eds.), *Perspectives on thinking, learning and cognitive styles* (pp. 197–226). Mahwah, NJ: Lawrence Erlbaum Associates.

3

Teachers, Students, and Title IX: A Promise for Fairness

Karen Zittleman
American University

Do we really need Title IX? And by the way, what is Title IX all about?
Why all this attention to girls?
Boys are the ones shortchanged. Girls get better grades.
Girls are more likely to get into college, while boys are more likely to get into trouble.

Many educators are confused about gender equity and the law. In fact, the statements at the beginning of this chapter were made by teachers. Is sex discrimination still a problem in our nation's schools? You bet. Traditional sexist stereotypes and blatant inequity prevail, limiting academic and social development. Consider the following:

"Freaky Fridays" are an unofficial ritual at one elementary school. Boys flip up girls' skirts, pull down their underpants, and snap their bra straps. The behavior is a rite of passage for boys to be considered part of the "in" crowd.

Another school constructed a state-of-the-art baseball field for the boys. It was large enough for both the junior and seniors to practice and play. There were dugouts, generous seating, lockers, a storage room, and a public address system. The girls, on the other hand, had no school field at all. They were told to share a field owned by a local church, without any of the facilities enjoyed by the males.

73

Unfortunately, such examples are not uncommon and reveal that gender bias is alive and well in our nation's schools. Despite evidence of the very real gender barriers that females as well as males continue to face, gender-stereotyped arguments about abilities and interests persist. Claims continue to be made, for example, that males outnumber females in doctoral degrees in fields such as physics and engineering because their spatial and mechanical aptitudes are superior to those of women and that sex hormones are the cause of these differences between males and females. One study found that 71% of male teachers believed that male students were more interested in the mechanics of computer technology and were more likely to attribute boys' success in technology to talent while dismissing girls' success as due to luck or diligence (American Association of University Women, 2000). These types of arguments have also been made repeatedly in an effort to deny women equal athletic opportunities, where critics assert that females are less interested than males in sports. Yet gender fairness is as important to a girl who dreams of becoming an astronaut as it is for a boy who wants to be an elementary school teacher. It reduces the gender disparities that are detrimental to classroom interactions and in testing; it encourages all students to pursue a variety of school subjects, putting no limit on what they can accomplish; and it gives students the opportunity to participate in all aspects of school sports and clubs. Although gender stereotypes and attitudes cannot be changed by laws, rights, opportunities, and treatment can be equalized.

This chapter discusses the following essential equity questions (EEQs):

- **Essential Equity Question 3.1:** What is Title IX and why do we need it?
- **Essential Equity Question 3.2:** How do schools comply with Title IX?
- **Essential Equity Question 3.3:** What emerging issues might affect Title IX?

Each EEQ includes two components: The What We Know component is a brief summary of Title IX and gender-related research. The Interactions component is based on research, and each Interaction suggests an activity that you can do to ensure learning. Interactions challenge you to *inter*sect what you have read with *actions* you can do, in or beyond class. The final interaction is an authentic assessment task—a real-world evaluation that gives you the opportunity to put your Title IX knowledge in action.

ESSENTIAL EQUITY QUESTION 3.1:
WHAT IS TITLE IX AND WHY DO WE NEED IT?

For more than 30 years, the federal law Title IX has prohibited sex discrimination in education. The law was enacted in 1972 as a broad proscription against discrimination in any federally funded education program or activity. It states "No person in the United States shall, on the basis of sex, be excluded from participation in, be denied the benefits of, or be subjected to discrimination under any education program or activity receiving Federal financial assistance" (Title IX of the Education Amendments of 1972, 20 U.S.C. Section 1681).

Title IX requires educational institutions to maintain policies, practices, and programs that do not discriminate against anyone on the basis of sex. It is the nation's educational promise that the talents of all its citizens—women and men, girls and boys—will not be restricted by discrimination. Today, Title IX provides legal protection against sex discrimination for approximately 70 million students and employees in all educational institutions receiving federal financial assistance (National Coalition for Women and Girls in Education, 2002; U.S. Department of Education, 2006). The law also covers institutions such as vocational training centers, public libraries, and museums. It was intended to ensure equal opportunity for women and girls in all aspects of education—from access to higher education to equal opportunities and fair treatment in elementary and secondary classrooms to equal opportunity in athletics. In this chapter, you will have the opportunity to understand the letter of the law—the legal requirements of Title IX—as well as to embrace the spirit of Title IX—a broader notion of equity that integrates gender with related issues of race, culture, disability, ethnicity, sexual orientation, and socioeconomic status. Access, achievement, and equity—isn't that what educational excellence is all about?

WHAT WE KNOW

A Look Back: The Beginning of Title IX. In 1970, Representative Edith Green and Senator Birch Bayh drafted legislation prohibiting sex discrimination in education and held the first congressional hearings on the education and employment of women. The original version of the bill proposed to amend Title VII of the 1964 Civil Rights Act (prohibiting discrimination in employment on the basis of race, color, religion, sex, or national origin) to cover employees in educational institutions. The measure also proposed to amend Title VI of the Civil Rights Act (prohibiting discrimination on the basis of race, color, or national origin in any program receiving federal financial assistance) to cover sex discrimination and to extend the Equal Pay Act to cover executives, administrators, and professionals. Honoring the requests of Black leaders and their supporters, who feared that the process of amending Title VI could weaken its coverage, Representative Green proposed a separate and new title, which became the now famous Title IX. Congress passed the bill on June 8, 1972. President Nixon signed Title IX into law on June 23, and it became effective on July 1, 1972 (Fischer, Schimmel, Stellman, & Kelly, 2002).

The Department of Health, Education, and Welfare took 3 years (1972–1975) to translate Title IX into specific regulations. Under these regulations, each institution has a responsibility to perform the following functions:

- Designate a Title IX coordinator to oversee compliance efforts and investigate any complaints of sex discrimination
- Notify all students and employees of activities of the Title IX coordinator
- Publicize its grievance procedures and nondiscrimination policies on sex discrimination

Although at least one employee must officially oversee Title IX protections, it is the shared responsibility of an entire school district, from top-level administration to individual staff, to foster compliance.

Why Do We Need Title IX?   Much progress has been made since Title IX was enacted on June 23, 1972—so much in fact that it is difficult for some to believe what education in the United States was like at that time. Did you know that female students were often barred from taking classes such as auto mechanics or criminal justice, and males could not take home economics? Or that some high school and college marching bands would not let women play? That athletic programs for girls consisted primarily of intramural sports and that boys would rarely consider cheerleading an option? Some schools would not even allow girls to serve on safety patrol. Pregnant and parenting students were even discouraged from attending school. Women seeking admission to the New York State College of Agriculture needed SAT scores 30 to 40 points higher than those of men. Males were shortchanged, too. They were not allowed to take classes such as home economics, child care, or family life, limiting their abilities to care for themselves and others. Males were also discouraged from pursuing traditionally female careers, such as nursing or elementary school teaching (National Coalition for Women and Girls in Education, 2002).

Three decades later, success can be seen in the participation and achievement of women and girls in education, athletics, and careers. Women are now the majority of college students, and though a modest improvement, more men (7%) are becoming nurses, up from 1% in 1972. Female enrollment in science and mathematics courses has increased dramatically in recent years. Girls are more likely to take biology and chemistry, trigonometry, and algebra. (However, boys still dominate physics and calculus.) Since its passage 30 years ago, Title IX has changed the athletic playing field significantly, creating greater opportunities for girls and women to play sports and receive scholarships. In 1972, fewer than 32,000 women competed in intercollegiate athletics. Women received only 2% of schools' athletic budgets, and athletic scholarships for women were nonexistent. Today, the number of college women participating in competitive athletics is nearly five times the pre–Title IX rate, and women are awarded 43% of athletic scholarships and 36% of athletic budgets. Title IX has had a tremendous effect on female athletic opportunities at the high school level as well. Before Title IX, fewer than 300,000 high school girls played competitive sports. Today the number has climbed to more than 2.8 million. Men's participation at both the high school and college levels has also increased (National Federation of State High School Athletic Associations, 2004; U.S. Department of Education, 2006). These are remarkable victories.

Unfortunately, Title IX remains a misunderstood law and gender bias is a pervasive problem in schools. Consider the following issues:

- In elementary school, both males and females report that they like math and science, and their test scores are comparable. Yet by the 12th grade, females report less positive attitudes and consider math and science harder subjects than do boys. Boys dominate physics and calculus courses and continue to outscore females on math and science standardized tests (more than 35 points on the math SAT; College Board, 2005; U.S. Department of Education, 2000).
- Girls are five times less likely than boys to consider a technology-related career and make up only 17% of computer science advanced placement test takers. Girls from all ethnic groups rate themselves considerably lower than boys on technological ability (National Coalition for Women and Girls in Education, 2002).
- Scoring gaps persist in high-stakes standardized testing, across all races and ethnicities, limiting women's access to educational institutions, financial aid, and careers. For example, males outperform females by 120 points on the Graduate Record Exam (Educational Testing Service, 2001).
- Vocational training programs channel girls and women into low-wage jobs. The National Women's Law Center (2002) recently reported that in cosmetology, child care, and health care programs more than 85% of students are females, whereas more than 90% of males are clustered in traditionally male—and higher paying—courses in technology and industrial trades, such as carpentry and plumbing.
- An American Association of University Women (2004) survey found that 83% of females and 79% of males experience some form of sexual harassment in school. Victims are more likely to want to avoid school or to even talk in class.
- Though a violation of Title IX, many school districts continue to require pregnant students to take off-campus classes and prohibit them from participating in regular programs or extracurricular activities. National Honor Societies have excluded pregnant young women on the grounds that premarital sex is immoral but have admitted young men who have engaged in the same behavior. Pregnancy and parenting are the major reasons that girls drop out of school, and only 30% of adolescent mothers earn a high school diploma by 30 years of age (National Coalition for Women and Girls in Education, 2002).
- Although athletics continues to be a beacon of female progress, it is also a symbol of continuing institutional opposition. In one school district, for example, the girls' field hockey team practiced on a poorly maintained field with bro-

ken glass, the same field deemed unsafe for the football team (U.S. Department of Education, 2001b).

• Women still have a long way to go to attain full equality with men in employment in educational institutions. A troubling pattern persists: As the rank on the career ladder increases, women become invisible. Women account for 73% of elementary and secondary school teachers but only 44% of school principals and less than 20% of superintendents. In higher education, women comprise 37% of faculty members and only 20% of full professors (U.S. Department of Education, 2006; National Coalition for Women and Girls in Education, 2002).

Few people are aware of the safeguards provided by Title IX, and many, if not most, schools nationwide are out of compliance. Gender bias and discrimination in the curriculum, classroom practices, assessment, and policies persists.

Why is enforcement of such a basic equal educational right so weak? One reason is that there has never been sufficient federal support to schools to enforce Title IX. Although Title IX mandates that schools appoint a Title IX compliance coordinator, no funds are provided to pay for such a coordinator. In most schools, the compliance officer has either not been appointed, or, if appointed, the position is seen as an add-on without training, real responsibility, or funding. Nor does the Office for Civil Rights receive adequate funding to fulfill its responsibilities to provide technical assistance to schools to correct violations. According to the 2000 Report to Congress, the Office for Civil Rights receives only $1 for each student in America's schools. A majority of funds appropriated to the Office for Civil Rights is devoted to case resolution and not to technical assistance (U.S. Department of Education, 2001b).

In those cases where educators and students learn about Title IX and gender equity, they have taken extraordinary actions to challenge unfairness: A valedictorian successfully overturned her school's decision to forbid her from giving a high school graduation speech because she was pregnant; a fourth-grade teacher and her students challenged a hospital-supported advertisement depicting girls sick from math class; and a high school football coach lobbied his school board to fund equitable sports facilities for female and male athletes.

INTERACTION 3.1:
Where Do You Stand on Title IX?

INTASC Principle 9: Reflection and Responsibility

Part of the legal responsibility of schools is to inform teachers and students of their rights under this law. Given all your time in schools, what do you already know about Title IX? Take this quick quiz to find out.

True	False	
___	___	1. Title IX requires that a girl be allowed to play on the football team if she is good enough.
___	___	2. Title IX requires that all classes have both females and males in them.
___	___	3. Title IX requires that when there is a disproportionately small number of women principals, women must be promoted before men.
___	___	4. Title IX encourages special programs for pregnant girls.
___	___	5. Title IX permits the use of separate vocational interest tests for females and males that provide occupational choices geared to the special interests of each sex.
___	___	6. Title IX requires that there be female coaches for girls' sports.
___	___	7. Title IX requires that as much money be spent on girls' as on boys' athletics.
___	___	8. Title IX prohibits the use of gender-biased textbooks.
___	___	9. Title IX requires that all club and extracurricular activities be coeducational.
___	___	10. Title IX requires that schools pay victims of sexual harassment.

The answer key: *All* items are false. How did you do? Are you a Title IX legal eagle? Or are you in need of a lesson in Title IX? In either case, please keep reading!

ESSENTIAL EQUITY QUESTION 3.2:
HOW DO SCHOOLS COMPLY WITH TITLE IX?

WHAT WE KNOW

Title IX prohibits any federally funded education program or activity from engaging in sex discrimination. It says: "No person in the United States shall, on the basis of sex, be excluded from participation in, be denied the benefits of, or be subjected to discrimination under any education program or activity receiving Federal financial assistance" (20 U.S.C. Section 1681). So, what does this really mean? The following questions are frequently asked about Title IX. The answers are intended to both increase your understanding of the law and encourage you to advocate for schools to follow the letter and spirit of the law.

What Educational Areas Does Title IX Cover? Title IX covers admissions and recruitment, treatment of students, and employment. Title IX prohibits sex discrimination in *admissions* to educational institutions that receive federal funds. Most public and private schools, vocational schools, and even museums are covered because they receive federal assistance, such as Title I funding, student loans, or research grants. Institutions covered under Title IX may not do any of the following acts:

- Limit the number or proportion of persons of either sex admitted
- Prefer applicants of one sex by ranking applicants separately by sex
- Treat male and female applicants differently because of their actual or potential parental, family, pregnancy, or marital status or make pre-admission inquiries into same
- Discriminate based on sex when recruiting students
- Use tests for admissions purposes that have a disproportionately adverse impact on the basis of sex *unless* (a) the test validly predicts success in the program or activity in question, and (b) alternative tests or criteria that do not have a disproportionately adverse impact are unavailable.

Treatment of students covers all students—female and male—at every educational institution receiving federal funds. Title IX clearly makes it illegal to treat students differently or separately on the basis of sex. All programs, activities, and opportunities offered by a school district must be equally available. In addition, school districts are required to remedy the effects of past discriminatory practices with affirmative measures when necessary. This might mean actively recruiting girls for competitive athletics and counseling students to explore nontraditional course and career options. Without such affirmative steps, equal access often produces little real change because past conditioning has been so strong. Under Title

IX, students must receive fair treatment in the following areas:

Athletics	Career education
Counseling and counseling materials	Course offerings
Discipline	Employee assistance
Extracurricular activities	Financial aid
Housing and facilities	Marital and parental status
Pregnant and parenting students	Scholarships and honors
Sexual harassment	Student health and insurance benefits

Title IX also prohibits sex discrimination in all aspects of *employment* in educational institutions, including employment criteria, advertising and recruitment, hiring and firing, promotion, tenure, pay, job assignments, training, leave, and fringe benefits.

What Kinds of Schools Are Covered by Title IX?   Title IX applies to all federally funded elementary and secondary schools, colleges, and universities. It also applies to programs and activities affiliated with schools that receive federal funds (such as internships or School-to-Work programs) and to federally funded education programs run by other entities, such as correctional facilities, health care organizations, museums, unions, and businesses.

Although Title IX's prohibition against sex discrimination is very broad, some schools and activities are not required to comply:

• The membership policies of the Girl and Boy Scouts, the YMCA and the YWCA, Campfire Girls, and other single-sex, tax-exempt youth service organizations whose members are chiefly under age 19

• University-based social fraternities and sororities

• Activities relating to the American Legion's Boys State, Boys Nation, Girls State, and Girls Nation conferences

• Father-son or mother-daughter activities, so long as opportunities for "reasonably comparable" activities are offered to students of both sexes

• Scholarships or other aid offered by colleges and universities to participants in single-sex pageants that reward the combination of personal appearance, poise, and talents

• Schools whose primary purpose is training for the U.S. military services or the merchant marine, though some choose to voluntarily follow the law

Is There a Penalty for Title IX Noncompliance?   Yes! Schools can lose federal funds for violating the law. Ironically, although most institutions are not in compliance with Title IX, no institution has actually lost federal money because of a government investigation. That's what lack of enforcement has done.

However, the Supreme Court acknowledged in *Franklin v. Gwinnett County Public Schools* (1992) that institutions could be held liable for individuals in those institutions who participated in sexual discrimination. In this landmark case, the Supreme Court also ruled that plaintiffs could sue for monetary damages. This ruling increased the willingness of lawyers to take on Title IX suits, and also issued a wake-up call to school districts about the possible consequences of noncompliance (Fischer et al., 2002). Some schools have indeed been forced to pay substantial damages and attorney fees in cases brought to court by individuals, demonstrating the power of what a student or teacher who has a lawyer.

How Should Title IX Be Enforced?   The U.S. Department of Education's Office of Civil Rights (OCR) is the federal agency officially charged with enforcing the civil rights laws that prohibit discrimination on the basis of race, national origin, sex, disability, and age in educational programs that receive federal financial assistance. About 5,000 complaints are filed each year, and approximately 10% are Title IX cases. To initiate an investigation, individuals must file a complaint with one of the 12 regional enforcement offices throughout the country within 180 days of the alleged discrimination. A complaint can be filed by anyone who believes that an institution covered by Title IX has discriminated against someone on the basis of sex. A person does not need to be a victim of the discrimination to file a complaint on behalf of another person or group facing sex discrimination. Anonymity is maintained, and institutions are prohibited from retaliating against any complainant. OCR also initiates voluntary compliance reviews of schools and offers technical assistance to help schools adhere to Title IX.

OCR consists of administrative offices that are located at the U.S. Department of Education's national headquarters in Washington, DC, and 12 enforcement offices around the country under four divisions. (See the resource section for a list of these agencies and their contact information.)

How Is a Grievance Filed?   Several options are available: 1. A complainant can file a grievance using the internal grievance process of the school district. Title IX regulations require schools to adopt and publish grievance procedures that allow for prompt and equitable resolution of complaints. Equity assistance centers or the other resources described at the end of this chapter can help schools comply with the law and create gender-fair learning environments. 2. Complainants can also file a complaint with OCR. Submission of a letter describing the nature and impact of the sex discrimination is all that is required to file the complaint. Complainants do not need to seek legal counsel to file a complaint and are protected from retaliation, thereby reducing the financial strain of fighting sex discrimination. To lessen the emotional strain, complainants can request confidentiality. However, many complainants do not know their rights under Title IX or what acts are considered illegal under Title IX. Lucky for you, after reading this chapter, you will be a well-informed Title IX advocate! 3. Another option for complaint is to file a suit in court.

The United States Supreme Court in *Cannon v. The University of Chicago* (1979) ruled that an individual has the right to file a private lawsuit under Title IX. In *Franklin v. Gwinnett* (1992) the court extended the reach of Title IX, allowing individuals to sue a school district for monetary damages.

Are Males Protected Under Title IX? Yes, both male and female students, faculty, and staff are protected from discrimination and harassment.

INTERACTION 3.2:
What's Your "IX IQ"?

INTASC Principle 9: Reflection and Responsibility

The following case studies are designed to deepen and apply your understanding of Title IX. For each vignette, decide if the situation complies with or violates the law. After your selection, the correct response and supporting court decisions or Title IX components are described. Keep track of your rights and wrongs. A scoring system at the conclusion will determine if you've made the Title IX grade.

Career Education: What Can I Be? Rebecca's friends nicknamed her "computer whiz" after she installed memory chips and a CD burner into her family's computer. Her high school offers a career education track, and Rebecca decided to explore her options as a computer technician at Career Day. She was disappointed, however, when speakers and materials promoted nursing and child care as good careers for females and computer repair and electrical engineering as male endeavors. She wondered if her goal was realistic and grabbed material on cosmetology. Has Title IX been violated?

____ Yes. Title IX ensures that recruitment and counseling are gender fair.

____ No. Title IX cannot prevent career counselors from matching males and females with traditional gender occupations.

Answer: Title IX requires recruitment practices that are free from sex stereotypes. Recruiting methods, such as posters, pamphlets, and career day speakers, must not treat females and males differently and must avoid stereotypes that suggest men or women are better at certain jobs. Discriminatory recruitment and counseling efforts often track students into courses and programs on the basis of sex rather than on individual interests and talents. Institutions must meet the following standards:

- Provide students with information about all career opportunities, not just traditionally female and male jobs

- Ensure that recruitment practices, classroom treatment, assignments, facilities, career assessment tests, career counseling, and evaluations are free from sex stereotypes
- Provide referrals to nondiscriminatory training programs, nondiscriminatory placement efforts, and training programs with equal opportunity employers

Single-Sex Schooling: Can Separate Be Equal? Principal Goldberg, troubled by his middle students' low scores on standardized test scores, decided to create a new school policy: All courses will be single-sex courses. His thinking was that boys can be boys and girls can be girls in single-sex courses. According to Principal Goldberg, single-sex classes eliminate budding distractions from the other sex and help students focus on learning. Class times will be also staggered to avoid boys and girls mingling in the hallways. They might eat lunch at the same time, but they can't sit at the same tables. Principal Goldberg had done his homework: Some research shows that girls talk more and perform better in all-girl math and science classrooms, which might especially help those girls who are "bad with numbers," and in language arts classrooms, boys could read books about snakes, spaceships, and war without offending girls. The bottom line: Principal Goldberg needs reading and math scores to improve or his school could lose federal funding—and he could lose his job.

But several teachers are worried that single-sex classrooms adversely affect healthy social development of adolescents, not to mention the idea that schools are microcosms of society where females and males can learn to live and work together. One teacher quietly wondered if single-sex classes in public schools were even legal. Does Principal Goldberg's policy on single-sex schools comply with Title IX?

_____ Yes. Title IX states that single-sex classes are needed to make up for the long-standing discrimination females have encountered in schools.

_____ No. Separate is rarely equal. Single-sex education has historically resulted in unequal opportunities and resources for girls and women. We are not so far from the days when girls were required to take home economics and boys were required to take shop.

Answer: No. Single-sex classes may be created for compensatory purposes; however, a school district must demonstrate that the program will counteract current or past discrimination and that a single-sex environment is necessary for that purpose. Importantly, gender stereotypes cannot be relied on to justify single-sex environments. For example, an all-girls math program may be sustainable if a school district can demonstrate that the program intentionally and directly remedies discriminatory practices they have faced in pursing an interest in math. If, however, a program lacks a compensatory justification, and instead teaches math in a diluted form based on stereotypes that girls are "bad with numbers," it is not in compliance with the law. Consequently, Principal Goldberg's single-sex policy is illegal.

Furthermore, participation in single-sex classes must always be voluntary. Voluntary means both that the federal government may not require local school districts to implement single-sex classes and that local school districts may not require students to participate. Additionally, the Equal Educational Opportunity Act of 1974 prohibits assignment of students to schools solely on the basis of sex: "The maintenance of dual school systems in which students are assigned to schools solely on the basis of race, color, sex, or national origin denies those students the equal protection of the law guaranteed by the Fourteenth Amendment." Principal Goldberg's policy requires participation in single-sex schools—a violation of the law.

Title IX currently does permit single-sex classes under the following circumstances:

- In music classes, schools may have requirements based on vocal range or quality, which may result in all-male or all-female choruses.
- In elementary and secondary schools, portions of classes that deal exclusively with human sexuality may be (but are not required to be) conducted in separate sessions for boys and girls.
- In physical education classes or activities, students may be separated by sex when participating in sports where the major purpose or activity involves bodily contact (e.g., wrestling, boxing, rugby, ice hockey, football, basketball). Students may also be grouped in physical education classes by ability if objective standards of individual performance are applied. This may result in all-male or all-female ability groups.

The effectiveness of single-sex schools is a big educational question mark. Some studies show that they are more effective for girls than boys, others show that only lower class students benefit, and still others show that such schools intensify gender stereotypes and homophobia. Critics point out that many of the academic successes of these schools may be due to smaller classes, engaged parents, and well-trained teachers, not to their single-sex makeup (Campbell & Sanders, 2002; Woody, 2002).

Pregnancy and Parenting: What Are You Expecting? Teresa, a 10th-grade student, is pregnant and comes to your office clearly distraught. "My guidance counselor told me last week that I have to attend a special school that offers classes about parenting skills. No college prep classes at all. I want to continue taking geometry and chemistry. And Mr. Simone, my history teacher, informed me on Monday that I shouldn't expect any special treatment just because I'm having a baby. When I asked him what that was suppose to mean, he explained 'No makeups. If you miss an assignment, a pop quiz—too bad. You girls have to learn that there are consequences to your actions.' Well, he let a student with mono do makeup work last semester. It's just not fair." Do you agree?

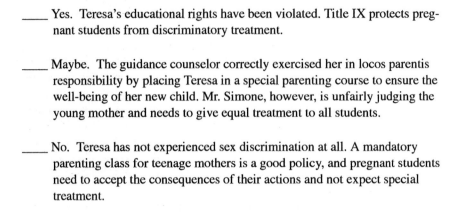

_____ Yes. Teresa's educational rights have been violated. Title IX protects pregnant students from discriminatory treatment.

_____ Maybe. The guidance counselor correctly exercised her in locos parentis responsibility by placing Teresa in a special parenting course to ensure the well-being of her new child. Mr. Simone, however, is unfairly judging the young mother and needs to give equal treatment to all students.

_____ No. Teresa has not experienced sex discrimination at all. A mandatory parenting class for teenage mothers is a good policy, and pregnant students need to accept the consequences of their actions and not expect special treatment.

Answer: Under Title IX, schools cannot treat students differently because of pregnancy, parenting, or marital status. Title IX prohibits schools from requiring pregnant students like Teresa to attend a separate school. Moreover, if Teresa chose to attend a separate school geared to the needs of pregnant and parenting students, that school would have to provide comparable learning opportunities. The recommended school in this scenario clearly does not. Mr. Simone's refusal to allow Teresa to make up work for health reasons while others are permitted to violates Title IX. Title IX includes specific guidelines related to this issue:

- Special programs: A school may not discriminate against any student in its educational program, including any class or extracurricular activity, because of the student's pregnancy, child birth, false pregnancy, miscarriage, or termination of pregnancy, unless the student requests voluntarily to participate in a different program or activity. Some schools offer special classes, programs, and extracurricular activities for pregnant students. A student can voluntarily choose to participate in such separate programs, but she has the right to attend the regular educational program if she so wishes. If a pregnant student selects a special separate program, the instruction she receives must be comparable to the instruction in the regular educational program.
- Homebound instruction: Schools may give instruction at home for students, who, for various medical reasons, cannot attend regular classes. Pregnant students who are physically unable to attend classes are entitled to homebound instruction.
- Medical disability: A school may ask a pregnant student to have her physician certify her ability to stay in the regular education program only if it requires a physician's certification for students with other physical or emotional conditions. Recipients must treat disabilities related to pregnancy the same way as any other temporary disability in any medical or hospital benefit, service, plan, or policy they offer to students. Pregnancy must be treated as justification for a leave of absence for as long as the student's physician considers it to be medi-

cally necessary. Following this leave, the student must be reinstated to her original status.

- Student health and insurance benefits: Student medical, hospital, accident, or life insurance benefits, services, or plans may not discriminate on the basis of sex. This would not bar benefits or services that may be used by a different proportion of students of one sex than of the other, including family planning services. Moreover, any school that provides full coverage health services must provide gynecological care. Institutions are not, however, required to offer abortions, though they may choose to do so.

Employment: Interview Jitters. Madison Pollack is interviewing for her dream job: teaching middle school science and directing the school's athletic program. Mr. Rodriquez, the school principal, seems impressed with her credentials. Madison feels confident and is glad to learn that Mr. Rodriquez and the school are committed to teachers and invest a great deal of resources into professional development. Mr. Rodriquez explains that he wants to ensure that this investment makes sense and inquires about Madison's long-range plans with the following questions: "Do you see yourself teaching at this school for a long time? Are you planning to marry or have children in the near future?" Madison's confidence wanes. If she answers a truthful "yes," will a job offer be jeopardized?

_____ Yes. School administrators must consider long-term staffing questions and are entitled to know about a potential teacher's long-term plans and job commitment. The questions are fair, and Madison should answer.

_____ No. It is illegal to consider marital and family status in employment decisions. Madison should avoid the questions.

Answer: The questions in this scenario are illegal. Before Title IX, school districts regularly gave hiring and promotion consideration to marital status and parenthood. For women, these were critical factors in being offered a job, and the "right" answer to ensure employment was, "No, I am not going to marry or have children." For male candidates, the question was less important and rarely asked. Now these questions are illegal. Interview questions must be related to job requirements. Questions about sex, race, religion, marital status, age, national origin, and disability are not allowed. Even requests for photographs along with applications are illegal. In *North Haven v. Bell* (1982), the Supreme Court affirmed that Title IX protects employees. Consequently, Title IX joins two other federal statutes, Title VII of the 1964 Civil Rights Act and the 1963 Equal Pay Act, to protect employees from sex discrimination.

Textbooks: The Characters of the Curriculum. Sadie is eager to begin her Introductory Physics course and already envisions constructing a hologram or space rocket as her final project. She even has her brother's graphic calculator to help with the difficult mathematical equations she'll encounter. Yet as Sadie flips through the pages of her textbook, her enthusiasm quickly erodes. There are neither pictures of women nor any mention of the contributions of female physicists. She wonders, "Do I really belong in a physics class?" Is the omission of women from the physics curriculum a violation of Sadie's education rights under Title IX?

_____ Yes. Title IX requires equal treatment of females and males in instruction and course offerings. When the contributions of women are omitted or minimized in the curriculum, females are discriminated against.

_____ No. Because of concern over potential conflict with First Amendment rights, Title IX does not address the use of specific texts or curriculum materials.

Answer. No. Protections under Title IX cannot violate the First Amendment right to freedom of speech. Consequently, Title IX does not cover textbooks. However, a school may establish its own curricular policy. Schools often decide that nonsexist, nonracist curricular materials provide a more effective education.

Financial Aid: Money Matters. As a secondary teacher, you are concerned with the manner in which scholarships and other financial awards donated by the local booster club and neighborhood businesses are distributed at graduation. You notice that nearly all of the awards are given to boys. You mention this to the principal, who explains that this has been the case for as long as anyone can remember. The organizations donating the scholarship funds use such categories as leadership skills and athletic accomplishments in choosing the recipients. The principal also admits that he tends to favor males over females when granting awards and argues that, though this is not exactly equitable, it is realistic because future financial burdens hit males more than females. Does this allocation of scholarships comply with Title IX?

_____ Yes. It is an unfortunate but realistic practice. Males are more likely to be leaders—in the classroom, on the athletic fields, and in the office—and inevitably will garner the lion's share of honors.

_____ No. It is illegal. You file a complaint with the Office of Civil Rights.

Answer. No. Title IX prohibits using sex as a criterion by which to grant awards, scholarships, or financial aid. Scholarship and aid must be awarded by objective criteria fairly applied without regard to sex. If it turns out that the most qualified students in a given year are predominately or entirely of one sex, that is acceptable, as long as the procedures and criteria have been fairly applied. But sex itself cannot be a criterion; this example is a violation of Title IX.

How should a school distribute scholarship awards? The fundamental principle is that the most qualified students receive scholarship aid, regardless of sex. If your school has one scholarship, then the most qualified student, female or male, should receive the award. If your school has five scholarships, then the top five students should be awarded those scholarships. It really does not matter if these top five students are all males, all females, or both. Simply stated, the awards go to the most qualified students.

There are, however, exceptions for athletic scholarships, foreign study awards, and single-sex scholarships established by will or trust:

- Athletic scholarships: An institution that awards athletic scholarships must provide "reasonable opportunities" for both sexes, in proportion to the number of students of each sex participating in interscholastic or intercollegiate athletics. Separate athletic scholarships for each sex may be offered in connection with separate male/female teams to the extent consistent with both the section on scholarships and the section on athletics.

- Scholarships for study abroad: The regulation exempts discriminatory student assistance for study abroad such as Rhodes Scholarships. Scholarship awards should be made equally available to both sexes.

- Single-sex scholarships: An institution may administer or assist in the administration of scholarships and other forms of student financial aid whenever a will, trust, or bequest specifies that the aid can go only to one sex, as long as the overall effect of making sex-restricted awards is not discriminatory. In short, the school should fund enough scholarship resources to honor both males and females equally.

Physical Education: Who Wants to Play?   As a physical education teacher you have grown to dislike coed classes, where students seem to abandon athletic skill development for social skill development. To avoid these coeducational problems, you try to separate the sexes so each can focus on athletic skills at their own level. You are pleased to learn that the local country club will now allow the school to use its golf course, but you worry that having female students swinging widely at the country club might lead to the end of the school's golf course privileges. You note that in a coeducational class more time is needed for teaching basic skills, but in the boys' class, more time is spent actually playing golf. It makes sense to have the boys register for the country club golf class while the girls register for the golf section that meets on the school field. You are amazed (and relieved) how the two classes fill up, but something still is troubling: are these all-boys and all-girls classes legal?

_____ Yes. Title IX requires that males and females be given equitable opportunities to learn and explore their athletic interests. The two-course solution allows both sexes to play golf and makes good pedagogical sense.

_____ No. Girls and boys may be separated under certain circumstances, but golf is not one. This violates the law.

Answer: No, this is not legal. Using skill levels to group students is legal, BUT using gender to group students usually is not. For example, if the teacher gave a skill test to each student to gauge golf skills, and then grouped students by ability as beginner, mid-level, and advanced, that would be legal. If all the boys were tested and found to be at the advanced level and all the girls tested and found to be beginners, that would be legal as well. But it is ability level—not an assumption of one gender being better in a sport—that must determine assignments. Obviously, some girls may be more skilled than boys, and an objective assessment of all students will best determine this, not sexist assumptions.

Title IX prohibits sex segregation in physical education classes except for the following:

• Students may be separated by sex within coeducational classes when participating in wrestling, boxing, rugby, ice hockey, football, basketball and other sports, the purpose or major activity of which involves bodily contact.

• Students may be grouped according to ability for instruction if the assessment is made using objective standards of individual performance.

• If students' religious beliefs prohibit them from participating in coeducational physical education, they may be excused from such classes or offered sex-segregated physical education.

Classroom Interactions: Having Your Say.   History has never been Hailey's favorite subject, but the current unit on the civil rights movement has really sparked an interest. In fact, she stayed up all night reading Fannie Lou Hamer's biography and even talked with her grandmother about sit-ins and bus boycotts. Every day in class, Hailey patiently waits for Ms. Friedman to call on her so she can share her ideas and ask questions. Hailey doesn't want to monopolize class time, so she even carefully writes down her top three questions. But Hailey is beginning to wonder if she'll ever have a chance to participate in the class discussion. Ms. Friedman almost always calls on the boys, even when Hailey raises her hand. Frustrated, Hailey decides that checking out a book from the library is her best chance at learning the answers. Is Ms. Friedman's discussion technique in violation of Title IX?

_____ Yes. Excluding females from classroom discussion creates different learning opportunities, a form of sex discrimination.

_____ No. The classroom is a busy place, with as many as a thousand teacher–student interactions in a day. To keep the classroom pace moving, teachers may unintentionally call on more active males.

Answer: Maybe. Teachers are often unaware of the way they interact with male and female students. Research shows that both female and male teachers are likely to call on male students more often. Whether inequitable instructional interaction is legal or not depends on the extent of the pattern of restriction or exclusion. Unintentionally calling on boys more frequently than girls is not illegal, though it may create an ineffective educational climate. However, a deliberate and consistent pattern of excluding students of one sex or restricting their opportunities for participation creates different educational opportunities and is illegal.

For equal opportunity in the classroom, teachers can develop other strategies for student participation besides hand raising—for example, writing each student's name on a card and using the cards to select students. Or set an expectation for full participation and call on students who don't raise their hands. Instead of a few students carrying the class, all students will be pulled into the learning process. Some students will feel intimidated anytime they are called on. Whether it is a lack of English language skill, a personal power strategy to shun the teacher's control, or even a cultural sign of respect, some students work to escape teacher contact. But in the American culture, success is related to acquiring a public voice. Students need to learn how to speak in class.

Sexual Harassment: Making the Grade. Christina, an 11th grader, confided in her guidance counselor, "I didn't do too well on a pop quiz in Mr. Armando's algebra class. Mr. Armando suggested I repeat the quiz after school in his office. I thanked him for the second chance, especially since I want to make honors this year. But then before I began the quiz, he started stroking my hair and whispering that I'd have to be 'nice' to him if I really wanted to bring up my grade. And then he asked me for a date. I felt really uncomfortable." Sexual harassment?

_____ Yes. Title IX protects against unwelcome sexual advances and requests for sexual favors.

_____ No. While Mr. Armando's behavior is suggestive, sexual harassment cannot be proven based on Christina's uncomfortable feelings. Without witnesses or evidence, this is a classic "he said–she said" scenario. Objective, rather than subjective, criteria are needed to exercise Title IX's protections against sexual harassment.

Answer: Yes. Educators wrestle every day with the challenge of helping students feel safe in schools, and they have both a legal and ethical responsibility to prevent and respond to harassment. What is sexual harassment? Is it what happens if a male student or teacher accidentally bumps into a girl in the hallway? Does it mean teachers can't hug students? That hand holding between students is wrong? Absolutely not! These are popular misconceptions. Sexual harassment is not an accidental jostle on the way to class, an encouraging hug, or a show of affection. Sexual harassment is unwelcome behavior of a sexual nature that interferes with a student's and a teacher's ability to learn, study, work, achieve, or participate in school activities. It includes the following behaviors:

- Insults and name calling
- Unwanted touching
- Offensive jokes
- Pressure for sexual activity
- Intimidation by words or actions
- Sexual assault or rape

Sexual harassment is a pervasive, harrowing part of everyday school life for students: Four of five students—male and female—report being harassed at school. Harassment ranges from sexual comments and gestures to inappropriate touching to rape. The consequences are troubling. Students who are harassed fear attending school, withdraw from friends and activities, and suffer sleep and eating difficulties (American Association of University Women, 2004).

Under Title IX, a school is required to have a policy against sex discrimination and notify employees, students, and elementary and secondary school parents of the policy. The law recognizes two broad categories of sexual harassment: quid pro quo and hostile environment. *Quid pro quo* is a Latin phrase meaning "this for that." This type of sexual harassment occurs when a person with authority over a student, such as a teacher or administrator, abuses that authority to get sexual favors. The scenario with Christina and Mr. Armando suggests a form of quid pro quo sexual harassment. Hostile environment consists of unwelcome sexual behavior so severe or widespread that it creates an abusive environment. This hostile behavior can be inappropriate spoken or written comments, or physical conduct. Here's an example:

Albert Feinstein is slender and not athletically inclined. In the locker room before gym class, his male peers tease him about his weight and clumsiness. Lately, they have taken to calling him "fag," "sissy," and "girl," and snapping their wet towels on his butt. Several times when Albert has opened his locker he has found a bra and girls' panties with his name written on them. After another boy 40 lb heavier than Albert pounced on him on a wrestling mat and simulated sexual intercourse, Albert began to skip gym class. Albert complained about these events to his physical education teacher, who replied, "Come on, Albert, loosen up and take it like a man."

A hostile environment usually involves a pattern of serious misconduct. An isolated incident generally does not make a hostile environment, unless that incident is very severe, such as unwanted sexual touching, sexual assault, or rape. On the other hand, one kiss on the cheek among young children would not create a hostile environment. The bottom line: Both quid pro quo and hostile environment demand that schools take prompt and effective action. In *Franklin v. Gwinnett* (1992), the Supreme Court extended the reach of Title IX, allowing students to sue a school district for monetary damages in cases of sexual harassment. The Gwinnett County case involved a Georgia high school student who was sexually harassed and abused by a teacher. The school district was instructed to pay monetary damages to the student—establishing a precedent.

Two relatively recent Supreme Court decisions make collecting personal damages from school districts more difficult. In *Gebser v. Lago Independent School District* (1998) and *Davis v. Monroe County Board of Education* (1999), the court ruled that a school district must show "deliberate indifference" to complaints about teacher and peer sexual harassment before a district would be forced to pay damages. Importantly, however, both *Gebser* and *Davis* made clear that the liability standards they established are limited to private actions for monetary damages. Nothing in either decision changes a school's obligation to take reasonable steps under Title IX to prevent and eliminate sexual harassment. Sexual harassment typically does not disappear when ignored—it only gets worse.

In March of 1997, the Office of Civil Rights released new guidelines for educators on Title IX, which make clear that one form of anti-gay harassment in schools—namely, harassment that creates a sexually hostile environment—is illegal under Title IX. Hostility and ridicule toward homosexual students may be actionable in court if they are sufficiently severe to limit or deny a student's ability to learn or participate in school programs. For example, in *Nabozny v. Podlesny* (1996), a gay student in Wisconsin was awarded a $900,000 judgment when his school district failed to end the violence he endured at the hands of classmates. This landmark case established that school districts must take action to protect gay students.

However, Title IX does not prohibit discrimination on the basis of sexual orientation. For example, if students heckle another student with comments based on the student's sexual orientation (e.g., "gay students are not welcome at this table in the cafeteria" or "we fear queers"), but their actions do not involve conduct of a sexual nature, their actions would not be sexual harassment covered by Title IX. Such behavior might well violate other school conduct policies.

Athletics: Leveling the Playing Field.   The superintendent has asked you to be the Title IX coordinator because the district's attorney just realized the district needed one. You and the high school's journalism teacher are good friends, and when you mention this new duty to her, she suggests that a student for the school paper write a story about Title IX and the responsibilities of the Title IX coordinator. You agree, realizing it's a great opportunity to educate students on their equity rights.

The day after the story comes out in the school newspaper, 10 girls who play on a club ice hockey team come to your office. They ask you to advocate making girls' ice hockey a varsity sport. The girls have already talked with the athletic director, who rejected the idea. The district eliminated the boys' ice hockey team last year because ice time at the city rink was too expensive. Consequently, there was no way the athletic director was going to even attempt to persuade the school board to fund a girls' ice hockey team. The girls claim that the district is just too cheap, citing that the girls' gymnastics team was eliminated last year to avoid replacing worn-out equipment. They are persistent and want to know what you are going to do to make the school district fund a varsity girls' hockey team. (New to the job, you quietly wonder how you will do this, too.) You tell the girls you need to investigate a few things before deciding whether or not you can fairly request funding for the team. And you promise to attend the girls' next club game.

At your request, the athletic director faxes data on girls' and boys' participation rates in athletics and wishes you luck in convincing the school board to fund a girls' ice hockey team the year after the board cut the boys' team. You look at the data and see that 52% of the students in your high school are girls and 48% are boys. You also discover that 40% of the school's athletes are girls and 60% are boys, but there are fewer boys' teams than girls' teams. Perplexed, you call the athletic direct and inquire why there are so many more boys participating in sports when there are fewer boys' teams. His answer: football. Is this high school in violation of Title IX? If so, what is the appropriate action to resolve the issue?

_____ Yes. Title IX requires a school to demonstrate that it offers equal opportunities for both males and females to play sports.

_____ No. Football necessitates big rosters, and the large number of males out for the sport unfairly limits the resources for female athletes. Consequently, football programs are exempt from Title IX.

Answer: Yes. Schools can show that they comply with Title IX if they can demonstrate any one of the following:

- Substantially proportionate athletic opportunities for male and female athletes
- A history and continuing practice of expanding opportunities for the underrepresented sex
- Full and effective accommodation of the interests and abilities of the underrepresented sex (schools do not necessarily need to offer identical sports, yet they need to provide an equal opportunity for females to play in sports of interest)

Were you able to pick out the key data in analyzing this scenario? The data reveal that the high school does not meet the "substantially proportionate" test: Because school enrollment is 52% female, 52% of athletes would be expected to be female. Moreover, because the district eliminated the girls' gymnastics team last year, despite interest, the district cannot show that it has a history and continuing practice of program expansion that is responsive to the developing interests and abilities of females. Finally, because there is an active girls' club hockey team that is interested in participating in varsity sports, the district cannot show that the current system fully and effectively accommodates girls' interest and abilities. The school's athletic program violates Title IX. The school could offer a girls' ice hockey team, or any girls' team of interest, to comply with the law. The school could also limit the number of players on the football team. Every school has choices about the size of their program and what sports are emphasized. Title IX is not intended to be a zero-sum game. The law is intended to ensure equality for both males and females.

As a general rule, institutions do not have to offer any particular sport. However, if an institution offers a contact sport (e.g., boxing, wrestling, rugby, ice hockey, football, basketball) to members of one sex, then it must also offer that contact sport to members of the other sex if (a) the opportunities for the excluded sex historically have been limited and (b) there is sufficient interest and ability among members of the excluded sex to sustain a viable team and a reasonable expectation of competition. If a school offers a noncontact sport to members of one sex, it must also offer that sport to members of the other sex if the previously cited conditions are true, unless members of the excluded sex do not have the skills to be selected for a single integrated team or to compete actively on such a team if selected. Schools also must ensure that male and female athletes are given equal treatment throughout the athletic program. Equal treatment includes the following areas:

- Coaching
- Game and practice times
- Medical and training facilities
- Equipment and supplies
- Locker rooms
- Practice and competitive facilities
- Publicity
- Recruitment of student athletes
- Travel per diem allowance
- Tutoring opportunities

It's important to note that schools do not have to provide exactly the same benefits and opportunities to specific men's and women's teams, as long as their treatment of male and female athletes is equal overall. Colleges and universities must also ensure that the overall share of athletic financial aid going to female athletes is about the same as the percentage of female athletes participating in the athletic program. Specifically, athletic aid for female athletes must be within 1%, or one scholarship (whichever is greater), of females' athletic participation rate, unless there are legitimate nondiscriminatory reasons to justify a larger disparity.

Scoring. This brief review of Title IX highlights the legal realities that surround today's classroom and the law's importance to teachers and students. It is your responsibility to stay current, not only on Title IX but also on the legal decisions that influence your actions inside and outside the classroom. Ignorance of the law is no defense. More positively, knowledge of fundamental legal principles allows you to practice preventative law—that is, to avoid or resolve potential legal issues before they become major ones. So how did you do on the quiz?

9–10 correct: Equity expert
7–8 correct: Soon-to-be legal eagle
5–6 correct: Promising advocate
0–4 correct: Fairness fumbler

ESSENTIAL EQUITY QUESTION 3.3:
WHAT'S NEXT FOR TITLE IX? EMERGING ISSUES

WHAT WE KNOW

Funding continues to be slashed for programs that support equity in education. In 1996, congress eliminated funds under the Title IV of the Civil Rights Act of 1964 that supported state Title IX coordinators and statewide gender equity training. The results are staggering. About half of the states have no employee designated to coordinate efforts to comply with Title IX, as required by the regulations (National Women's Law Center, 2002). Further, although 10 regional federally funded Equity Assistance Centers continue to provide gender, race, and national origin equity assistance to local school systems, the centers have received no funding increase in the last 5 years, despite a significant increase in requests for services following the loss of state department of education programs. Additionally, the Women's Educational Equity Act, the only federal program that focuses specifically on increasing education opportunities for women and girls, has had its funding eliminated.

Another challenge is the growing movement to roll back Title IX protections, especially in athletics. Opposition to gender equity in sports often comes from football coaches and athletes who fear that putting more resources into women's programs will mean taking away money from football. When Title IX was first passed, the National Collegiate Athletics Administration led a campaign to have football exempted from gender equity requirements, arguing that football teams produce profits that fund other sports. However, few football teams make a profit, and most run at a large deficit. In 1999, only 41% of football programs broke even (National Coalition for Women and Girls in Education, 2002). Opposition also arises from men's sports that generate low revenues and media attention, such as wrestling, golf, and gymnastics, arguing that as more women become athletes, there are fewer opportunities for men to play. This argument proves false. Female athletes at the high school level have increased substantially since Title IX—from 295,000 to nearly 3 million—but the number of male athletes has also grown and now approaches 4 million, an increase of nearly 500,000 athletes. Yet females are only 42% of high school athletes, and their participation rates are still below male pre-Title IX levels (National Coalition for Women and Girls in Education, 2002).

Following a contentious review of Title IX by a federal commission and faced with overwhelming support for the law, the U.S. Department of Education issued a "clarification" letter reaffirming Title IX policies. The department further proposed to better educate schools on Title IX requirements and committed to more stringent enforcement (U.S. Department of Education, 2004). The department's support of Title IX was considered a major victory for Title IX advocates concerned with a possible rollback of the law's protections. Enforcement efforts are focusing on the public information campaign to help schools comply with Title IX through the law's three-prong test. Calling the elimination of teams a "disfavored practice," the federal letter further promised to work with schools to find compliance remedies that do not cut teams, male or female. The letter also promised to "aggressively enforce Title IX standards, including implementing sanctions for institutions that do not comply" (U.S. Department of Education, 2004). As previously discussed, Title IX's most severe sanction—defunding an institution—has never been enforced. You may also hear the plaintive cry, "But what about the boys?" Are attempts to level the educational playing field for girls harmful to boys? Is education a "zero-sum game" where helping one group must come at the expense of another? This polarizing political ideology—known as the Backlash—blames the academic problems of boys on efforts to ensure equal educational opportunities for girls. Make no mistake: Boys merit our attention. Boys lag behind females in reading and writing, account for two thirds of all students served in special education, have a higher dropout rate, are less likely to attend college, and receive lower report card grades (U.S. Department of Education, 2001a, 2006). Yet these Backlash arguments create a false opposition between girls and boys, suggesting that helping one must come at the expense of the other. We often associate gender equity with equalizing the educational, athletic, and career playing field for girls. Title IX benefits everyone—girls and boys, women and men. Elimination of discrimination against women and girls has received more attention because females have historically faced greater gender restrictions and barriers in education. As Representative Patsy Mink noted, "Discrimination against women in education is one of the most damaging forms of prejudice in our Nation for it deprives a high proportion of our people of the opportunity for equal employment and equal participation in national leadership" (Congressional Record, 1971).

Yet gender bias is a double-edged sword. To much of the world, boys appear to be the favored gender, heir apparent to society's rewards. They are the recipients of the lion's share of teacher time and attention and the featured figures in most textbooks. Sitting atop high standardized test scores, they haul in the majority of scholarship dollars, claim more than half of the openings in the most prestigious programs, and are destined for high salaries and honored professions. Sometimes this extra attention is welcome; sometimes the spotlight is uncomfortable. Although boys rise to the top of the class, they also land at the bottom. Labeled as problems in need of special control or assistance, boys are more likely to fail a course, miss promotion, or drop out of school. Prone to take risks, they jeopardize not only their academic futures but also their lives as they dominate accident, suicide, and homicide statistics (Sadker, 2002). In fact, because the educational failures of boys are so visible and public, schools invest extra resources on their behalf. Girls suffer silent losses, but boys' problems are loud enough to be heard throughout the school. Clearly sexism is not a girls'-only issue. Until educational sexism is eradicated, all children will be shortchanged and their gifts lost to society.

INTERACTION 3.3:
Your Turn: Making the Case for Title IX (Authentic Assessment)

INTASC Principle 9: Reflection and Responsibility

INTASC Principle 10: Relationships and Partnerships

Ready to put your Title IX knowledge to the test? The following observations and questions will help you uncover clues to Title IX compliance in a school. They are not all-inclusive but serve as a springboard to your Title IX detective work. You are encouraged to adapt these or create additional ones. Your case will be built on documenting efforts to comply with the law as well as observations of attitudes related to Title IX and gender equity displayed by faculty, staff, students, and parents.

This activity is not a formal investigation, nor is it intended to be a threat of impending legal action. It is a social action research activity designed to motivate students and schools toward overall achievement of gender equity and Title IX compliance. You are encouraged to work with your school to make necessary changes and to seek outside help, if needed. You will find a list of resources at the end of this chapter. We can fulfill the promise of Title IX.

Share these Title IX compliance findings with your class. You may also choose to invite school administrators and other teachers. Try a variety of reporting methods, such as presenting statistics with graphs, creating a collage of Title IX artifacts or a mural depicting the school's equity climate, composing an equity song for the school, recreating through mime an equitable or inequitable behavior you uncovered, or simulating a gender-fair or biased interaction. Tap into your creativity and reflect on the following questions:

Compliance Checklist

To gather evidence, observe classrooms and extracurricular events; interview faculty, administrators, and your peers; and reflect on your own experiences in school.

Title IX coordinator
Is a Title IX coordinator assigned to your school? Is the name and telephone number of the Title IX coordinator made available to students, teachers, parents, and community members? How?

Title IX policy
Does your school district have a written policy on Title IX?

Suspensions and disciplinary referrals
Are gender patterns proportionate to the student body enrollment?

Course titles and descriptions
Do course titles and descriptions avoid referring to one sex?

Enrollment patterns by gender for each subject area and course
Note gender equitable and inequitable patterns.

Gender segregation patterns
Are males and females segregated in the classroom, in the lunchroom, on the playground? Is this segregation school, teacher, or student initiated?

Gifted and talented programs
Do enrollments reflect the student population? Do females and males receive similar opportunities?

Special education programs
Do enrollments reflect the student population? Do females and males receive similar opportunities?

Data collected on dropouts
Are there gender differences?

Counseling materials
Do counseling and guidance materials provide a balanced range of choices for females and males? Are these materials free from gender stereotypes?

Test scores and report card grades
What tests are used as part of the school's standard counseling services? Do results reveal gender differences? Do report card grades show gender differences?

Extracurricular participation patterns
What clubs and activities are available to students? What is the membership by gender? Is the number of females and males participating in an activity proportional to their school enrollment? For example, are the chess club and computer club predominately male? Are cheerleaders primarily female? Are females and males allowed to join all the school's extracurricular activities? Take a look at the leadership positions in these activities to see if gender balance exists. *Who runs for office?*

Athletics
Are participation rates for girls' and boys' programs in proportion to their respective school enrollment? What are total athletic expenditures for each gender? Are facilities, equipment, practice time, and game schedules comparable? Are the training, experience, professional qualifications, and number of coaches equitable? Are the mascots, emblems, and team names free from gender bias?

Physical education
Are girls and boys encouraged to participate in activities that have traditionally been expected for members of the other gender? Do girls and boys have equal access to facilities and equipment?

Treatment of pregnant and parenting students
What program options are available for pregnant students?

What programs are available for parenting teens?

Is participation in special programs voluntary?

If homebound instruction is provided for students with various medical disabilities, is this instruction available to pregnant students for reasons of medical disability?

> If your school requires a doctor's certificate for pregnant students to participate in or be excused from school activities, or to take a leave of absence, does your school also require a doctor's certificate for students with other medical disabilities?
>
> Are your school's criteria for honors and awards applied equally to married or pregnant students without differentiation on the basis of sex?

1. What did you expect to find about Title IX compliance in your school? Were your expectations confirmed or challenged?
2. How easy or difficult was it to find an item or information?
3. Describe people's reactions when you asked for certain items or information.
4. How would you assess the school's overall compliance level with Title IX? In what areas is gender equity achieved or encouraged? In what areas is gender bias revealed?
5. What steps will you take, individually and collectively, to strengthen gender equity and Title IX compliance in the school and to further your understanding of equity in education? Create pledge cards, contracts, or action plans that encourage advocacy. How can students and teachers assist each other to keep their commitments?

Although there has been progress during the past 30 years under Title IX, many battles still must be fought to eradicate sex discrimination in education and to enable females and males to realize their full potential. These barriers must be eliminated, and strong advocacy and enforcement of Title IX is necessary to open the door to equal educational opportunity. After 30 years of this important law, educators still fall short of the educational landscape that the late Representative Edith Green and former Senator Birch Bayh envisioned when they sponsored Title IX—namely, complete elimination of the "corrosive and unjustified discrimination against women" in education (Congressional Record, 1971). Educators must recommit to making the letter and the spirit of Title IX a reality across all areas of education and for all students.

RESOURCES

American Association of University Women

Hostile Hallways: Bullying, Teasing, and Sexual Harassment in School. Available at http://www.aauw.org/research/girls_education/hostile.cfm. This report investigates sexual harassment in public schools and explores differences in responses by gender, race/ethnicity, grade level, and area (urban, suburban, or rural).

A License for Bias: Sex Discrimination, Schools, and Title IX. Available at http://www.aauw.org/research/titleix.cfm. This publication examines uneven efforts to implement the 1972 civil rights law that protects more that 66 million students and millions of employees from sex discrimination in schools and universities. The analysis of non-sports-related complaints filed between 1993 and 1997 pinpoints problems that hamper enforcement and includes recommendations from Congress, the Office for Civil Rights, and educational institutions.

Single Sex Schools

"Challenging the System: Assumptions and Data Behind the Push for Single-Sex Schooling," by P. Campbell & J. Sanders, in *Gender in Policy and Practice: Perspectives on Single Sex and Coeducational Schooling* (A. Datnow & L. Hubbard, Eds.), 2002, New York: Routledge. Available at http://www.josanders.com/pdf/SingleSex.pdf.

Two respected educational scholars on single-sex education compare findings on whether girls learn better apart from boys. The article discusses early history, reasons why some advocate for or against it, and the mixed results for achievement, and the authors challenge the popular idea that single-sex education is better for girls than coeducation.

Equity Assistance Centers

http://www.ed.gov/about/contacts/gen/othersites/equity.html. The 10 Equity Assistance Centers are funded by the U.S. Department of Education under Title IV of the 1964 Civil Rights Act. They provide assistance in the areas of race, gender, and national origin equity to public school districts to promote equal educational opportunities.

I Exercise My Rights

http://www.titleix.info/index.jsp. I Exercise My Rights is a public service, informational campaign designed to educate the public about Title IX. Many people have never heard of Title IX. Most people who know about Title IX think it applies only to sports, but athletics is only one of 10 key areas addressed by the law. These areas are access to higher education, career education, education for pregnant and parenting students, employment, learning environment, math and science, sexual harassment, standardized testing, and technology. This Web site explains Title IX in easy-to-understand language and uses real case studies as examples. In addition, it provides ways to find out about Title IX in your local community and offers links to many governmental and educational organizations that promote gender equity in schools.

K12 Associates

http://www.k12associates.com/k12associates.html. K12 Associates helps elementary and secondary schools improve student achievement by building a climate in which students can learn. Students, staff, and parents learn to reduce bullying, sexual violence, harassment, and discrimination that is based on race or ethnicity, gender, disability, or sexual orientation and other protected categories.

WEEA Digest

WEEA Digest: What About the Boys? by M. Kimmel, 2000, Newton, MA: WEEA. Available at http://www.edc.org/WomensEquity/pdffiles/males.pdf. Explores the issues that boys face both in education and in our society.

National Coalition for Girls and Women in Education

Title IX at 30: Report Card on Gender Equity. Available at http://www.ncwge.org/. This collection of statistics and analyses marks the progress made and challenges still to confront after 30 years of Title IX legislation. The following educational areas are reviewed: access to higher education, athletics, career education, employment, learning environment, math and science, sexual harassment, standardized testing, technology, and treatment of pregnant and parenting students.

National Women's Law Center

Check It Out: Is the Playing Field Level for Women and Girls at Your School? Available at http://www.nwlc.org/pdf/Checkitout.pdf. Women and girls continue to make tremendous contributions to sports, and they, in turn, reap great academic, economic, social, and health benefits. Yet more than 25 years after the enactment of Title IX, too many schools still are not providing their female students with equal athletic opportunities. *Check It Out* is an important tool for women and girls at all levels of education, as well as for others interested in making sure that athletic opportunities are distributed fairly. The publication explains Title IX's requirements as applied to athletics and allows readers to examine their own schools' athletics programs to see whether males and females are treated equally.

Do the Right Thing: Understanding, Addressing, and Preventing Sexual Harassment in Schools. Available at www.nwlc.org. Designed for teachers, parents, and other nonlegal types, this manual focuses on sexual harassment of students and the legal obligations placed on schools to address it.

Putting the Law on Your Side: A Guide for Women and Girls to Equal Opportunity in Career Education and Job Training. Available at http://www.nwlc.org/pdf/ptl.pdf. For girls in middle or high school, or women in postsecondary or job training programs, this publication explains the laws that apply to career education and offers advice about how to deal with sex discrimination in such programs.

United States Department of Education's Office of Civil Rights

http://www.ed.gov/about/offices/list/ocr/know.html. The Office of Civil Rights provides complete Title IX regulations along with specific guidelines for preventing and addressing sexual harassment and achieving equity in athletics. A case resolution manual is also available online, with step-by-step guidelines for filing a complaint with the office.

Office of Civil Rights National Headquarters

U. S. Department of Education
Office for Civil Rights/Customer Service Team
Mary E. Switzer Building
330 C Street, SW
Washington, DC 20202
Telephone: 202-205-5413; 1-800-421-3481
FAX: 202-205-9862
TDD: 202-205-5166
E-mail: OCR@ed.gov

EASTERN DIVISION	SOUTHERN DIVISION
Office for Civil Rights, Boston Office	**Office for Civil Rights, Atlanta Office**
U.S. Department of Education	U.S. Department of Education
J. W. McCormack Post Office and Courthouse	61 Forsyth St. S.W.
Room 707, 01-0061	Suite 19T70
Boston, MA 02109-4557	Atlanta, GA 30303-3104
(617) 223-9662; FAX (617) 223-9669	(404) 562-6350; FAX (404) 562-6455
TDD (617) 223-9695	TDD (404) 331-7236
E-mail: OCR_Boston@ed.gov	E-mail: OCR_Atlanta@ed.gov
Serves: Connecticut, Maine, Massachusetts, New Hampshire, Rhode Island, Vermont	*Serves:* Alabama, Florida, Georgia, South Carolina, Tennessee

Office for Civil Rights, New York Office

U.S. Department of Education

75 Park Place, 14th Floor

New York, NY 10007-2146

(212) 637-6466; FAX (212) 264-3803

TDD (212) 637-0478

E-mail: OCR_NewYork@ed.gov

Serves: New Jersey, New York, Puerto Rico, Virgin Islands

Office for Civil Rights, Dallas Office

U.S. Department of Education

1999 Bryan Street, Suite 2600

Dallas, TX 75201

(214) 880-2459; FAX (214) 880-3082

TDD (214) 880-2456

E-mail: OCR_Dallas@ed.gov

Serves: Arkansas, Louisiana, Mississippi, Oklahoma, Texas

Office for Civil Rights, Philadelphia Office

U.S. Department of Education

Wanamaker Building, Suite 515100

Penn Square East

Philadelphia, PA 19107

(215) 656-8541; FAX (215) 656-8605

TDD (215) 656-8604

E-mail: OCR_Philadelphia@ed.gov

Serves: Delaware, Maryland, Kentucky, Pennsylvania, West Virginia

Office for Civil Rights, District of Columbia Office

U.S. Department of Education

1100 PA. Ave, N.W., Rm. 316

P.O. Box 14620

Washington, D.C. 20044-4620

(202) 208-2545; FAX (202)-208-7797

TDD (202) 208-7741

E-mail: OCR_DC@ed.gov

Serves: North Carolina, Virginia, Washington, DC

MIDWESTERN DIVISION

Office for Civil Rights, Chicago Office

U.S. Department f Education

111 N. Canal Street,

Suite 1053

Chicago, IL 60606-7204

(312) 886-8434; FAX (312) 353-4888

TDD (312) 353-2540

E-mail: OCR_Chicago@ed.gov

Serves: Illinois, Indiana, Minnesota, Wisconsin

WESTERN DIVISION

Office for Civil Rights, Denver Office

U.S. Department of Education

Federal Building, Suite 310, 08-7010

1244 Speer Boulevard

Denver, CO 80204-3582

(303) 844-5695; FAX (303) 844-4303

TDD (303) 844-3417

E-mail: OCR_Denver@ed.gov

Serves: Arizona, Colorado, Montana, New Mexico, Utah, Wyoming

**Office for Civil Rights,
Cleveland Office**

U.S. Department of Education

600 Superior Avenue East

Bank One Center, Room 750

Cleveland, OH 44114-2611

(216) 522-4970; FAX (216) 522-2573

TDD (216) 522-4944

E-mail: OCR_Cleveland@ed.gov

Serves: Michigan and Ohio

**Office for Civil Rights,
San Francisco Office**

U.S. Department of Education

Old Federal Building

09-801050 United Nations Plaza, Room 239

San Francisco, CA 94102-4102

(415) 556-4275; FAX (415) 437-7786

TDD (415) 437-7783

E-mail: OCR_SanFrancisco@ed.gov

Serves: California

**Office for Civil Rights,
Kansas City Office**

U.S. Department of Education

10220 North Executive Hills Boulevard

8th Floor, 07-6010

Kansas City, MO 64153-1367

(816) 880-4200; FAX (816) 891-0644

TDD (816) 891-0582

E-mail: OCR_KansasCity@ed.gov

Serves: Iowa, Kansas, Missouri, Nebraska, North Dakota, South Dakota

**Office for Civil Rights,
Seattle Office**

U.S. Department of Education

915 Second Avenue

Room 3310, 10-9010

Seattle, WA 98174-1099

(206) 220-7900; FAX (206) 220-7887

TDD (206) 220-7907

E-mail: OCR_Seattle@ed.gov

Serves: Alaska, Hawaii, Idaho, Nevada, Oregon, Washington, American Samoa, Guam, Trust Territory of the Pacific Islands

REFERENCES

American Association of University Women. (2000). *Tech-savvy: Educating girls in the new computer age.* Washington, DC: Author.

American Association of University Women. (2004). *Hostile hallways: Bullying, teasing, and sexual harassment in school.* Washington, DC: Author.

Campbell, P., & Sanders, J. (2002). "Challenging the system: Assumptions and data behind the push for single-sex schooling." In A. Datnow & L. Hubbard (Eds.), *Gender in policy and practice: Perspectives on single-sex and coeducational schooling* (pp. 31–46). New York: Routledge.

Cannon v. The University of Chicago (1979). 441 U.S. 677.

College Board. (2005). *College Board Services 2005.* New York: College Board.

Congressional Record 117 2658. (1971).

Davis v. Monroe County Board of Education (1999). 526 U.S. 629.

Educational Testing Service. (2001). *Differences in the gender gap: Comparisons across racial/ethnic groups in education and work.* Princeton, NJ: Author.

Fischer, L., Schimmel, D., Stellman, L., & Kelly, C. (2002). *Teachers and the law* (6th ed.). Boston: Allyn & Bacon.

Franklin V. Gwinnett County Public Schools (1992). 526 U.S. 60.

Gebser v. Lago Independent School District (1998). 524 U.S. 274.

Nabozny v. Podlesny (1996). No. 95-3634, 1996 WL 4208031, 7th Circuit.

National Coalition for Women and Girls in Education. (2002). *Title IX at 30: Report card on gender equity.* Washington, DC: Author.

National Federation of State High School Athletic Associations. (2004). *NFHS 2002-2003 high school athletics participation survey.* Retrieved July 1, 2005, from http://www.nfhs.org/scriptcontent/VA_Custom/SurveyResources/2003_04_Participation_Summary.pdf

National Women's Law Center. (2002). *Title IX and equal opportunity in vocational and technical education: A promise still owed to the nation's young women.* Retrieved June 22, 2004, from http://www.nwlc.org/pdf/TitleIXCareerEducationReport.pdf

North Haven v. Bell (1982). 456 U.S. 512.

Sadker, D. (2002). An educator's guide to the gender war. *Phi Delta Kappan, 84*(3), 235–240.

United States Department of Education. (2000). *Trends in educational equity for girls and women.* Washington, DC: U.S. Government Printing Office.

U.S. Department of Education. (2001a). *Elementary and secondary school compliance reports.* Washington, DC: U.S. Government Printing Office.

U.S. Department of Education. (2001b). *OCR annual report to congress, 2000.* Washington, DC: U.S. Government Printing Office.

U.S. Department of Education. (2004). *Notice of intent. Nondiscrimination on the basis of sex in education programs or activities receiving federal financial assistance* (67 Fed. Reg. 31,098). Retrieved March 13, 2004, from http://www.ed.gov/legislation/FedRegister/proprule/2004-1/030904a.html

U.S. Department of Education. (2006). *Digest of education statistics, 2005.* Washington, DC: U.S. Government Printing Office.

Woody, E. (2002). Constructions of masculinity in California single gender academies. In A. Datnow & L. Hubbard (Eds.), *Gender in policy and practice: Perspectives on single-sex and coeducational schooling* (pp. 280–303). New York: Routledge.

4

Citizenship Education for the 21st Century—A Gender Inclusive Approach to Social Studies

Margaret S. Crocco
Teachers College, Columbia University

Andrea S. Libresco
Hofstra University

This chapter is an effort to help preservice and in-service teachers and others think about how gender equity issues intersect with social studies. Attention is also paid to how gender, defined to include both boys and girls, relates to diversity. Our approach addresses four essential equity questions (EEQs), outlined later, for both elementary- and secondary- level teachers in training. The activities offered as part of the chapter can be done with students enrolled in social studies methods classes and can also be adapted for use with students in elementary and secondary classrooms and for professional development workshops.

The central premise informing our work is the idea that the field of social studies was created by educators early in the 20th century to help promote the development of effective citizens. Deliberations about individual identity, citizenship rights and responsibilities, and obligations to one's community are all at the heart of this subject. We believe that social studies education involves preparing students with the knowledge, skills, and dispositions necessary to lead informed, productive, and engaged lives as present and future citizens of a democracy. As a result, social studies education often leads to action that promotes the values of democracy, a subject we address in the last EEQ. The following EEQs are addressed in this chapter:

- **Essential Equity Question 4.1:** Who are our students?
- **Essential Equity Question 4.2:** Whose story gets told in my social studies classroom?
- **Essential Equity Question 4.3:** Which instructional and assessment approaches advance gender equity in social studies classrooms?
- **Essential Equity Question 4.4:** What kinds of citizens do we want to be—what do we know and believe about the implications of the citizenship mandate for social studies education?

Each EEQ includes two components: What We Know and Interactions. The What We Know component is a brief summary of gender-related research in social studies. Interactions are based on the research and suggest an activity that you can do to promote learning. Interactions challenge you to *inter*sect what you have read with *actions* you can do, in or beyond class. The final interaction is an authentic assessment task—a real-world evaluation giving you the opportunity to put your social studies and gender equity knowledge to work.

ESSENTIAL EQUITY QUESTION 4.1:
WHO ARE OUR STUDENTS?

WHAT WE KNOW

This EEQ starts from the assumption that nothing is more central to good pedagogy than knowing and understanding one's students. That doesn't mean, of course, that students aren't individuals or that all members of a group think alike, have similar values, or do things the same way. But knowing something about who our students are and something about their backgrounds and cultures can be quite helpful to successful teaching. Good teachers know their students as well as their subject matter, and they know how to translate the subject matter into effective learning activities for their particular students. This also means that teachers are reflective about who they are and how the differences between their own identities and those of their students may help or hinder the process of learning for their students.

Our Nation's Population. The U.S. Census Bureau has indicated that the population of this country is becoming increasingly diverse. For example, the Bureau predicts that the White population of this country will decline as a portion of the total from 76% in 1987 to 62% in 2040. During this same period, the Black population will rise from 12% to 15%. The Asian, Pacific Islander, and Native American population will grow the fastest, tripling to 24% from its 1987 level of 8%. During this same time, the Hispanic population will more than double by 2020, totaling 115 million people. These changes will result from different levels of natural increase and the effects of immigration. By the middle of this century, the "average" American will trace his or her roots to Africa, Asia, the Hispanic world, the Pacific Islands, or Arabia—almost anywhere but White Europe.

These developments are not confined to major metropolitan areas but reflect changes that are occurring in virtually every community in the United States. Furthermore, even teachers working in very homogeneous areas are preparing students for lives that will surely be lived in places and times with greater diversity than exists today in smaller communities. Thus, it is important that teacher educators prepare teachers and teachers prepare students for dealing with diversity of all types, including the diverse expectations many ethnic and religious groups hold for their daughters and sons.

In many classrooms, therefore, diverse and contradictory expectations may exist concerning what it means to be a young man or woman. Nevertheless, we take it as axiomatic that classrooms are gendered environments. Teachers need to be knowledgeable about how culture shapes gender-role expectations, because this knowledge will help them in understanding their students better and responding to their educational needs. Because social studies teachers take society—past, present, and future—as their subject matter, these differences in socialization, attitudes, and expectations will undoubtedly surface in discussions taking place in their classrooms.

How Do I See My Students? How Do I Define My Classroom Community?
In thinking about the diversity of students in a classroom, how useful is it to strive for color-blindness or gender-blindness? Are these reasonable aims? In other words, if a teacher tries to ignore race, ethnicity, and gender in the classroom, what's at stake? Do teachers benefit their students when they ignore their social location or wear "gender blinders" or "race blinders" in the classroom?

Let's look at this another way—from the standpoint of planning curriculum and pedagogy for students: If you know, for example, that many girls do better with activities structured toward cooperation rather than competition, do you teach to that strength (i.e., in cooperative rather than competitive learning modalities)? Or do you adopt the view that teaching strategies should help compensate for the weaknesses of the students? Can you do both at the same time? Why would this constitute the best pedagogy?

For example, it may be the case that some of the young women rarely speak during discussions in your social studies class. As the teacher, what do you want to do about that? What you do will undoubtedly depend on whether you think it is a problem if some students are silent during class. Is participation in classroom discussion an important skill in a social studies classroom? We certainly think so because it's an ability associated with being a good citizen—that is, to learn to speak one's mind in a reasoned fashion.

Research has shown that boys dominate classroom discussion (see Orenstein, 1995; Sadker & Sadker, 1994). Boys respond more quickly, loudly, and frequently to teacher-posed questions than do girls. As a result, boys may effectively shut many girls out of the conversation because of an aggressive classroom discussion style.

As a teacher, if you want to control this dynamic, it is important to keep in mind the importance of wait time in classroom discussion. You can do that by counting to five before calling on any raised hands; allowing for a second wait time by counting another 5 seconds after a student responds; using small group work; and monitoring the gender of those you call on for answers, trying to let one girl speak for every boy who speaks. This balancing act will benefit both boys and girls. The boys will learn to be patient, to be better listeners, and not to call out; the girls will learn to speak up and recognize that their voices are important to class discussions, too.

How else can you structure the discussion in a way that gives balanced time to the girls and boys, to the quieter students and the more outspoken ones? Think about learning strategies that provide a space for even the quietest students to speak up. It has sometimes been said that Asian American students don't contribute a great deal to classroom discussion, given a cultural view that takes the teacher's authority and expertise as the most important voice in the classroom. How can you encourage their participation? Would small group discussion, cooperative learning, or fishbowl conversations work as alternative ways of generating student participation? Do such contributions always need to come through discussion? In other words, could written reflections in student journals substitute for participation in discussion?

Finally, do you reward students who contribute to discussion and penalize those who don't? Some teachers develop techniques for scoring discussions; others decide they do not want to add or subtract points to a student's grade for classroom participation. What do you think about that issue?

In considering the community of the classroom, Nel Noddings, in her books, *Caring* (1984) and *The Challenge to Care in Schools* (1992), offered some general principles for thinking about the relationships built there. As teachers of social studies, you should model behavior that confirms your commitment to helping all students succeed. Knowing something about who your students are, the ways they may be alike, and the ways they may be different will help achieve the ends of gender-equitable and effective learning for all students.

Who Am I?   Learning about societies—American and others, past and present—lies at the heart of social studies. Identifying where a person is situated within his or her society involves figuring out social location. As a teacher, analyzing your own social location helps demonstrate the many ways in which you—and everyone else—are a composite of various traits (e.g., gender, race, social class, religion, ethnicity, language differences, geography). In other words, everyone has a multicultural self. Depending on the setting, these traits can make you feel part of the mainstream or on the margins. Different identity traits may be more or less salient to certain environments and certain situations. For example, in schools, verbal forms of intelligence often make a person successful. On an athletic team, kinesthetic intelligence is an advantage to some people and a disadvantage to others. Gender, like race, is a trait that is almost always shaping the ways in which social interactions are conducted, especially in schools and classrooms.

As a teacher, you will inhabit a social space called the classroom and share that space with students. Figuring out who your students are requires that you take a good look at yourself as a teacher. Acknowledging your social location may help you understand the limitations of your own perspective on some topics. Moreover, recognizing the interplay between social location and perspective taking is an important social studies skill.

Social Location and Social Studies Teaching. We believe that taking the social location of students into consideration in planning curriculum and pedagogy implies a set of good design principles for teaching:

1. Yes, it is important to remember that every student is an individual.
2. It's also useful to know certain generalizations about groups (e.g., Muslims do not eat pork, Blacks have been discriminated against in American society).
3. Not every generalization about a group will apply to each individual member of that group. Not all Asian Americans are good in science and math or even excel in school generally.
4. Avoiding stereotyping, either bad or good, as the previous example suggests, is important in recognizing that every student is an individual.
5. Assuming, for example, that all women are passive and shirk competition because women are inherently shy and retiring is a formula for trouble and suggests an essentialist notion about the meaning of being a woman. If you look at women's identities and roles throughout the world, you will find that, in some cultures, women are believed to be the more aggressive sex, whereas in others, they are believed to be the passive one. It is our view that socialization is the key to understanding who a girl (or boy) becomes as an adult.
6. Above all, in planning curriculum and pedagogy, it's important to keep in mind the idea that curriculum should provide both a window and a mirror (Style, 1988) for all students in the classroom and that good pedagogy means mixing it up. This means that using a variety of teaching strategies is the best way to create effective learning opportunities for all students, whatever their gender, race, intellectual aptitude, language background, and so forth.

INTERACTION 4.1:
Getting to Know Me

INTASC Principle 4: Variety of Instructional Strategies

Do some autobiographical writing, maybe a page or two, about how and why you came to be a teacher of social studies. Are there teachers in your family? What attitudes have your family members expressed about your decision to become a teacher?

Reflect on all the teachers you have ever had: How were they divided in terms of gender at each level—elementary school, high school, and college? Were the administrators in your schools mostly men or women? What about race? Have you ever had a person of color as a teacher, professor, or administrator? Share experiences with the class. Try to analyze the reasons for the patterns you uncover.

INTERACTION 4.2:
Educating Girls

INTASC Principle 2: Human Development and Learning

Consider the following statement from the *New York Times,* in its lead editorial on November 28, 1998: "Educating girls … is a good investment, producing lower birth rates, healthier children and a better-schooled and richer population all around" (p. A14). Why do you think the newspaper made this statement?

INTERACTION 4.3:
The Social Location of the Teacher

INTASC Principle 3: Diversity in Learning

Draw a circle in the center of a blank piece of paper. Draw spokes from the central circle to other circles and write your name in the center circle. Then, label each of the outer circles with a feature of your personal identity: gender, race, social class, religion, ethnic background, regional or national background, educational level, sexual orientation, marital status, family relations (e.g., brother, sister, mother, father), age, disability—whatever is important to you in defining who you are. Tease out all the different dimensions of your personal identity that come into play in the classroom when you enter the social space of the classroom. Write or discuss with a partner what difference you think this will make in your teaching and interactions with students (Style, 1996).

INTERACTION 4.4:
Gender and Education Worldwide

INTASC Principle 1: Subject Matter Knowledge

Discuss the role of education in the lives of women in the United States and around the world. You might begin with consideration of the educational aspirations of the students in your classroom. If you're student teaching in an elementary school, have the students poll their parents to discover how many of their mothers and fathers went to college. Today, women make up a larger portion of college students than do men. What about your student body? Do they aspire to college after high school graduation? Are there differences by gender in these aspirations? What about the community in which these students live? What defines the boundaries of their world and their experiences? Should social studies education open them up to broader communities? How important to these students is knowledge about broader communities, such as the nation, the state, and the world?

Not all women in the world have access to free, public, K–12 schooling. You may want to explore these national differences by using online and print media. One fascinating angle you might want to pursue is the relationship between education and fertility. It's been shown that as women's education increases, the number of children they bear goes down. These are the kinds of findings that you may want to discuss with your students. For comparative data on women and education, go to the United Nations's CyberSchoolBus web site to find statistical information about education in the countries mentioned: http:// www.cyberschoolbus.un.org/ infonation/info.asp

INTERACTION 4.5:
Women and Work

INTASC Principle 1: Subject-Matter Knowledge

Women who teach are also workers. In the United States in the 19th century, most teachers were men. Women did not have high expectations for their own educations. Gradually, during the 19th century, writers such as Benjamin Rush and Catharine Beecher encouraged women to pursue their educations so they could teach the next generation—inside and outside the house— to be good citizens. However, as teaching became "feminized," women were paid significantly less than men for the same teaching jobs. In fact, until the middle of the 20th century, many school districts stipulated that women teachers could not marry or get pregnant if they wanted to keep their jobs (Carter, 2002).

Interview a few female practicing teachers. Ask them about how their gender shapes their work or their prospects for advancement to department chair or school principal. Investigate the percentages of women who hold the following categories of education-related jobs in the United States:

- Elementary school principals
- High school principals
- Superintendents
- Assistant professors
- Associate professors
- Full professors
- College presidents of 2-year institutions
- College presidents of 4-year institutions

For historical background on women and their paid labor in the United States, you might want to read Alice Kessler-Harris's *Women Have Always Worked: A Historical Overview* (1981). Lead a discussion about women and work. Consider what you know about how women's opportunities for work have changed over the last century and reflect on the challenges of being a working woman today in terms of day care, household responsibilities, and pay equity. Describe how the following ideas fit your cognitive framework on this subject: *glass ceiling, glass escalator, pink collar ghettoes, double day,* and *sexual harassment.*

ESSENTIAL EQUITY QUESTION 4.2:
WHOSE STORY GETS TOLD IN MY SOCIAL STUDIES CLASSROOM?

WHAT WE KNOW

This question starts from the premise that knowledge is a social construction. In other words, people—in this case, mainly scholars of one sort or another—have created what counts for knowledge in Western society. Knowledge construction is a rational enterprise, and since the 17th century the standards of rationality have taken as their model science, which supplanted religion during the modern era as the arbiter of evidence, knowledge, and truth. The disciplines of history and political science, sociology, and anthropology all attempted to follow the model of science to prove their own validity. This effort was not always successful because propositions made in the humanities and social sciences tend not to be verifiable in the same manner that experimentation provides proof for scientific hypotheses. By contrast, most humanities and social science disciplines are "normative"—that is, propositions rest on values that are not susceptible to scientific proof.

Knowledge Construction.   Knowledge construction takes different forms in different disciplines. In this chapter, we focus on knowledge construction in history. We start by reviewing some obvious facts, beginning with the commonsense point, although sometimes dimly understood by students, that no one-to-one correspondence exists between the past (i.e., the complete) lived experience of all peoples during any one period in human *history* and what gets recorded as *History* (the representation of the past that is a tiny slice of that larger whole of past lived experience). As the celebrated historian Gerda Lerner (1984) liked to say, what transforms *history* into *History* doesn't happen randomly. We explore these ideas in more detail in the following sections and consider what the criteria have been that influenced this process of change.

Notions of Significance.   Over the period of history's evolution from the days of the Greek writer Herodotus, the father of history, to the professionalism of history in the United States in the 19th century, key considerations have governed the extraction from the larger whole of past experience to the distillation represented by recorded history. Often, the process of extraction and distillation is explained in terms of the concept of historical significance or importance. In other words, the events and developments that make it into history are what society deems important to remember. You are probably asking, "Important, how? In what sense do we mean something is important?" This is the pivotal question. You might also ask, "Important to whom?"

In what is, we admit, a gross oversimplification, the following formulation might be offered: In the ancient civilizations of the Middle East, historical matters often involved religion; in Greek and Roman history, military and political events garnered great attention; and, in medieval times, religion and politics were a central focus. But, in general, history followed power. Historical significance was determined by the people, activities, and instruments of power in a society. Since the democratization of the Western world order of the 18th century, scholars have gradually broadened the scope of what gets covered to include new fields of investigation, such as social history, labor history, African American history, and women's history. In other words, history has slowly begun to include the everyday lives of ordinary, working people in its sweep, but these developments have largely been 20th century phenomena. In sum, what a society deems important and, thus, what makes its way into history is governed by the values of that society.

Many women's historians, political scientists, sociologists, and anthropologists have noted the tendency to deal with power only in the public realms of life: typically, government and politics, economics and business. Because many women have been restricted from participation in these realms, their stories have taken place in the private realms of life, where little public record has been made of their experiences and contributions. Of course, a few exceptions exist, such as Queen Elizabeth, Marie Antoinette, and the like. But generally, women have lived their lives influencing the course of the world and its culture apart from the corridors of power that are represented in history books. They have done what Peggy McIntosh refers to in her speeches as "the making and mending of the social fabric." But in doing so, their stories have been left out of recorded history.

The Feminist Critique. Feminist scholars, both men and women, have suggested that the values governing selection of material that becomes part of the canon within the humanities, especially history, reflects a highly gendered set of values, which privilege public domains of activity over private life. Two books that help explain the process of knowledge construction from a feminist perspective are *Transforming Knowledge,* by Elizabeth Minnich (1990), and *The Creation of Patriarchy,* by Lerner (1984). Minnich's book deals broadly with many disciplines; Lerner focused on the origins of patriarchy, or male domination, in Western history. In Lerner's first chapter, she provided an excellent introduction to the issues of history versus History, which we're discussing here. In the appendix, she provided some useful definitions that help students understand how patriarchy has operated in Western civilization and the ways in which patriarchy has actually benefitted some women at the expense of others.

In applying these intellectual developments to education during the 1970s, scholars committed to sex equity focused on the problems of textbooks, which almost universally perpetuated stereotypes about women and men. Teacher educators such as Janice Trecker, Mary Kay Tetreault, and Myra and David Sadker took a look at popular textbooks to see what coverage women received in them. In an article published in 1971 in the National Council for the Social Studies journal *Social Education,* Trecker talked about the role schools played in perpetuating stereotypes of women. She posed the following question: Are the stereotypes that limit girls' aspirations present in high school history texts? Her answer was a resounding "yes" (p. 148). In the 1980s, Tetreault's (1986) study of another 12 popular high school American history textbooks found that copy devoted to women did not exceed 8% in any text surveyed and was less than 5% in more than half the books. A few years later, the Sadkers (1995) took a look at Prentice Hall's 1992 *A History of the United States* by Boorstin and Kelley. They found a text that had four males for every female. Less than 3% of the thousand pages of history were about women; only eight women had as many as 25 lines (about a paragraph or two) written about them.

In the 1990s, Jane Bernard-Powers (1995) reported that the K–12 curriculum "had not been receptive to change," commenting:

But in the K–12 social studies curriculum women of all classes, races, and ethnicities; women who are differently abled; women who are heterosexual; and women who are lesbian are still in the margins of the text, or invisible— along with their perspectives, experiences, and connections to each other, to men, and to children. (p. 192)

Bernard-Powers (1995) also discussed the role of curriculum standards and frameworks in retarding the process of curriculum transformation. Today, educators might add that high-stakes testing has pushed the curriculum in many fields in more traditional directions. Curriculum frameworks shape textbooks, Bernard-Powers pointed out, and this continues to undermine the process of gender-balancing the social studies curriculum, because women's stories, lives, and experiences are so often taken to be less significant than military, political, and economic power in our society. When gender intersects with race, the results are even worse, according to Darlene Clark-Hine, a Black historian, who made the following statement to an audience of social studies educators about her analysis of four history textbooks: "The authors ... consistently fail[ed] to provide an appropriate social, political, or cultural context for the Black Woman. People of color were marginalized and the dominant narrative requires a total re-conceptualization" (1990, as quoted in Bernard-Powers, 1995, p. 197).

Periodization. In this chapter, we discuss some of the issues raised by scholars around what's called "transforming curriculum" for gender balancing and multicultural considerations. Several models exist that the teacher educator or teacher might find useful which will be discussed below. One of the interesting dilemmas posed by women's history scholars has to do with the process of periodization, a staple feature of historical representation of the past. Scholars put large blocks of time together in what are called "periods" of history. These divisions help those who read and study the past to understand the large themes or developments that characterize a large span of time, perhaps as much as 500 years. In traditional history, labels such as the Renaissance, a time of tremendous creative flowering in the arts, letters, and scientific study, are familiar to many people.

Women historians suggest, however, that traditional periodization has ignored women's history and that when women are included in the sweep of history the labels don't always make sense as measured against women's experiences. For example, the Renaissance, according to Kelly (1984), was a period of retreat and retrenchment for women's liberties and social prerogatives from the more open and flexible period of the late Middle Ages. But reperiodization is no easy task because these labels are cemented in our collective consciousness. In fields other than history, reconceptualization is also a challenge. For example, the familiar stage theories of moral (Lawrence Kohlberg) and cognitive (William Perry) development were based on a sample of young White men and have been criticized as not being appropriate for women's development in these domains. But changing familiar labels is difficult.

Transforming Curriculum. Reconceptualization poses challenges for teachers interested in incorporating the study of women into history. New questions must be asked. Teachers need to be careful that the conventional periodization of history doesn't blind them to what was happening to diverse women or pressure them to force women's history into an ill-fitting garment. In Crocco's (1997) article "Making Time for Women's History," she used an antebellum example that suggests the manner in which this period can be taught from a variety of perspectives—political, economic, or social—either to enhance or constrain the attention given to women during those decades. In another case, "Women's History of the 1920s" (Crocco, 1995), she gave a 20th century example that also illustrates how women's history can be woven into the conventional portraits of an era found in standard secondary textbooks. Many other examples are available in the literature today. A textbook series that does an excellent job of incorporating women's and multicultural history throughout the full sweep of American history is *A History of Us* by Joy Hakim (1993). What comes across in such works (see also Takaki's, 1993, *A Different Mirror: A History of Multicultural America*) are the roles of positionality and perspective in history. As shown in EEQ 4.1, every historical actor operates from a particular social location or position that shapes his or her perspective on life. Positionality and perspective taking in history suggest that different individuals, situated in radically different places, may have very different interpretations of the meaning of past or present experience.

Of course, history is only one of the disciplines or subject matters taught as part of the social studies. Challenges have occurred in other disciplines from women scholars who have highlighted the partialities and misrepresentations that occur in a domain of knowledge when the experiences of the part (men) have been substituted for those of the whole (men and women). As we have seen, much of the research on cognition and moral reasoning was done with all-male student samples. In the past 20 years, scholars such as Carol Gilligan (*In a Different Voice*, 1982) and Mary Belenky and colleagues (*Women's Ways of Knowing*, 1997b) have revised the theories of Kohlberg and Perry, respectively, about moral reasoning and cognition.

In economics, sociology, anthropology, and political science, a number of scholars have investigated the effects of globalization and development of third-world countries on women, the different socialization processes of girls and boys, and gendered definitions of citizenship, to name just a few topics. This scholarship is, however, more readily available on the university level. Teachers at the K–12 level will have to be inventive in bringing gender and diversity questions to bear on teaching social science disciplines. They could ask about the effects of economic or political change on women or raise the question of gender (and race and class) whenever discussing politics, probing to see if the overall picture represented in texts applies equally to men and women. Since the 1980s, the gender gap in voting has been much discussed. Teachers can explore this topic online at the Center for American Women and Politics of the Eagleton Institute at Rutgers University or do a Lexis-Nexis search on this subject. The point is to bring gender into the classroom as a frame of reference no matter what social studies topic is being explored.

So when we ask the question "Whose story gets told in my classroom?" we are moving into the realm of gender-balancing the curriculum—that is, bringing a gender perspective into the classroom. When we add considerations of diversity to the mix, as most multicultural education scholars encourage, then we look at gender in relation to race, diversity, physical challenges, and sexual orientation. Teachers should ask themselves the following questions: Are any of these categories of persons invisible in my curriculum? Why is this so? How do I bring these stories into the classroom? Where will I find time to do it all? Remember, balancing the curriculum is a holistic process. That means you should look at everything you teach and find opportunities to raise questions about gender and diversity as appropriate and effective. Clearly, only doing this 5% or 10% of the time doesn't seem equitable; doing it 100% of the time may be a long-term goal for teachers over the course of several years. But incremental change toward a balanced curriculum for gender and diversity ought to be the immediate task at hand.

Mary Kay Tetreault's Approach. For a detailed presentation of what Tetreault calls the stages of thinking about women in history, see Tetreault (1986, 1987). She described the following stages of curriculum transformation (Tetreault, 1986):

1. Male history: The absence of women is not noted. There is no consciousness that the male experience is a "particular knowledge" selected from a wider universe of possible knowledge and experience. It is valued, emphasized, and viewed as the knowledge most worth having.
2. Contribution history: The absence of women is noted. There is a search for missing women according to a male norm of greatness, excellence, or humanness. Women are considered as exceptional, deviant, or "other." Women are added into the traditional structure of the discipline but the structure and methodology are not challenged. In this sort of "contribution history," women such as Queen Elizabeth, Molly Pitcher, and Marie Curie "stand in" for all the other missing women in history.
3. Bifocal history: Human experience is conceptualized primarily in dualist categories: male and female, private and public, agency and communion. Emphasis is on a complementary-but-equal conceptualization of men's and women's spheres and personal qualities. There is a focus on women's oppression and misogyny. Women's efforts to overcome that oppression are presented.
4. Feminist history: Scholarly inquiry pursues new questions, new categories, and new notions of significance that illuminate women's traditions, history, culture, values, visions, and perspectives. The public and the private are seen

as a continuum in women's experiences. Efforts are made to reconceptualize knowledge to encompass the female experience. The conceptualization of knowledge is not characterized by disciplinary thinking but becomes multidisciplinary.

5. Multifocal, relational history: A multifocal, gender-balanced perspective is sought which serves to fuse women's and men's experiences into a holistic view of human experience. At this stage scholars are conscious of particularity, while at the same time identifying common denominators of experience. They must begin to define what binds together and what separates the various academic disciplines. Scholars have a deepened understanding of how the private as well as the public form a continuum in individual experiences. ... Efforts are made to reconceptualize knowledge to reflect this holistic view of human experience. The conceptualization of knowledge is not characterized by disciplinary thinking but becomes multidisciplinary. In this sort of history, families and communities as well as nation states and mass political organizations are considered appropriate topics for exploration; men's lives as well as women's lives are studied using tools drawn from the arts and literature as well as from economics and politics. (pp. 215–217)

Bias in Textbooks.   We've already considered the meaning of bias in relation to prejudice and stereotyping of other people. In this section, we consider the different forms of bias often found in curriculum materials. Sadker and Zittleman (2002) have identified these forms of bias as follows:

• Invisibility: Certain groups have been underrepresented in education, by the media, and in materials. The significant omission of women and people of color has become so great as to imply that these groups are of lesser value, importance, and significance in our society.

• Stereotyping: By assigning traditional and rigid roles or attributes to a group, materials and activities stereotype and limit the abilities and potential of that group. Stereotyping denies everyone knowledge of the diversity, complexity, and variation of any group of individuals.

• Imbalance/Selectivity: The media and text materials have perpetuated bias by presenting only one interpretation of an issue, a situation, or a group of people. This imbalanced account restricts the knowledge of students regarding the varied perspectives and alternative possibilities.

• Unreality: Materials, media, and books have frequently presented an unrealistic portrayal of history and contemporary life experience. Controversial topics have been glossed over and discussions of discrimination, sexual harassment, and prejudice have been avoided.

• Fragmentation/Isolation: By separating issues related to people of color and women from the main body of schooling, instruction has implied that these issues are less important than and not a part of the cultural mainstream.

• Linguistic bias: Materials and conversation reflect the discriminatory nature of the dominant language. Masculine terms and pronouns, ranging from *our fore-fathers* to the generic *he,* have denied the participation of women in our society.

• Cosmetic bias: Textbook publishers are aware that educators and reform movements are demanding better, fairer, and more comprehensive materials in education. To rewrite texts requires thorough research and infusion. Occasionally, publishers and authors minimize the process by creating an illusion of equity. Two common shortcuts are to place large pictures of nontraditional people (in the beginning of the book or at the front of major chapters) with little evidence of content inclusion and to add special focus sections that discuss yet segregate tasks of underrepresented groups with exceptional or stereotypic stories (p. 62).

INTERACTION 4.6:
Arrangement of History Events

INTASC Principle 1: Subject-Matter Knowledge

History deals with chronology; its essence is the consideration of time and shaping of past events into periods or epochs that help people make sense of the long chronicle of the past by breaking it into segments for greater sustained understanding by students. What historians call periodization is essential to the process of making History from history by selecting some events from the past that seem to go together and arranging them into periods that are given names that conceptualize the larger changes at work in any given block of time. Devise a timeline of 20th century U.S. history that does not rely on wars as the key markers for the century. Do the same for the 19th century. Was this difficult? What other events, episodes, and developments did you turn to in place of military history to structure your timeline?

INTERACTION 4.7:
Oral History Project

INTASC Principle 4: Variety of Instructional Strategies

Take an oral history from another person in your class. Interview the person for 60 to 90 minutes. (For help in getting started on oral history see www.lib.berkeley.edu/BANC/ROHO/1minute.html. This site provides the "One-Minute Guide to Oral Histories" by Carole Hicke.) Look over the transcript of your interview with the goal of developing themes to periodize the person's life, outside the conventions of childhood, school years, adolescence, adulthood, and so on. Come up with an original set of periods that break the life you've just learned about into coherent parts with main themes for each.

Compare the periods of your interviewee's life to traditional political/military periodization found in a text. Which periodization works better for describing the particular life you have studied? Would the lives of people of differing genders, races, ethnicities, classes, abilities, and sexual orientations lend themselves to different periodizations? Why or why not? How well are these different histories represented in History? Is this hard? What gets left out? Emphasized? Deemphasized? Is the operation of selectivity of emphasis clear to you after engaging in this process? Could bias play a role in your selection and emphasis?

INTERACTION 4.8:
Detecting Bias in Texts

INTASC Principle 1: Subject-Matter Knowledge

Assume that you find the following statements in your history book. Circle the letter A if you think the statement is essentially accurate or the letter D if you think it is basically inaccurate or distorted.

A   D   1. Alone in the wilderness, the frontier family had to protect itself from wild animals and unfriendly Indians.

A   D   2. The Chinese were willing to work for what other laborers considered very low wages.

A   D   3. Japanese Americans, interned in concentration camps during WWII, were victims of hysteria brought on by the war.

A   D   4. Not until 1920 did the Constitution give all American women the right to vote.

A   D   5. The president wears many hats. He can be Chief of State, Commander-in-Chief, Chief Diplomat, Party Chief, Chief Legislator, or Chief Executive, sometimes all in the same day!

A   D   6. The availability of birth control information was, perhaps, more important for changing women's lives than was suffrage.

After completing this exercise on your own, share your responses with your classmates. As you will note, the wording of these sentences can convey meanings that may not reflect all sides of the story. For example, in labeling Indians as unfriendly, the first sentence is told from the frontier family's point of view and does not look at westward expansion from the Native Americans' perspective. In the second example, the word *willing* suggests that the Chinese immigrants were happy to accept substandard wages, when the reality was that they had little real choice, given the discrimination they faced. The third sentence seems accurate, given that hysteria could characterize the post-Pearl Harbor mood of the country; however, while hysteria is an explanation for internment, it is not the only explanation. Prejudice and racism may certainly be contributory factors when one notes that only the racially distinct group was incarcerated without due process. Sentence four also seems accurate enough, until one probes deeper. The use of the word *give* implies that suffrage was achieved without any struggle, when, in fact, women were hauled off to jail, went on hunger strikes, and were force fed in prison. In addition, it is worth noting that although the 19th Amendment gave all women the constitutional right to vote, Black women in the South were not beneficiaries of that right until the struggles of the civil rights movement led to federal legislation and a constitutional amendment, both enforced by the federal government. The fifth sentence reveals a gender bias in language in the use of the pronoun *he*. Although the nation has, to date, had only male presidents, when speaking of an office holder generically, either gender should be referred to; the language used to describe the possible president, then, must be gender neutral.

Perhaps the texts from which the first five statements were taken contain more explanatory information that balances each of the single sentences presented here; context is important, to be sure. But the skills being taught here—reading with a critical eye, being attentive to particular language, analyzing the perspectives represented—are skills that teachers and students need to be equipped with as they approach any text. The final sentence, assessing the impact of birth control vis-à-vis suffrage on the lives of women, is the only one not taken from a text, namely because the impact of birth control is rarely addressed in any depth in most texts. In fact, birth control has had a profound effect on women's health, reproductive patterns, and work lives, not to mention its effect on family size, demographics, and men's work lives. This sentence reminds us that, in addition to analyzing our texts for bias, we must also be attentive to sins of omission—that is, whole topics left out or watered down because they are deemed too controversial.

The examples commit a sin of omission, themselves. They do not address the issue of class. As Loewen (1995) pointed out in *Lies My Teacher Told Me: Everything Your American History Textbook Got Wrong*, neither do most textbooks. One way to explore the issue of social class in history is to read and discuss the Bertolt Brecht poem, "Questions from a Worker Who Reads." This poem is available online on many web sites. As the title suggests, it asks a series of questions including

"Who built Thebes of the seven gates?" It goes on to address the following point: "In the books you will find the names of kings" and then asks another probing question: "Did the kings haul up lumps of rock?" Read the whole poem and discuss how Brecht would answer the question "Who makes history?" What are the implications of this poem for the teaching of history? What kind of content information do we need to have as teachers to honor the spirit of the poem?

It is important to allow students to take action when they discover their texts are biased. Most students cannot write in their texts; however, adhesive notes can achieve the same effect. Students can write "corrections" or include supplementary material (such as information from the varied oral histories they conduct) to balance the bias in their school texts. Thus, students will not feel that, having detected biases, they are stuck with them. In addition, they will have the satisfaction of knowing that their adhesive notes will be read and thought about by future students who use the imperfect text.

- How reflective of present-day texts is this activity?
- To what extent do you find bias when you analyze texts in your field placement?
- Which types of bias do you find?
- What can this exercise tell your students about how to approach their textbooks?
- What proportion of your teaching should include a textbook?
- What other sources can be used to supplement a textbook?

INTERACTION 4.9:
Detecting Bias in Tests

INTASC Principle 1: Subject-Matter Knowledge

Now that your antennae are up with respect to bias, it is worth checking other materials used in your classroom. Assess teacher-made and state history tests by creating categories of analysis, perhaps looking for a representation of social, economic, and political history, then doing an item analysis of both the multiple-choice and the writing portions of the tests. Are the tests you construct, and those of the teachers you observe, attentive to issues of bias? Do your tests and any standardized tests you are required to use reflect a range of perspectives and the stories and experiences of a variety of people?

INTERACTION 4.10:
Detecting Bias in the Classroom

INTASC Principle 6: Communication Skills

Review the bulletin boards in the classrooms in which you observe. What kinds of historical figures are highlighted? All the presidents? Any women? People of color? Which of the forms of bias that Sadker and Zittleman (2002) talk about as present in texts are present on the walls of the classrooms and hallways? Create a list of materials you would want for your ideal classroom. Analyze this list for forms of bias. How can your ideal list be achieved if your materials budget is small?

INTERACTION 4.11:
Women's History Month—To Celebrate or Not to Celebrate?

INTASC Principle 1: Subject-Matter Knowledge

Depending on what month you undertake an analysis of bulletin boards, your results may be quite different. An investigation done in February may reveal many more Black figures than any other month, owing to Black History Month; similarly, Women's History Month in March may yield an unusual number of female faces. A question worth pondering, then, is whether setting aside special months devoted to particular groups is the most desirable method of addressing gender and diversity in the social studies curriculum. To which of Tetreault's stages does the celebration of Women's History Month correspond? What are arguments for and against focusing on separate months for particular groups versus integrating the histories of groups throughout the curriculum? What do you think is the better approach for addressing gender and diversity in the social studies curriculum?

ESSENTIAL EQUITY QUESTION 4.3:
WHICH INSTRUCTIONAL AND ASSESSMENT APPROACHES ADVANCE GENDER EQUITY IN SOCIAL STUDIES CLASSROOMS?

WHAT WE KNOW

Most of the time in any "Methods of Teaching Social Studies" course is devoted to examining and creating curriculum and approaches to instruction and assessment that will best serve all students. This EEQ starts from the assumption that constructivism is the best means toward that end. When we speak of constructivism, we mean an educational practice where meaning is intimately connected with experience. Students come into a classroom with their own experiences; they reformulate their existing cognitive maps only if new information or experiences are connected to knowledge already in memory. Inferences, elaborations, and relationships among old perceptions and new ideas must be personally drawn by the students for new ideas to become integrated as useful parts of their memories. Rote memorization of information that has not been connected with learners' prior experiences will be forgotten quickly. In short, learners must actively construct new information that enters their existing mental frameworks for meaningful learning to occur.

Constructivist Approaches to Teaching Social Studies.   Constructivism differs from the traditional knowledge reproduction model of teaching that is practiced in many American classrooms, whether grade school or college level, and is driven by teacher talk and heavily dependent on textbooks for the structure of the course. In these traditional classrooms, the idea is that a static body of information exists that students acquire from the teacher. The notion that students learn by making their own meaning, is underscored by the finding of Alleman and Brophy (1993) that what college students remember of their elementary social studies classes are the activities and concepts they created and learned directly from their experiences in those classes.

What do you remember from your K–12 social studies classes? To what extent did the teachers you had from kindergarten through high school follow the constructivist approach, even if they didn't call it that? What kinds of specific activities do you think would be consonant with a constructivist approach? What types of teaching would be dissonant?

Gender Equity and Social Studies Knowledge.   Although the attention to gender in social studies education began in the 1970s with a focus on the silence in history books about women's lives, the topic of gender in the 21st century encompasses so much more. Equally important as issues of representation in texts and curricular content decisions are issues involving methodology. Studying how women learn must also be a component of any analysis of gender and social studies education.

Women who express themselves, as Gilligan (1982) wrote, "in a different voice" from that of men; women as learners different from men, with, what Belenky et al. (1997b) called "different ways of knowing;" women who may identify more with what Noddings (1984) termed an "ethic of care" than with a framework of rights are all women who need a greater variety of methods of instruction than those traditionally offered in secondary and postsecondary education.

Belenky and her colleagues (1997b) added new depth to the understanding of ways many women learn. Their work focused on women's preference for connected knowing (consciously subjective, relational, integrative, and empathic) as contrasted with the separate knowing (objective, dispassionate, and abstract) often fostered in formal education environments. Their interviews with college women revealed that a loss of voice is common among them, as many talked of being so afraid of saying something stupid that they chose to say nothing at all. Therefore, classes where professors started with students' experiences made students feel more powerful than those that began with an assumption of the professor's knowledge and the students' ignorance.

Some of the women in the study commented on their discomfort with "experts" who tried to assert dominance over less knowledgeable people either by assaulting them with information or by withholding it. Belenky and her colleagues (1997b) also challenged the conventional wisdom regarding critical thinking. Few of the women interviewed found argument to be a congenial form of conversation because they had often been battered with words and reasons. Assailing opponents' logic and attacking their evidence seems to occur less often among women, and teachers complain that women students are reluctant to engage in critical debate with peers in class, even when explicitly encouraged to do so.

Many feminist theorists argue that women should not have to emulate male models of learning that don't work for them. Adrienne Rich (1979) wrote that we should not be training women students to think like men, arguing, "Men in general think ... in disjuncture from their personal lives, claiming objectivity where the most irrational passions seethe" (p. 244). Rich charged women in a world dominated by men to "think critically, refuse to accept the givens, and listen for the silences, ... to define a reality which resonates to *us*, which affirms *our* being, which allows the woman teacher and the woman student alike to take ourselves, and each other, seriously: meaning, to begin to take charge of our lives" (p. 245).

Other feminist theorists warn against a kind of masculine empathy where one projects one's own personality onto the object of contemplation. For Noddings (1984), empathy "does not involve projection, but reception ... I do not project, I receive the other into myself, and I see and feel with the other" (p. 30). Noddings's conception fits nicely with Belenky's et al.'s (1997a) metaphor of teacher as midwife. The midwife teacher is, of course, in direct opposition to the model, critiqued by Freire (1970), of banker-teacher, where static knowledge is deposited in impoverished students, empty receptacles waiting to be filled. To prevent knowledge from being the private property of the teacher, Freire advocated the problem-posing method, where both students and teachers engage in the process of thinking and talk about what they are thinking in a public dialogue.

Gender Equitable, Effective Teaching in Social Studies.   This method suggests a kind of joint inquiry model where a variety of materials are employed and no one has exclusive access to knowledge. Some methods of instruction, including document-based questions (DBQ), Socratic seminars, and graded discussions fulfill these twin principles of making knowledge from a variety of sources available to students and giving students opportunities to refine their thinking by engaging in public dialogue. (For a fuller explanation of these methods, see the section on Key Concepts later in this chapter.)

Once there is an emphasis on employing a variety of materials, it is a logical corollary to use materials from a variety of perspectives in our classrooms. Even elementary students can exchange their reliance on a single narrative of history for a prism containing a variety of perspectives to arrive at a more fully realized vision of historical truth. Quite a few (e.g., Levstik & Barton, 2005) case studies at different grade levels make this point: even young students can grasp the concept of perspectives and multiple stories in history.

It is important to put these perspectives in a context that students can follow; otherwise, teachers will just bombard them with ever-more information without any overarching themes. Many teachers find that developing what have been called *essential questions*, broad questions that raise important issues to guide each unit of study, addresses this problem of adding more data to already overflowing courses. The documents and perspectives studied, then, are in the service of larger themes, rather than remaining isolated pieces of unrelated data.

If you intend to use the Internet regularly to access primary sources, it is worth thinking about whether or not this will enhance constructivism and equity. At first glance, activities associated with the Internet tend to have a constructivist look. Teachers spend little time giving direction and students are very active. Students are eager to help each other, and teachers spend most of their time facilitating student work. Students seem comfortable and motivated as they click from site to site. A closer look at the Internet assignments, however, suggests that teacher practice has not changed in constructivist directions. In general, the assignments expect students to answer a number of factual questions at the knowledge retrieval level. The addition of the Internet to the classroom has not yet increased the frequency with which students are expected to go beyond fact finding.

In terms of gender equity, the jury on the Internet is still out. Although we know that boys are more likely to take computer courses, and are more comfortable with computers than are girls, the Internet may change the gender imbalance. The numbers of girls and women using the Internet are rising, and they tend to see the Internet as an important means of communication. As to how gender plays out in social studies classes that use the Internet, more research is certainly needed.

The jury is not out when it comes to class equity. That there is a digital divide, that not all students have Internet access at home, has negative implications. Only students whose parents can afford the Internet have the opportunity to work on Internet research projects outside of school and perhaps get significant help from their parents. And the gap continues at school. Although a school's poverty rate is a strong predictor of how much Internet access it offers its students, money isn't the only factor that is drawing dividing lines.

A growing body of research shows that teachers tend to infuse technology into lessons less with low-achieving students than with high achievers. Many teachers say they would like to integrate more technology into classes for lower achievers, but the realities of teaching make it difficult. With tight time constraints, such as 45-minute periods in many high schools, some teachers feel they have to forgo technology use to make sure they cover the prescribed curriculum—a more time-consuming task with students who have weaker skills or less motivation. Similar difficulties often lead teachers of bilingual students to limit the use of technology in their classes, too, according to advocates for students who are still learning English.

INTERACTION 4.12:
Acquiring Reliable Knowledge—Acknowledging Perspective

INTASC Principle 4: Diversity of Instructional Strategies

In this exercise, have students write about a memorable event in their lives, hand in their writing, and then go home and interview a classmate about her or his memories of the same event. As students compare the two versions, have them note the differences in perspective and in fact. Brainstorm a list of primary sources that could resolve any discrepancies in the two versions, posing the question "How do historians acquire reliable knowledge?" Finally, read the picture book *Seven Blind Mice* (Young, 1992) aloud to the students, getting at the issue of looking at something (in this case, an elephant) from a variety of perspectives before passing judgment on it. This book has the same theme as the story of the blind men and the elephant, where each of the men investigates only one aspect of the elephant and, thus, draws an incorrect conclusion about it. An added angle in the book is that each of the different-colored mice imagines the "strange something" as being the same color as itself, paralleling how we see things through our own lenses of vision, making assumptions based on who we are. This point can be expanded through a reading of *The True Story of the Three Little Pigs* (Scieszka, 1989). The wolf's story is that he was just borrowing a cup of sugar when he sneezed and blew the houses down. Nevertheless, he is arrested and the story ultimately appears in *The Daily Pig,* ignoring the wolf's version of events, raising the issue of whether the various forms of media are sources of reliable information. This is an excellent opportunity to have students gather information from a variety of sources on an issue of the day and make judgments about what really happened.

INTERACTION 4.13:
The Triangle Shirtwaist Factory Fire

INTASC Principle 4: Diversity of Instructional Strategies

Students can take an event in history and write about it from a paired perspective in the format of a dialogue poem. The following is an excerpt from a student poem (in Balantic & Libresco, 1997):

I work for the Triangle Shirtwaist Company
I work for the Triangle Shirtwaist factory

I am in charge of two hundred girls

I work along side two hundred other women workers

All my girls care about is their next break

Mr. Manager, can't I even go to the bathroom?

If I turn my back, they will slack off

Why must we be locked in?

Students can also respond to the following quotes and make up their own statements about perspective in history:

History is longer, larger, more various, more beautiful and more terrible than anything anyone has ever said about it.—James Baldwin

A mountain appears to have different shapes from different angles of vision. It doesn't follow from this that the mountain has no shape at all or an infinity of shapes. What matters is the angle of vision. The best historians make sure they view the mountain from all angles in order to see all the variables and to find representative realities.—E. H. Carr

History is messy.—Jeannette Balantic, social studies teacher

Teachers can carry this issue of perspective into the literature they read with the students that raises social studies issues, comparing different works for their attention to gender roles. One such comparison that bears fruit is contrasting *The Giving Tree* (Silverstein, 1964), where the theme of total selflessness of a female character, the tree, morphs into a theme (perhaps unwittingly on the part of Silverstein) of exploitation, with *Piggybook* (Browne, 1986) where an exploited wife and working mother takes action to rectify her exploitation. How did students see Silverstein's classic prior to reading *Piggybook*?

INTERACTION 4.14:
Conducting Meaningful, Inclusive Discussions

INTASC Principle 4: Diversity of Instructional Strategies

Find a text that you think presents complex ideas and is worthy of discussion. One such text might be Emily Style's "Curriculum as Window and Mirror," which can be accessed at http://www.wcwonline.org/seed/curriculum.html. You might begin with a focus on a particular quote (e.g., the section where Style suggested an alternative to the Golden Rule, replacing, "do unto others as you would have them do unto you" with "do unto others as they would have you do unto them") asking which philosophy they think is better for a teacher to hold. It may be tempting to begin with a question about the biggest issue in the piece, that of window and mirror; however, starting with the major point often leads participants to talk in generalities rather than in specifics. Use of a particular quote that is relevant to, but is not itself, the main point is also less off-putting and allows more students to enter the discussion. Although many of the questions for Socratic seminars evolve on the spot, sample questions that demonstrate constructive participation and are appropriate for any Socratic seminar may include the following:

- Here is my view and how I arrived at it; how does it sound to you?
- Do you see gaps in my reasoning?
- Do you have different data?
- Do you have different conclusions?
- How did you arrive at your view?
- Are you taking into account something different from what I have considered?

It is important to note that moderating discussions on complex issues is not an activity that ought to be reserved only for secondary students. A rich Socratic seminar could be undertaken with fifth graders with a text like Lois Gould's (1980) *X*, a story of a how a couple tries to bring up a baby whose gender is unknown by avoiding all gender stereotyping.

INTERACTION 4.15:
Controversial Issues

INTASC Principle 4: Diversity of Instructional Strategies

Take turns moderating a National Issues Forum (NIF), a conversation where people of different backgrounds, using nonpartisan briefing books, share their opinions, concerns, and knowledge on an issue of the day. Participants (your colleagues, your students, community members) explore several possible ways for society to address the given problem by analyzing pro and con arguments for each choice and trying to put themselves in the shoes of those who support or disagree with each choice. Deliberative forums help people to see issues from different points of view; forum participants use the discussion process to discover rather than to persuade or advocate. (NIF books are also available in abridged editions, suitable for middle school students.) A moderator's guide can be accessed at the NIF Web site: http://www.nifi.org/. The guide helps moderators to ask questions that involve all participants and to think beyond their own point of view. Some of these questions include the following:

- What is valuable to us? How has this issue affected you personally? What things are most valuable to people who support this option?

- What are the costs or consequences associated with the various options?
- What are the tensions or conflicts in this issue that we have to "work through"?
- Can we detect any shared sense of purpose or how our interdependence is grounds for action?
- What trade-offs are we willing to accept? What are we willing to do as individuals or as a community to solve this problem?

You may wish to use these questions to explore a policy question dealing with issues of diversity and gender; the booklet that deals with affirmative action is titled *How Can We Be Fair? The Future of Affirmative Action* (1995) and can be ordered at the NIF site.

The emphasis during and after the forums is on the process of deliberative discussion; consequently, the guide includes questions to ask at the end to explore systematically what has been learned individually and as a group for the purposes of future deliberation and action. Be sure to use the following questions as a guide at the conclusion of your own forum:

Individual reflections questions:

- How has your thinking about the issue changed?
- How has your thinking about other people's views changed?
- How has your perspective changed as a result of what you heard in this forum?

Group reflection questions:

- What didn't we work through?
- Can we identify any shared sense of purpose or direction?
- What trade-offs are we, or are we not, willing to make to move in a shared direction?

Next step reflection questions:

- What do we still need to talk about?
- How can we use what we learned about ourselves in this forum?
- Do we want to meet again?

INTERACTION 4.16:
Teaching With Documents

INTASC Principle 4: Diversity of Instructional Strategies

First, discuss the content of the following document. Then, address the pedagogy. Generate questions that help students comprehend and analyze Table 4.1. What essential question might this data generate? What other kinds of statistics and documents would you like to add to a DBQ that includes this table? For what grade levels would this document be appropriate? How would you run a discussion on the gender issues implicit in the document? How would you handle any derogatory comments about women if they arise?

TABLE 4.1
Ratio of Female-to-Male Median Earnings

Year	Year-round full-time workers	Full-time workers	Year	Year-round full-time workers	Full-time workers
1999	72.2	76.5	1989	68.7	70.1
1998	73.2	76.3	1988	66.0	70.2
1997	74.2	74.4	1987	65.2	70.0
1996	73.8	75.0	1986	64.3	69.2
1995	71.4	75.5	1985	64.6	68.2
1994	72.0	76.4	1984	63.7	67.8
1993	71.5	77.1	1983	63.6	66.7
1992	70.8	75.8	1982	61.7	65.4
1991	69.9	74.2	1981	59.2	64.6
1990	71.6	71.9	1980	60.2	64.4

Source: U.S. Bureau of the Census and U.S. Bureau of Labor Statistics.
Note: Data in columns 2 and 5 are based on median annual earnings for all workers age 15 or older who worked 50–52 weeks in a year and at least 35 hours in a week, including the self-employed; before 1989, earnings covered civilian workers only. Data in columns 3 and 6 are based on median weekly earnings for wage and salary workers age 16 or older who worked at least 35 hours in a week.

INTERACTION 4.17:
Solving a History Mystery

INTASC Principle 4: Diversity of Instructional Strategies

A good example of a history mystery in our time is the death of John F. Kennedy. He was definitely shot, but the list of possible culprits in the assassination is both endless and bizarre, and there are myriad documents available regarding the assassination (especially on conspiracy theorists' sites). A comprehensive example of a history mystery from the past is Bennett's *What Happened on Lexington Green: An Inquiry into the Nature and Methods of History* (1967). This booklet, replete with primary source documents, asks students to weigh pieces of evidence and analyze their reliability to discover who fired the first shot in the American Revolution. You certainly don't have to include as many documents as Bennett did; 15 documents is probably an upper limit for the history mysteries you develop.

Try out *A. Pintura: Art Detective*, an online game about art history and art composition that can be found at http://www.eduweb.com/pintura/. In the game, you play a 1940s detective with a degree in art history. A distraught woman asks you to identify the artist who made a painting she found in her grandfather's attic. To do so, you must examine paintings (primary source documents) by famous artists from Gauguin to Van Gogh. Each example highlights an art concept, such as composition, style, or subject. You may also want to examine PBS's *History Detectives* series, which traces the authenticity of one document or artifact on each program (see http://www.pbs.org/opb/historydetectives/).

Beware of many so-called history mysteries you find on the Internet. They are often just trivia questions devoid of primary source documents. One site worth exploring, however, is a history site published by the State of Wisconsin (http://www.ecb.org/history/mystery.htm) where elementary students are encouraged to create and solve their own history mystery by thinking of a question about Wisconsin history and then using primary sources to research the answer. One of the students submitted the following question: "What would a day in the life of a 10-year-old boy be like in a cabin in the 1800s in Wisconsin?" He used the following outline to organize his project:

- Question—one that is important to you
- The plan—sources to be investigated
- Investigation—where to go to find the clues; record observations
- Analysis—information provided by sources; what remains unclear
- The answer—determine whether the answer is definitive or still a mystery based on conflicting clues; ask, "Is there a new mystery?"

Use a search engine like www.google.com to peruse and critique some history mystery sites on the Internet. What would you change to improve them?

INTERACTION 4.18:
Conducting Oral "history" and Situating the Stories in "History"

INTASC Principle 4: Diversity of Instructional Strategies

If you go to http://ourworld.compuserve.com/homepages/pennycolman/resou2.htm, you will find advice from Penny Colman (2002), an author of nonfiction children's books on women in history, on how to conduct oral history. She points out that among the 131 images in her book, *Girls: A History of Growing Up Female in America*, "you will find a picture of me as a young girl on page 159 and of my sister on page 171. This is my invitation to readers of all ages to insert their own pictures and stories into the text. Since the book is chronological, readers can easily situate themselves and their relatives and friends into this true story of growing up female in America. My image is of an accordion, as readers make *Girls: A History of Growing Up Female in America* get fatter and fatter. My message is: We are all history makers!"

Follow Colman's advice and develop questions for and conduct an oral history interview; then situate the interview in the sweep of American history. For an example of this method, see Andrea Libresco's "Doing 'Real' History: Citing Your Mother in Your Research Paper" (2001). On an elementary level, see David Weitzman's (1975) *My Backyard History Book* for a variety of oral and community history activities.

ESSENTIAL EQUITY QUESTION 4.4:
WHAT KINDS OF CITIZENS DO WE WANT TO BE—WHAT DO WE KNOW AND BELIEVE ABOUT THE IMPLICATIONS FOR SOCIAL STUDIES EDUCATION OF THE CITIZENSHIP MANDATE?

WHAT WE KNOW AND BELIEVE

As we move through the early years of the 21st century, citizens of the United States are increasingly aware of the degree to which this period of world history will be defined by its global nature. Ours is truly a world in which local actions have global ramifications and global events affect Americans quite directly. New ways of thinking about our citizenship rights and obligations, our global interconnections as a nation-state, and even educators' professional responsibilities to ensure coverage for world events in social studies classrooms have been altered as a result of the impact of the events surrounding September 11, 2001.

A commitment to democratic education cannot end at the classroom door. Citizenship doesn't happen only on election day. Social studies teachers bear a responsibility to enact democracy in their classrooms, schools, and communities. In addressing this last EEQ, we address our values and beliefs about social studies education and the large scope that this enterprise entails. We refer to the National Council for the Social Studies statement made in *Expectations of Excellence* (1994) and reprinted here along with the "Ten Thematic Standards" that should guide curriculum development at all levels. As you will note in reviewing them, global citizenship plays an important role. Our thinking about what these standards and commitments entail leads us to pose certain questions that beginning and experienced teachers should consider:

- If we consider citizens as members of a global as well as national and local community, then what are our responsibilities?

- Do our obligations to promote democratic education end at the door to our classroom?
- Are there distinctive ways in which social studies educators have tried to promote democratic decision making in their classrooms?
- What do these questions have to do with gender and diversity issues?

We offer a brief statement of our views on these matters, but in keeping with the open-ended, inquiry-oriented approach found throughout this chapter, we encourage you to explore these questions on your own.

A commitment to social justice requires social studies teachers to become informed about equity issues; teachers cannot act on issues, or expect students to do so, if teachers do not know about them. As singer-activist Harry Chapin said, "To know is to care; to care is to act; to act is to make a difference." Therefore, teachers have to model the behavior of wide-awake citizens informed about issues of the day. Elementary and secondary teachers alike need to get information from a variety of sources across the political spectrum, and they need to educate themselves about conditions in local, national, and global communities. They should "talk back" to the newspapers and magazines they are reading and engage in discussion groups with other adults about what is going on locally, nationally, and globally. They should act on their views, writing letters to the editors of newspapers, congressional representatives, and friends and family about the issues that excite their passions. Finally, they need to keep students abreast of their efforts to inform themselves and to act on the information they have deemed reliable. If they want an attentive society, they need to model the behaviors of one.

We agree with Parker's (1991) assessment when he wrote, "Curriculum renewal in a society striving to express the democratic ideal is necessarily different than curriculum renewal in totalitarian societies" (p. 45). If the social studies curriculum is going to be renewed, then participatory citizenship, its ideal, needs to factor into what gets taught and how it gets taught. As Parker noted, "A proper education for participation, and one that is well within the reach of the social studies curriculum at every grade, emphasizes learning to participate in public discussions of the public's problems" (p. vi). This understanding suggests to us that social studies teachers must promote active, participatory learning experiences in their classrooms and schools. But Parker wisely points out that action must be based on knowledge. An excellent resource for teaching about the democratic basis of this society is the project called "We the People: The Citizen and the Constitution," which is available through the Center for Civic Education (1999). Other excellent models of materials devoted to deliberation and discussion of public issues are the regularly updated materials of the National Issues Forum, published by Kendall Hunt publishers, and the "Choices" materials, available through Brown University (www.choices.edu).

Social studies renewal in the 21st century needs to attend more fully to matters of gender and diversity. Thus far, the field has not embraced this mandate at the grassroots level as fully as it should. Parker (1996) called on the field to enact advanced ideas about democracy, which include the commitment to respect diversity. If they take this mandate seriously, then social studies educators must engage in active promotion of equity and justice for all members of the community, including students and fellow citizens, here in the United States and outside its borders. Some refer to such a stance as a commitment to social justice.

The key issue for us is that social studies educators at all levels should be engaged in informed deliberation about these issues. Educators will not all agree, we know, about the scope of what comes under the heading of social studies education, which is and always has been a controversial enterprise. Because it is normative and rests on values and the interpretation of values in action, we know that some teachers, schools, and communities will come to different conclusions about even so fundamental an issue as equity. That is why it is important to recognize that this chapter addresses the subject of gender balancing the curriculum from the standpoint of both equity and effectiveness. We must underscore the point that teaching with an eye to gender and diversity produces more effective learning in students. We suspect most teachers will recognize the truth in this statement. How far you will travel with us, however, in promoting a vision of global citizenship tied to social action for social justice is probably less certain.

The work of social studies educators must involve the task of moving the institutions with which they are associated toward greater equity and fairness for all individuals, boys and girls, and fellow citizens of this nation and planet. Accomplishing these goals, even in a small way, means moving the curriculum outside the classroom and school by bringing national and global issues inside the classroom. One manageable way of doing this with a particular emphasis on gender and diversity might be to look at the media and its socialization of gender roles and treatment of diversity. So many boys and girls get their notions about what it means to be men and women from the media. Likewise, depictions of racial and ethnic groups can often be quite stereotypical in popular culture. Educating students to critical media literacy will help undermine the corrosive effects on both young men and women of these images. (See Cortes, 2000, for some useful ideas on this subject.)

In considering the topic of global citizenship, an excellent place to start is with the "Universal Declaration of Human Rights." For the complete text in a variety of languages on the official United Nations Web site devoted to this document, see www.unhchr.ch/udhr/index.htm. Attention to the gendered dimension of this document was given in 1998 and resulted in "A Declaration of Human Rights in a Gender Perspective," which is available at http://www.pdhre.org/involved/cladinfo.html.

In the United States, people often take for granted the notion of human rights. But this is a modern concept, one not fully realized, especially for women, in many parts of the world. Even in the United States, many recent immigrants come from cultures in which women's rights are not seen as human rights. This situation also applies to groups other than women in this society, such as gays and lesbians, the poor, and members of racial and ethnic minorities. See, for example, the recent report by Human Rights Watch (2001), *Hatred in the Hallways*, about the ways in which schools can be hostile places, even violent places, for gay, lesbian, and transgender students. Crocco (2001, 2002) has argued that teachers, especially social studies teachers committed to democratic citizenship education, have an obligation to disrupt abusive, violent, and prejudicial behavior wherever they encounter it in their schools. Thus, teachers' values as social studies educators suggest that their mission is a global one, but their first steps must be local, making whatever communities they work in and live in fairer, more just, and more equitable environments for all.

INTERACTION 4.19:
The Personal Is Political

INTASC Principle 4: Diversity of Instructional Strategies

Be a sociologist in your own home and in your own school and select an issue that, although others might classify it as merely personal, you believe has larger political implications. Discuss the issue with a group of other students in class and select one issue for the group to investigate further and document. Then decide how to inform others of your findings and suggest a course of action.

INTERACTION 4.20:
More Controversial Issues

INTASC Principle 4: Diversity of Instructional Strategies

This discussion method was mentioned in addressing EEQ 4.3 as an exemplar for running an inclusive and thoughtful discussion. The methods and materials are, perhaps, even more relevant in this EEQ addressing citizenship because the purpose of NIF is to help people of diverse views find common ground for action on issues that concern them deeply. NIF has prepared booklets on a range of current issues (for a full list of issues, go to their Web site: http://www.nifi.org/); those that intersect with gender and diversity include topics on the family, day care, immigration, affirmative action, racial and ethnic tensions, and abortion. Take turns moderating discussion of an issue, using the guidelines in EEQ 4.3. It is worth noting the emphasis on process throughout the materials. The NIF moderator's guide explains that participants conduct this difficult work through a deliberative dialogue by taking the following actions:

- Understand the pros and cons of every option, its costs and consequences
- Know the strategic facts and how they affect the way the group thinks about each problem

- Go beyond the initial position people hold to their deeper motivations—the things people consider to be most valuable in everyday life
- Weigh carefully the views of others; appreciate the impact various options would have on what others consider valuable
- Work through the conflicting emotions that arise when various options pull and tug on what people consider valuable
- Move from first reactions and mass opinions toward a more shared and stable public judgment where a public voice emerges, different from personal preference or special interest pleadings
- Understand the implications of how citizens sense their interdependence on the issues and its implications for community action.

INTERACTION 4.21:
Gender and Schooling Questionnaire

INTASC Principle 4: Diversity of Instructional Strategies

Fill out the following "Gender Bias Checklist" and discuss your results to determine what responsibilities the teachers, students, and administrators have to address any gender bias you and your classmates uncover.

Gender Bias Checklist

Directions: Place a checkmark next to every situation that you think is an example of gender bias.

_____ 1. A teacher turns to the boys when a piece of audiovisual equipment isn't working.

_____ 2. A teacher compliments the girls more than the boys about how they look and what clothes they are wearing.

_____ 3. A teacher utters the following sentence in science class: "The scientific advances of man in the 20th century are amazing!"

_____ 4. The school has better coaches and equipment for the boys' teams.

_____ 5. The school has many more boys than girls in auto mechanics class.

____ 6. A teacher hears some boys call a girl "bitch" in the hallway and keeps walking.

____ 7. A teacher hears some boys call a boy "fag" in the hallway and keeps walking.

____ 8. Bathroom graffiti saying, "For a good time, call *girl's name*," is not removed for a month.

____ 9. A teacher uses sports analogies exclusively to illustrate points in class.

____ 10. There are more boys than girls taking advanced science and math classes.

____ 11. There are more girls than boys taking advanced placement English literature.

____ 12. The boys in a class interrupt more than the girls do.

____ 13. There are more girls than boys in the government, yearbook, and drama clubs.

____ 14. One in three girls plays on teams, as opposed to one in two boys.

____ 15. Boys are disciplined and called on more often than are girls in a teacher's class.

____ 16. There are more boys than girls in special education class.

____ 17. More boys than girls drop out of the school.

____ 18. The bulletin board in an American history class displays only the presidents.

____ 19. When group work is done in a class, the girls tend to get the recorder roles.

____ 20. When group labs are done, the boys tend to hold and control the equipment.

INTERACTION 4.22:
Hostile Hallways

INTASC Principle 4: Diversity of Instructional Strategies

Spend some time in the hallways of a school when classes are changing and observe the behavior of the students toward one another, as well as the reactions (or lack thereof) of the teachers and administrators to any incidents of bias or harassment. Record your data and discuss the teacher's role in addressing these behaviors.

INTERACTION 4.23:
Defining Citizenship Through Children's Literature

INTASC Principle 4: Diversity of Instructional Strategies

Students as young as second grade can engage in critical thinking. They can make informed judgments, the most important citizenship skills in a democracy. In the primary grades, much of students' research is found in the literature they read and the conversations they have with community members. Their models of good citizens come from their picture books and their neighborhoods; the problems they work on arise from their classrooms and their immediate environs. Still, these 7- and 8-year-olds can do the stuff of citizenship by identifying and describing the characteristics of good citizens, giving examples of behaviors of good citizens, defending what they see as the most important behaviors of good citizens, and applying their knowledge of good citizens to judge the actions of characters in literature and in real life.

Before examining the following lessons (Libresco, 2002), make your own list of good citizens and their behaviors; in addition, compare your list to those found in primary materials used in the school in which you observe or work. How are the conceptions of citizenship in these lessons broader than those in traditional primary classrooms and materials?

Lesson 1: Defining Good Citizenship

- Key question: What are the most important behaviors of good citizens?
- Objectives: Students will be able to
    1. Identify and describe the characteristics of good citizens
    2. Give examples of behaviors of good citizens
    3. Defend what they see as the most important behaviors of good citizens
    4. Apply their knowledge of good citizens to judge the actions of characters in literature and in real life.

- Motivation: Teacher and students read situations (see Handout 1) and discuss whether or not each is an example of good citizenship. As they do so, they develop a class list of behaviors of good citizens that include items such as "keep their community beautiful," "help their community members without doing their work for them," "express their views in a variety of ways," "stand up for people's rights," "listen to others," "inform themselves," "vote," and so on.
- Development: Teacher and students discuss in greater depth any conflicting information they have about citizens; for example, the situations the students seem to have the most consternation about are numbers 15, 16, and 17 on Handout 1, which deal with expressing one's point of view more forcefully and even, possibly, engaging in civil disobedience. Higher level thinking questions are asked, allowing students to grapple with the relationship of citizenship to questioning authority:
  - Do good citizens sometimes raise issues that may be difficult to solve?
  - May good citizens suggest new ideas to someone in power (like the principal)?
  - Can it ever be a sign of good citizenship to break the law?
  - Was Martin Luther King, Jr. a good citizen?
  - Do good citizens always obey authority or are there times when they may question authority?
- Application: Teacher reads Dr. Seuss's *Yertle the Turtle* aloud, asking students to look for good and bad citizens in the story and give reasons for their classifications. The story revolves around a dictator, Yertle, who commands the other turtles to stack themselves into a throne for him so that he can be ruler of all the turtles. The bottom turtle, Mack, pleads on behalf of himself and the other turtles, talking of starving and being in pain and basing his argument on the rights of turtles. When Yertle wants to make his throne higher than the moon, Mack reaches his breaking point. He burps, and that burp jostles the throne, sending Yertle into the mud and setting the other turtles free, as Dr. Seuss suggests, all creatures, animal and human, should be. Students are quick to identify Yertle as a bad citizen and Mack as a good one; however, when asked to compare their assessments to their earlier definitions of good citizens, the students become less certain. Higher level thinking questions are asked, allowing students to assess the roles of authorities, activists and bystanders.
  - Is Mack being a good citizen when he talks back to and overthrows Yertle who is in charge?
  - Are the other turtles in the stack good citizens or not? (Interestingly, the students I have worked with notice that Mack uses the pronoun *we*, and they suggest that he is speaking on behalf of the other turtles; therefore, most students feel that the other turtles, too, are good citizens.)
  - How innocent are bystanders?
- Follow-up: The teacher can follow up the literary example with real-world ones, presenting students with historical and current examples of protesters to assess whether or not they exhibit the behaviors of good citizens. Students can

also analyze another character from literature to assess her or his citizenship. A different Dr. Seuss story may be used here, "What Was I Afraid Of?" from *The Sneetches and Other Stories*, where the main character is afraid of a pair of pale green pants with nobody inside them because he doesn't know anything about the pants and is prejudging them. From this story, the students can discover perhaps the most important attribute of a good citizen, namely, the commitment to acquiring reliable information and then acting on it.

Handout 1: WHAT IS GOOD CITIZENSHIP?

Directions: Read each situation below. If you think it is an example of good citizenship, write *YES*. If you do not think it is an example of good citizenship, write *NO*.

SITUATIONS   *GOOD CITIZENSHIP: YES or NO?*

1. Picking up trash in the hall   _____

2. Helping another student understand the
   homework assignment   _____

3. Shoving to get on the bus first   _____

4. Writing a letter to the school newspaper to
   express your view   _____

5. Teasing someone based on that person's looks   _____

6. Telling someone to stop teasing another person   _____

7. Turning off the water while you brush your teeth   _____

8. Running in the halls at school   _____

9. Listening to the principal's announcements   _____

10. Reading the school newspaper to find out
    what's going on in school   _____

11. Wearing a button that reads, "Reduce.
    Reuse. Recycle."   _____

12. Voting for a candidate for student
    government   _____

13. Joining a club in school   _____

14. Volunteering to help clean up the local beach   _____

15. Presenting the principal with a petition, signed
    by lots of kids, which asks for an after-school
    sports club   _____

16. After noticing there was no recycling bin in your
    classroom, asking questions until a recycling bin
    is placed in the class   _____

17. After noticing that a local restaurant won't serve
    Black customers until all of the White people have
    been served, organizing your friends and your
    parents to do what you think Martin Luther King, Jr.,
    would have done and break the law by sitting in at
    the lunch counter and refusing to move until they
    change their unfair practices   _____

Lesson 2: Identifying Good Citizen Role Models

- Key question: Whom would you nominate for good citizenship awards?
- Objectives: Students will be able to:
  1. Discuss activities that contribute to the betterment of the community
  2. Evaluate the activities of community helpers in literature
  3. Evaluate the activities of community helpers in their communities
- Motivation: Students brainstorm a list of activities they feel contribute to the betterment of the community. Responses may begin with general behaviors (helping others); however, the teacher should move students to more specific examples (e.g., the neighbor who shovels the elderly neighbor's walk every snowstorm, the neighbor who works at the soup kitchen once a week, the person who organized the clothing drive, the families who agree to get one fewer holiday gift for each other every year so that they can donate money to those in need, the neighbor who worked tirelessly to get a stop sign put in, the family who won't buy certain products because they're made by companies that exploit children, the friend who is a literacy volunteer, the parent who writes letters to her congressperson about important issues).

- Development: Students research other examples of good citizens in fiction and nonfiction. The following sources may be used individually, in pairs, in reading groups, or (especially in the case of the video) as whole-class activities.

Fiction resources include:

Brown, M. (1982). *Arthur's Halloween.* Boston: Little, Brown. After gathering reliable information, Arthur and his friends discover that their neighbor is not a witch, and, together, they clean her yard.

Browne, A. (1990). *Piggybook.* New York: Knopf. When Mom leaves, Dad and sons realize how much she did for them; they resolve to pull their weight and share jobs.

Bunting, E. (1989). *Wednesday Surprise.* New York: Clarion. A girl teaches her grandmother to read.

Cooney, B. (1982). *Miss Rumphius.* New York: Scholastic. A woman makes the world more beautiful by planting flowers.

Cowen-Fletcher, J. (1994). *It takes a village.* New York: Scholastic. The entire village watches out for a child.

Houston, G. (1991). *My great aunt Arizona.* New York: HarperCollins. A woman has an exponential effect on a town by staying to teach rather than traveling around the world.

King Mitchell, M. (1998). New York: Aladdin Paperbacks. *Uncle Jed's barbershop.* A man uses hard-earned money to help others in trouble and delays his own dream of owning a barbershop.

Lionni, L. (1987). *Frederick.* New York: Knopf. A mouse imagines beautiful images to help his friends get through the winter.

Pfister, M. (1992). *The rainbow fish.* New York: North South Books. A beautiful fish ultimately shares his prized possessions.

Polacco, P. (1991). *Applemondo's dreams.* New York: Philomel. A boy's dreams change the village and the people.

Polacco, P. (1996). *The tree of the dancing goats.* New York: Simon & Schuster. Jewish and Christian neighbors reach out to each other.

Silverstein, S. (1964). *The giving tree.* New York: Harper & Row. A tree gives all it has to a boy.

Thurber, J. (1972). *The great Quillow.* New York: Harcourt Brace. A tiny toy maker defeats a giant and saves a town.

Untermeyer, L. (1962). *One and one and one.* New York: Crowell-Collier Press. Four animal friends build a home together.

Nonfiction biography resources include:

Borden, L., & Kroeger, M. K. (2001). *Fly high! The story of Bessie Coleman.* New York: Margaret McElderry.

Brill, M. T. (2001). *Margaret Knight: Girl inventor.* Brookfield, CT: Millbrook Press.

Christensen, B. (2001). *Woody Guthrie: Poet of the people.* New York: Knopf.

Hoose, P. (2001). *We were there, too! Young people in history.* New York: Farrar, Strauss, and Giroux.

Rappaport, D. (2001). *Martin's big words: The life of Martin Luther King, Jr.* New York: Jump at the Sun.

Rockwell, A. F. (2000). *Only passing through: The story of Sojourner Truth.* New York: Knopf.

Sullivan, G. (2001). *Helen Keller (in their own words).* New York: Scholastic.

Other nonfiction resources include:

The Earth Works Group. (1990). *50 simple things you can do to save the Earth.* Kansas
    City, MO: Andrews and McMeel. Actions kids can take to clean up the environment.
Gibbons, G. (1996). *Recycle! A handbook for kids.* New York: Little, Brown, & Co.
Harlow, R., & Morgan, S. (2002). *Garbage and recycling: Young discoverers: Environmen-
    tal facts and experiments.* New York: Houghton Mifflin. Explains about biodegradable
    garbage and recycling and has suggestions for how young recyclers can help.
Showers, P. (1993). *Where does the garbage go?* New York: HarperCollins. Explains what
    used to happen to solid waste, what goes into landfills, and how recycling works today.
50 Simple Things You Can Do to Save the Earth. (48 minute video). (1992). Chicago: Chur-
    chill Media. Actions kids of all ages have taken to clean up the environment in 5–8 min-
    ute segments.
Weekly Reader, Time for Kids, Scholastic News, and local newspaper articles.

After doing their research, the students return to the brainstormed list and add
any new qualities or behaviors that describe a good citizen. Teacher and students
then turn the list into a good citizen nomination form that will include examples of
good citizen behaviors. Students bring home several forms and distribute to parents
and neighbors. Students may, of course, fill one out themselves.

• Application: When forms have been returned to the students, they will, in
groups, evaluate the nominees and select the top picks. Students must be able to
give reasons for their selections orally and in writing. The class will develop a
book that recognizes these good citizens with a photograph of each, a profile written by students (individually, in pairs, or in groups) and an illustration. The class
will plan a ceremony for these good citizens at which the book is read and, if de-
sired, a student-designed award/certificate can be presented to the honorees.

• Follow-up: Students can nominate characters in books, well-known citizens, and historical figures for good citizenship awards.

INTERACTION 4.24:
Analyzing the Media With Respect to Gender and Diversity

INTASC Principle 4: Diversity of Instructional Strategies

Because teachers and students get much information from the media, it is worth analyzing what people see and hear to ascertain the reliability of that information. Develop a tally form for recording the number and type of characters on entertainment
programs and in advertisements with respect to gender and diversity. Analyze the
portrait of America these programs give teachers and students. Then investigate the
information people get from print sources, television, radio, and the Internet. What
kinds of political biases are people exposed to on network and cable television? How
do these biases affect views of the world? How diverse are the views represented in

the materials people regularly read, listen to, and watch? If they are not diverse, what supplemental materials do teachers and students need beyond mainstream media outlets? For further discussion on the media and its often problematic relationship to democracy, see Fallows (1996) and Cappella and Jamieson (1997).

INTERACTION 4.25:
Document-Based Analysis as Integral to Citizenship

INTASC Principle 1: Subject-Matter Knowledge

If you refer to the Chapin quote earlier in the chapter, you will find that the first step in making a difference is acquiring knowledge. You cannot expect students to work for social justice as adults if they are not exposed to information and methods of analyzing that information. Thomas Jefferson, too, recognized the necessity of purposefully seeking data. He said, "If a nation expects to be ignorant and free, it expects what never was and never will be."

As mentioned in EEQ 4.3, when students analyze documents, they are in charge of weighing evidence and making their own meaning about historical events and current world conditions. Table 4.2 focuses on the condition of women in the world. This data can be found online at the United Nations' CyberSchoolBus web site.

What do you learn about women in the world from an analysis of these documents? What questions would you ask to help students analyze the documents? What other kinds of documents would you seek out for your students on this topic? How could you help your students move from acquiring this knowledge to social action?

Use these documents as a springboard to write a journal entry about your own knowledge of conditions in the world for diverse groups of people. What plan of action do you need to acquire more information about political, social, and economic

TABLE 4.2

Country	Life Expectancy at Birth (years, 1990–99)		Adult Illiteracy Rate (%, 1995) Total	Adult Illiteracy Rate (%, 1995) Female	Sex Ratio (females per 100 males, 1999)
	Female	Male			
Afghanistan	46	45	68.5	84	95
China	72	68	18.5	27.3	94
India	63	62	48	62.4	94
United States of America	80	73	—	—	103

Source: Statistics and indicators are provided by the United Nations Statistics Division from the World Statistics Pocketbook and Statistical Yearbook, except capital cities and languages.

conditions? Once you have taken the first steps to acquiring information, how will you go about assessing the reliability of the information? How will you decide what to do with this new information—as a teacher and as a citizen?

INTERACTION 4.26:
Assessing Learning (Authentic Assessment)

INTASC Principle 8: Assessment

INTASC Principle 1: Subject-Matter Knowledge

1. Search for and select picture books and age-appropriate biographies that focus on good citizens from diverse backgrounds. Create activities that connect the literature to the different conceptions of citizenship with which you want students to become familiar.
2. Create a unit on women of the world today. Gather documents and develop activities for your students to learn about and act on world conditions in terms of gender equity. Look into the materials offered by the United Nations, among others, for help with this project.

INTASC Principle 3: Diversity in Learning

3. Devise a chart that lists gender stereotypes for both men and women. Come up with at least 10 different stereotypes for each group. Write an essay explaining how such stereotypes may evolve from generalizations about a group. Indicate in your essay how such stereotyping may be harmful to members of each group.
4. Once you've looked at some of the dimensions of gender in the classroom from the previous activities, write an ethnography—a descriptive accounting with lots of detail—about how you think gender operates in a particular social studies classroom. This means playing the role of the participant observer as anthropologists do when they visit a society that they wish to study. Pay careful attention to what is going on in this classroom as you work with, observe, and interact with students and teachers. Put on your gender-investigator hat and try to step outside the interactions and activities to determine the subtle and not-so-subtle ways in which gender roles and gender-related expectations shape the behavior you're witnessing. For example, is the teacher a male or a female? What difference do you think gender might make in what you see occurring? Count the number of times the girls get called on by the teacher; then count the number of boys called on. Do you detect any difference in the kinds of interactions the teacher has

with male and female students? Overall, who talks more in the classroom—girls or boys? What about the topics being studied? Are women present in the curriculum? Compose an ethnographic account that focuses on the ways in which gender operates in this classroom.

5. Write a letter to the editor of your local newspaper suggesting the importance of diversity education for influential members of your community (e.g., politicians, teachers, doctors, nurses, social service workers) highlighting the changing demographics of your region or state.

INTASC Principle 9: Reflection and Responsibility

6. Write a speech you might deliver to your department arguing for or against the celebration of Women's History Month.

RESOURCES

Web Sites

A Geographic Guide to Uncovering Women's History in Archival Collections: http:// www.lib.utsa.edu/Archives/links.htm

Making of America: http://moa.cit.cornell.edu/moa/

The Eleanor Roosevelt and Human Rights Project: http://www.gwu.edu/~erpapers/

U.S. National Archives and Records Administration: http://www.archives.gov/index.html

Women in the World Curriculum Materials: http://www.womeninworldhistory.com/wiwhc.html

American Women's History: A Resource Guide: http://www.mtsu.edu/~kmiddlet/history/women.html

Universal Voices: Online Human Rights Internet Guide: http://www.uwm.edu/Dept/CIS/humanrights/hrwomen.html

Selected Women and Gender Resources on the World Wide Web: http://www.library.wisc.edu/libraries/WomensStudies/others.htm

Women's Studies/Women's Issues Resources Site: http://research.umbc.edu/~korenman/wmst/links.html

National Women's History Project: http://www.nwhp.org/

Do History (associated with Laurel Thatcher Ulrich's *Diary of Martha Ballard*): www.dohistory.org

National Issues Forum: www.nifi.org/

National Standards in Social Studies—NCSS Expectations of Excellence: Curriculum Standards for Social Studies: These 10 thematic strands should be woven into the social studies curriculum at each level, elementary, middle, and high school (search "standards" at www.socialstudies.org):

1. Culture
2. Time, Continuity, and Change
3. People, Places, and Environments
4. Individual Development and Identity
5. Individuals, Groups, and Institutions
6. Power, Authority, and Government
7. Production, Distribution, and Consumption
8. Science, Technology, and Society
9. Global Connections
10. Civic Ideals and Practices

Media

It's Elementary: Talking about Gay Issues in Schools, Debra Chasnoff and Helen
  Cohen, Women's Educational Media, New Day Films, 77 minutes
Slim Hopes: Advertising and the Obsession with Thinness, Jean Kilbourne, Media
  Education Foundation, 30 minutes
Still Killing Us Softly III, Jean Kilbourne, Media Education Foundation, 34 minutes
Tough Guise: Violence, Media, and the Crisis in Masculinity, Jackson Katz, Media
  Education Foundation, 82 minutes

Recommended Reading

American Association of University Women. (1993). *Hostile hallways: The AAUW survey
  on sexual harassment in America's schools.* Washington, DC: Author.
American Association of University Women. (1999). *Gender gaps: Where schools still fail
  our children.* New York: Marlow.
American Social History Project. (2000). *Who built America? Working people and the na-
  tion's economy, politics, culture, and society.* New York: Worth Publishers.
Barton, K. C. (1997). History—It can be elementary: An overview of elementary students'
  understanding of history. *Social Education 61,* 13–16.
Besner, H. F., & Spungin, C. J. (1995) *Gay and lesbian students: Understanding their
  needs.* Washington, DC: Taylor & Francis.
Bigelow, B., & Diamond, N. (1988). *The power in our hands.* New York: Monthly Review Press.
Brophy, J., & VanSledright, B. (1997). *Teaching and learning history in elementary
  schools.* New York: Teachers College Press.
Connell, R. W. (1996). Teaching the boys: New research on masculinity, and gender strate-
  gies for schools. *Teachers College Record, 98*(2), 206–235.
Delpit, L. (1995). *Other people's children: Cultural conflict in the classroom.* New York:
  W. W. Norton.
Eisner, E. W. (1994). *The educational imagination: On the design and evaluation of school
  programs.* New York: Macmillan.
Engle, S., & Ochoa, A. (1988). *Education for democratic citizenship: Decision making in
  the social studies.* New York: Teachers College Press.

Evans, R. W., & Saxe, D. W. (1996). *Handbook on teaching social issues: NCSS Bulletin 93*. Washington, DC: NCSS.

Fosnot, C. T. (1989). *Enquiring teachers, enquiring learners: A constructivist approach for teaching*. New York: Teachers College Press.

Hahn, C. (1980). Social studies with equality and justice for all: Toward the elimination of sexism. *Journal of Research and Development in Education, 13*(2), 103–112.

Hahn, C. (1999). *Becoming political: Comparative perspectives on citizenship education*. Albany: State University of New York Press.

Hahn, C. (2001). Democratic understanding: Cross-national perspectives. *Theory into Practice 40*(1), 14–22.

Kimmel, M. (2000). *The gendered society*. New York: Oxford University Press.

Kimmel, M. (2000). *The gendered society reader*. New York: Oxford University Press.

King, J. E., Hollins, E. R., & Hayman, W. C. (1997). *Preparing teachers for cultural diversity*. New York: Teachers College Press.

Ladson-Billings, G. (1994). *Dreamkeepers: Successful teachers of African American children*. San Francisco: Jossey-Bass.

Lee, E. D., & Okazawa-Rey, M. (Eds.). (1998). *Beyond heroes and holidays: A practical guide to K-12 anti-racist, multicultural education and staff development*. Washington, DC: Network of Educators on the Americas.

Levstik, L. (1989). Building a sense of history in a first-grade class. In J. Brophy (Ed.), *Advances in research on teaching 4: Case studies of teaching and learning in social studies* (pp. 1–31). Greenwich, CT: JAI Press.

Logan, J. (1993). *Teaching stories*. St. Paul: Minnesota Inclusiveness Program.

Makler, A., & Hubbard, R. S. (2000). *Teaching for justice in the social studies classroom: Millions of intricate moves*. Portsmouth, NH: Heinemann.

McCormick, T. (1994). *Creating the nonsexist classroom: A multicultural approach*. New York: Teachers College Press.

Merryfield, M., & Crocco, M. S. (Eds.). (2003). Teaching about women of the world [Special issue]. *Social Education, 67*(1).

Miedzian, M. (1992). *Boys will be boys: Breaking the link between masculinity and violence*. New York: Anchor Books.

Munro, P. (1999). Widening the circle: Jane Addams, gender, and the re/definition of democracy. In M. Crocco & O. L. Davis, Jr. (Eds.), *"Bending the future to their will": Civic women, social education, and democracy* (pp. 73–92). Lanham, MD: Rowman & Littlefield.

Nieto, S. (1999). *The light in their eyes: Creating multicultural communities*. New York: Teachers College Press.

Noddings, N. (1997). Social studies and feminism. In E. W. Ross (Ed.), *The social studies curriculum: Purposes, problems, and possibilities* (pp. 59–71). Albany: State University of New York Press.

Oakes, J., & Lipton, M. (1999). *Teaching to change the world*. New York: McGraw-Hill.

Oliver, D., & Shaver, J. (1966). *Teaching public issues in the high school*. Boston: Houghton Mifflin.

Olson, L. (1997). *Made in America: Immigrant students in our public schools*. New York: The New Press.

Omi, M., & Winant, H. (1994). *Racial formation in the United States: From the 1960s to the 1990s* (2nd ed.). New York: Routledge.

Paley, V. G. (1997). *White teacher*. Cambridge, MA: Harvard University Press.

Reardon, B. (2001). Education for a culture of peace in a gender perspective. Paris: UNESCO.

Seager, J. (2000). *State of women in the world atlas.* New York: Touchstone.

Sleeter, C., & Grant, C. (1988). *Making choices for multicultural education: Five approaches to race, class, and gender.* Columbus, OH: Merrill.

Stein, N., & Sjostrum, L. (1994). *Flirting or hurting? A teacher's guide to student-to-student sexual harassment in schools (Grades 6 through 12).* Wellesley, MA: Center for Research on Women.

Tatum, B. (1997). *Why are all the Black kids sitting together in the cafeteria? and other conversations about the development of racial identity.* New York: Basic Books.

Tetreault, M. K. (1986). Integrating women's history: The case of United States history high school textbooks. *The History Teacher, 19*(2), 211–252.

Tetreault, M. K. (1987). Rethinking women, gender, and the social studies. *Social Education, 51*(3), 170–178.

VanSledright, B., & Brophy, J. (1989). Storytellers, scientists, and reformers in the teaching of U.S. history to fifth graders. In J. Brophy (Ed.), *Advances in research on teaching* (pp. 195–243). Greenwich, CT: JAI Press.

Wade, R. (2000). *Building bridges: Connecting classroom and community through service-learning in the social studies.* Washington, DC: NCSS.

Yankelovich, D. (1992, October 5). How public opinion really works. *Fortune, 126*(7), 102–106.

APPENDIX: KEY CONCEPTS

Bias: The concepts *generalization, stereotyping*, and *essentialism* are also linked to the notion of *bias*, or a distorted perspective towards a category of other persons. Bias interferes with the way people see the world and other people. If teachers are biased toward their students, if they bring a set of preconceived notions or stereotypes about, for example, what women can and cannot do in the classroom and in life, they will have difficulty developing the capacities of all students, male and female, in their classrooms.

Bottom-up history: An interpretation of the past from the often neglected perspective of the experiences of "ordinary" (i.e., non-elite) men and women of a variety of races and ethnicities and class backgrounds.

Connected knowing: Describing a way many women learn, Mary Belenky and her colleagues' (1997a) work on connected knowing focuses on many women's preference for consciously subjective, involved, integrative, and empathetic learning situations as contrasted with separated knowing (objective, removed, and abstract), which is fostered in many formal education environments.

Constructivism: The basis of constructivism is that students learn by actively constructing new information onto their existing mental frameworks. According to Jacqueline and Martin Brooks (1993), teachers in constructivist classrooms exhibit the following behaviors: (1) become one of many resources from whom the student may learn, not just the primary source of information; (2) engage students in experiences that challenge previous conceptions of their existing knowledge; (3) allow student responses to drive lessons and seek elaboration of students' initial responses, allowing student thinking time after posing questions; (4) encourage the spirit of questioning by asking thoughtful, open-ended questions, encouraging thoughtful discussion among students; (5) use cognitive terminology such as *classify, analyze,* and *create* when framing tasks; (6) encourage and accept student autonomy and initiative, being willing to let go of classroom control; (7) use raw data and primary sources, along with manipulative, interactive physical materials; (8) don't separate knowing from the process of finding out; (9) insist on clear expression from students because, when students can communicate their understanding, then they have truly learned. It should be apparent from this list of behaviors that they are inherently compatible with feminist and multicultural ideas of seeking out a variety of voices and perspectives on any given topic.

Cooperative learning: Grouping techniques in which students work together toward a common learning goal in small heterogeneous (with regard to gender, race, ethnicity, and ability) groups of about four or five students, cooperative learning teams are designed to achieve both cognitive and affective objectives.

"Declaration of Human Rights in a Gender Perspective": A statement that incorporates advances made to human understanding of human rights since passage in 1948 of the Universal Declaration of Human Rights, with particular attention paid to progress in the last 20 years of including women's experiences in any consideration of human rights.

Democratic decision making: A phrase used by many social studies educators to capture the deliberative and communal sense of how decisions are reached in a representative democracy. In social studies classes, experiences should be provided to students that model such communal decision making, either through voting or achieving consensus.

Discipline: Defined as "a branch of knowledge, instruction, or learning, such as history or English or biology," discipline is broken into portions that become the subject matter of schooling across the K–12 curriculum. What's typically taught in college under the heading of "political science" is often quite different from high school civics, for example. In each academic discipline, knowledge is selected, arranged, codified, verified, organized, and transmitted to future generations for the purpose of maintaining and developing a disciplinary tradition.

Document-based questions (DBQ): The DBQ is designed to enable students to work like historians and good citizens, analyzing and synthesizing evidence from a variety of sources and media, developing a thesis of their own based on the data. Although thesis development is often seen as a skill that only secondary students can master, with the proper instruction, elementary students can draw conclusions based on their analysis of different pieces of data at the appropriate reading level.

The types of documents that might be included as historical sources include personal, historical, and public records; diaries and letters; art, literature, and music; charts and graphs; maps; speeches; news articles; interviews; photographs; and political cartoons. Many of these documents are available in supplementary books that often come with texts; in addition, the Internet has a wealth of primary sources that students can locate, that teachers can bookmark for their students, or that teachers can find in advance and edit according to the reading level of their students. Many sites contain scanned copies of historical records and educational activities. Try starting with your state's archives, the National Archives (www.nara.gov) and the Library of Congress (www.loc.gov). It is worth noting that the variety of sources includes both public and private documents, thereby increasing the opportunity for hearing multiple and diverse perspectives. It is also the case that, by doing the analysis themselves, students make their own meanings, as opposed to assuming that their teacher or their text has the definitive answer.

DBQs are appropriate for all students, from elementary school through high school. They prepare students to consider multiple perspectives and interpretations, recognize points of view and bias, reconcile differing positions, recognize their own frames of reference and contemporary viewpoints that color their interpretations, evaluate the strength of particular arguments, engage in higher level thinking, enhance their analytical skills, and develop confidence in their ability to acquire knowledge. K–3 teachers can assess their pupils' abilities to draw information from a photograph and then move to a written document as students become more proficient readers. Older and more experienced students generally work with more documents and engage in higher level analytical skills and more complex tasks.

Essential questions: Wiggins and McTighe (2005) argue that students should be engaged in answering essential questions where the themes of the unit and the course are not hidden from them; rather, they are shared from the beginning. The content of the course is, then, in the service of grappling with these overarching questions worthy of discussion. Therefore, when students ask the inevitable question, "Why do we have to know this?" you should be able to answer. If you do not have an answer, you shouldn't be teaching that content.

Essentialism: The imputing of certain traits that are believed to be inherent in a particular group and individual members of that group is essentialism.

Gender-balancing the curriculum: The effort to introduce women's lives, experiences, and perspectives into a particular domain of knowledge, especially in schools and universities, as the word *curriculum* implies. In doing work that is sensitive to the ways in which culture socializes both boys and girls to particular gender role models, teachers consider how gender assumptions shape curriculum for both groups. For example, is the study of literature or fine arts considered a female pursuit?

Gender equity: By gender equity, we mean treating both boys and girls in a fair and equitable fashion. Sometimes, this may mean treating them the same; at other times, this may involve taking into consideration each group's strengths and weaknesses in planning curriculum and pedagogy. Should our strategies play to the strengths of certain students or attempt to remediate their weaknesses? We believe that the best curriculum and pedagogy build both approaches into the curriculum (e.g, using both competitive and cooperative learning strategies). We use Emily Style's (1988) metaphor of "curriculum as window and mirror" (p. 6) to get across our perspective that we think about these issues from a both-and rather than an either-or perspective. In the past, education tilted toward male norms, ways of knowing, content, and so forth. In the future, we hope to do a better job in balancing what we do in the classroom, taking gender and diversity issues into consideration to a far greater extent than has been the case until now. In discussing EEQ 4.2, we give some examples of what this approach to curriculum as window and mirror might look like in practice.

Generalization: A proposition asserting something to be true of the greater part of a class or group. To generalize is to infer a general principle or trend from facts, statistics, or the like.

Global citizenship: Many social studies educators believe that the demands of civic responsibility and engagement extend beyond national borders. Although not replacing national citizenship, this idea is seen as supplementing the way in which individuals conceive of their identities in a shrinking world.

Graded discussion: Teachers are understandably reluctant to have too many discussions. One reason for this disinclination is because they want to give assignments that can be evaluated for grades. Graded discussions can address this problem. The rubric you develop (and this can be done with student input) can let your students know what discussion behaviors you value. Some rubric categories might evaluate students on the extent to which their preparation is evident in the quality of their comments during the discussion. Other categories might assess students' listening skills. Still others might address students' interaction skills: Do students speak to the whole class or only to the teacher? Do students build on the remarks of their fellow students? Do students' comments indicate thoughtfulness both regarding the topic and with respect to their classmates?

History vs. history: The distinction between what has been recorded about the past and the totality of lived experience that has occurred in the past.

History mystery: Similar to the DBQ, a history mystery presents students with a variety of sources so that they can research a question in history to which they do not know the answer. The sources are, in effect, clues, and the student detectives piece together the clues to develop a hypothesis about the issue under discussion. James Davidson and Mark Lytle (1992) published a college-level text, *After the Fact: The*

Art of Historical Detection, with chapters containing specific problems historians have encountered as well as the evidence they have used to come to different conclusions. These college-level problems can be modified for secondary students. At the elementary level, most past events are a bit of a mystery to students who have not yet studied history in school; there are, therefore, many opportunities to pose problems, cut up pieces of evidence, and let students work at solving the mystery. As is the case with the DBQ, students are in charge of weighing evidence and making their own meaning about historical events.

Inquiry approaches: No doubt you're learning about this approach in your social studies methods classes. What we want to stress here is the inherent compatibility of these teaching approaches with feminist and multicultural ideas about positionality and perspective taking. These strategies put student discovery, often with primary source documents of one sort or another, at the heart of the learning process. This form of teaching readily exposes the degree to which disciplinary knowledge results from a process of social and intellectual construction.

Knowledge reproduction model: The idea that there is a fixed world of knowledge that the student must come to know is the basis for the knowledge reproduction model where teachers serve as pipelines and seek to transfer their thoughts and meanings to the passive student. There is little room for student-initiated questions, independent thought, or interaction between students. John Dewey (1933) analogized this model to a student being treated as "a cistern into which information is conducted by one set of pipes that mechanically pour it in, while the recitation is the pump that brings the material out again through another set of pipes. Then the skill of the teacher is rated by his or her ability in managing the two pipelines of flow inward and outward" (p. 261).

Knowledge transformation model: The idea that students learn by making their own meaning is the basis of the knowledge transformation model. Philip Jackson (1968) described this model as one whose central questions involve "how the knowledge ... is being used by the learner, how it relates to what was learned before, how it becomes personalized by being translated into the learner's own language, how it applies to new situations ... the focus is no longer on the power of memory alone. It now encompasses levels of mental functioning which customarily fall under the rubrics of 'judgment' and 'understanding'" (p. 71).

Multiple perspectives: This phrase suggests the concept that different actors in the past and present will have different viewpoints about past or contemporary events depending on where they were/are situated in terms of social location. Much history teaching today emphasizes the notion that constructing a story about the past involves inquiry into a variety of perspectives about past events.

Oral history: This data collection project may be defined as any firsthand account of an event. Students who record oral histories may benefit from connecting a real person to a specific event as well as to the larger sweep of history. The activity can also provide a sense of personal engagement in a stream of events, as well as in one's local community. This technique allows for multiple perspectives and can balance the history of famous people with the histories of extraordinary, ordinary people.

Participatory citizenship: This is the notion that being a citizen in a democracy entails acting out the privileges and responsibilities of citizenship chiefly by means of voting but also in terms of other forms of active engagement in civic and community life.

Periodization: The arrangement of historical time into segments that give definition to the long sweep of chronology that comprises history to try to make some sense of the meaning of that flow of time.

"The personal is political": This phrase, crystallized by the women's movement of the 1960s and 1970s, suggests that our individual experiences, feelings, and possibilities are not just a matter of personal preferences and choices but are defined, molded, and limited by the broader political and social setting. The "personal is political" means, therefore, that people's personal lives are, in considerable, part politically delimited and determined, so to improve their particular experiences, people must collectively address political relationships and structures.

Preconceptions and misconceptions: By introducing these concepts into a chapter on gender equity and social studies, we are emphasizing that students bring prior learning into classrooms that often interferes with their understanding of concepts teachers try to teach. For example, if a child is taught to believe that women are inferior to men, he or she will find it difficult to accept ideas of the suitability of much of women's history to the curriculum. Likewise, if a student brings racially or religiously prejudiced ideas into the classroom, teachers may have a difficult time teaching tolerance to that young person. But this may function on a more innocent level as well. One of our favorite examples of this phenomenon is the frequent misconception, shared by young and old alike, that Africa is a country and not a continent. Teachers need to disabuse students of this misunderstanding if they are going to be successful in developing a new, better understanding of Africa and its diverse countries and populations.

Prejudice: Prejudice is defined as an unfavorable opinion or feeling formed beforehand or without knowledge, thought, or reason. Most people are aware of racial prejudice called racism, but other forms of prejudice exist. Prejudice against women is often called sexism. The assumption that every person is sexually attracted to members of the opposite sex is called heterosexism. Negative attitudes toward Jews are called anti-Semitism. Other prejudices have been labeled ableism and ageism. Explore with students the meaning of these latter terms and how they may be reflected in people's behavior.

Service learning: Service learning combines service to the community with student learning in a way that improves both the student and the community (National Service-Learning Clearinghouse, servicelearning.org).

Simulation: Activities designed to provide real-world problem-solving experiences in the form of a game, simulations often provide a representation of some phenomenon, event, or issue that actually exists or existed in the world. They enable many students to relate easily to and become highly interested in a problem that they might not otherwise take very seriously; in addition, they allow students to assume more control over their own learning and to be less dependent on the teacher. In addition, simulations tend to encourage role plays and the chance to put oneself in another's shoes. These skills also address the different ways of knowing that encompass both traditional and nontraditional modes of cognition because both male and female students exhibit a wide range of different, and not always predictable, learning styles.

Social location, positionality, perspective taking, situatedness: These are all terms that address a common view that human beings begin their cognitive, moral, and imaginative processes from a starting point that is typically influenced by, but cannot be reduced to, the social location each person inhabits in this world. That is, people's life experiences and thus their ways of seeing the world are shaped by attributes such as class, race, religion, gender, ethnicity, age, and so forth. How you were socialized, what you believe to be important, and how you view the world are greatly influenced by these attributes. In classrooms, social location, even from a young age, shapes the experience of learning and engagement with peers, ideas, and teachers. We believe that the invisible hand of male dominance, what some might call patriarchy or sexism, has shaped the academic enterprise to a degree that is often not understood, even by those who work in schools and classrooms on a daily basis.

Socratic seminar: This teaching method is quite similar to the previous term and is derived from Socrates' belief that the surest way to attain reliable knowledge is through the practice of disciplined conversation where opinions and ideas are examined logically, often by a question and answer method, to determine their validity. In a Socratic seminar, participants seek deeper understanding of complex ideas in a rich text through rigorously thoughtful dialogue, rather than by memorizing bits of information. At the end of a successful Socratic seminar, participants often leave with more questions than they brought with them. A Socratic seminar opens with a question posed by the leader (can be a teacher or a student) or solicited from participants as they acquire more experience in seminars. An opening question has no right answer; instead, it reflects a genuine curiosity on the part of the questioner. A good opening question leads participants back to the text as they speculate, evaluate, define, and clarify the issues involved. Responses to the opening question generate new questions from the leader and participants, leading to new responses. In this way, the line of inquiry in a Socratic seminar evolves on the spot rather than being predetermined by the leader. When participants realize that the leader is not looking for right answers but is encouraging them to think out loud and to exchange ideas openly, they discover the excitement of exploring important issues through shared inquiry. Like the graded discussion, the Socratic seminar is supportive of students making their own meaning. They are encouraged to refer back to sources when needed during the discussion because a seminar is not a test of memory. Students are not learning a subject; rather, their goal is to understand the ideas, issues, and values reflected in the text they are analyzing. A Socratic seminar points out the difference between dialogue and debate. Whereas the former is collaborative with multiple voices working toward shared understanding, the latter is adversarial, where two opposing sides try to prove each other wrong. Predicated on open-mindedness, dialogue is designed to enlarge and possibly change a participant's point of view, whereas debate defends assumptions as truth and can create a close-minded attitude, a determination to be right. In dialogue, one searches for strengths in all positions; in debate, one searches for weaknesses in the other position. Dialogue assumes that many people have pieces of answers and that cooperation can lead to a greater understanding; debate assumes a single right answer that somebody already has.

Stereotyping: The process of making a simplified and standardized conception or image invested with special meaning and held in common by members of a group. Many writers on stereotypes (see, e.g., Stephan, 1999) acknowledge that stereotypes and generalizations have a lot in common. Both are forms of attributing characteristics to classes of objects, something people do as a function of language every day. With a certain category people associate a plan of action: For example, chairs are for sitting, holidays are for resting, food is for eating, and so on. In the case of *stereotyping*—that is, attaching a set of traits to a group of people—people overgeneralize (i.e., assume that every person belonging to certain group behaves a certain way or has the same qualities). Sometimes this process of overgeneralizing happens when people interested in gender equity talk about boys and girls. They talk or act in a way that seems to suggest that all boys and all girls behave, think, and act in prescribed ways. It's important to recognize that among all boys and among all girls, among all men and among all women, diversity exists. That's why we believe it is important to tackle issues of both gender and diversity in this chapter. The traits we attach to a group are sometimes negative ones. Stereotyping people presents a problem because it reduces the complex reality of a group of people to a limited set of traits that are used to define that group, but it presents an even bigger problem when the traits associated with a group are negative.

REFERENCES

Alleman, J., & Brophy, J. (1993). Teaching that lasts: College students' reports of learning activities experienced in elementary school social studies. *Social Science Record, 30*(2), 36–48.

Balantic, J., & Libresco, A. (1997). Women's issues in the progressive era. In *Social studies resource guide* (pp. 10–15). Albany: New York State Department of Education. Retrieved on June 12, 2006 from http://llemsc32.nyscd.gov/guides/social/partII4.pdf

Belenky, M. F., Clinchy, B. M. Goldberger, N. R., & Tarule, J. M. (1997a). Toward an education for women. In D. Flinders & S. J. Thornton (Eds.), *The curriculum studies reader* (pp. 306–324). New York: Routledge.

Belenky, M. F., Clinchy, B. M. Goldberger, N. R., & Tarule, J. M. (1997b). *Women's ways of knowing: The development of self, voice, and mind.* New York: Basic Books.

Bennett, P. (1967). *What happened on Lexington Green? An inquiry into the nature and methods of history.* Washington, DC: Office of Education, Bureau of Research. (Eric Document Reproduction Service No. ED 032 333)

Bernard-Powers, J. (1995). Out of the cameos and into the conversation. In J. Gaskell & J. Willinsky (Eds.), *Gender in/forms curriculum: From enrichment to transformation* (pp. 191–209). New York: Teachers College Press.

Brooks, J., & Brooks, M. (1993). *In search of understanding: The case for constructivist classrooms.* Alexandria, VA: Association for Supervision and Curriculum Development.

Browne, A. (1986). *Piggybook.* New York: Alfred A. Knopf.

Cappella, J., & Jamieson, K. H. (1997). *Spiral of cynicism: The press and the public good.* New York: Oxford University Press.

Carter, P. (2002). *Everyone's paid but the teacher.* New York: Teachers College Press.

Center for Civic Education. (1999). *We the people: The citizen and the Constitution.* Calabasas, CA: Author.

Colman, P. (2002). *Girls: A history of growing up female in the United States.* New York: Scholastic.

Cortes, C. (2000). *The children are watching: How the media teach about diversity.* New York: Teachers College Press.

Crocco, M. S. (1995). Bibliography on women's history related to the Nineteenth Amendment. *Social Education, 59*(5), C3.

Crocco, M. S. (1997). Making time for women's history ... .When your survey course is filled to overflowing. *Social Education, 61*(1), 32–37.

Crocco, M. S. (2001). The missing discourse about gender and sexuality in the social studies. *Theory into Practice, 40*(1), 65–71.

Crocco, M. S. (2002). Homophobic hallways: Is anyone listening? *Theory and Research in Social Education, 30*(1), 217–233.

Davidson, J. M., & Lytle, M. H. (1992). *After the fact: The art of historical detection.* NY: McGraw-Hill.

Dewey, J. (1933). *How we think.* Boston: D. C. Heath.

Dewey, J. (1954). *The public and its problems.* Athens: Ohio University Press.

Fallows, J. (1996). *Breaking the news: How the media undermines democracy.* New York: Pantheon Books.

Freire, P. (1970). *Pedagogy of the oppressed.* New York: Continuum.

Gilligan, C. (1982). *In a different voice: Psychological theory and women's development.* Cambridge, MA: Harvard University Press.

Gould, L. (1980). *X.* New York: Stonesong Press.

Hakim, J. (1993). *A history of us.* New York: Oxford University Press.

Human Rights Watch. (2001). *Hatred in the hallways: Violence and discrimination against lesbian, gay, bisexual, and transgender students in US schools.* New York: Author.

Jackson, P. (1968). *The teacher and the machine.* Pittsburgh: University of Pittsburgh Press.

Kelly, J. (1984). *Women, history, and theory: The essays of Joan Kelly.* Chicago: University of Chicago Press.

Kessler-Harris, A. (1981). *Women have always worked: A historical overview.* New York: The Feminist Press.

Lerner, G. (1984). *The creation of patriarchy.* New York: Oxford University Press.

Levstik, L., & Barton, K. C. (2005). *Doing history: Investigation with children in elementary and middle schools* (3rd ed.). Mahwah, NJ: Lawrence Erlbaum Associates.

Libresco, A. S. (2001). Doing real history: Citing your mother in your research paper. In F. L. Stevens (Ed.), *Homespun: Teaching local history in grades 6–12* (pp. 163–169). Portsmouth, NH: Heinemann.

Libresco, A. S. (2002). Nurturing an informed citizenry: Three lessons for second graders. *Social Studies and the Young Learner, 15*(1), 11–16.

Loewen, J. (1995). *Lies my teacher told me: Everything your American History text got wrong.* New York: The New Press.

Minnich, E. (1990). *Transforming knowledge.* Philadelphia, PA: Temple University Press.

National Council for the Social Studies. (1994). *Expectations of excellence: Curriculum standards for social studies.* Washington, DC: Author.

National Issues Forum Institute. (1995). *How can we be fair? The future of affirmative action.* Dubuque, Iowa: Kendall/Hunt Publishing.

National Service Learning Clearinghouse. "What is Service Learning?" [online]. Accessed on June 10, 2006

Noddings, N. (1984). *Caring: A feminine approach to ethics and moral education.* Berkeley: University of California Press.

Noddings, N. (1992). *The challenge to care.* New York: Teachers College Press.

Orenstein, P. (1995). *Schoolgirls.* New York, Anchor.

Parker, W. C. (1991). *Renewing the social studies curriculum.* Alexandria, VA: ASCD.

Parker, W. C. (Ed.). (1996). *Educating the democratic mind.* Albany, NY : State University of New York Press.

Rich, A. (1979). *On lies, secrets, and silence: Selected prose, 1966–1978.* New York: W.W. Norton.

Sadker, D., & Zittleman, K. (2002). Gender bias in teacher education texts: New (and old) lessons. Teacher education textbooks: The unfinished gender revolution. *Educational Leadership, 60*(4), 59–63.

Sadker, M., & Sadker, D. (1995). *Failing at fairness.* New York: Touchstone.

Scieszka, J. (1989). *The true story of the three little pigs* by A. Wolf. New York: Scholastic.

Seuss, Dr. (1958). *Yertle the turtle.* New York: Random House.

Seuss, Dr. (1961). *The sneetches and other stories.* New York: Random House.

Silverstein, S. (1964). *The giving tree.* New York: Harper & Row.

Stephan, W. (1999). *Reducing prejudice and stereotyping in schools.* New York: Teachers College Press.

Style, E. (1988). Curriculum as window and mirror. In M. S. Crocco (Ed.), *Listening for all voices: Gender balancing the school curriculum* (pp. 6–12). Summit, NJ: Oak Knoll School.

Style, E. (1996). Circles of our multicultural selves. *Transformations, 6*(2), 64–84.

Takaki, R. (1993). *A different mirror: A history of multicultural America.* Boston: Little, Brown.

Tetreault, M. K. (1986). Integrating women's history: The case of United States history high school textbooks. *The History Teacher, 19,* 211–252.

Tetreault, M. K. (1987). Rethinking women, gender, and the social studies. *Social Education, 51*(3), 170–178.

Trecker, J. (1971). Women in U.S. history high-school textbooks. *Social Education, 35*(2), 249–261.

Weitzman. D. (1975). *My backyard history book*. Canada: Little, Brown.
Wiggins, G., & McTighe, J. (2005). *Understanding by design* (2nd ed.). Alexandria, VA: Association for Supervision and Curriculum Development.
Young, E. (1992). *Seven blind mice*. New York: Philomel Books.

5

A Gender-Inclusive Approach to English/Language Arts Methods: Literacy With a Critical Lens

Shirley P. Brown
Educational Consultant

Paula Alidia Roy
Writer and Consultant

When someone with the authority of a teacher, say, describes the world and you are not in it, there is a moment of psychic disequilibrium, as if you looked into a mirror and saw nothing. (Rich, 1984, p. 199)

Anyone who has spent time in American schools, and in English/language arts classrooms, knows that gender plays a significant role in everyday interactions among students, teachers, and staff. We take for granted that boys and girl play out "naturally" different roles, approved and validated as cultural mores by the community, including parents and teachers. Consider the beloved rituals of school life: elementary school children who line up by gender; secondary school dances for which tickets are sold to heterosexual couples; football players and their cheerleaders acting out a version of domestic coupling as the girls serve the boys a pregame breakfast or scamper from house to house toilet papering players' yards; at grade levels from primary through high school, the casual, daily fusillade of homophobic slurs directed "in jest" and with deadly seriousness at any boy or girl who appears to cross the rigidly assigned and maintained gender lines ("faggot," "dyke," "homo," "that's so gay"); sexual harassment that passes as flirting; the shrugging off of rude and violent behavior as "boys will be boys" or the adult mantra accepted with almost religious fervor—"hormones." These behaviors are such a part of school life that they go unnoticed and unchallenged, except when they cross a line that involves school rules. Even then, there is little or no institutional analysis of the cultural norms that empower such attitudes and behaviors.

As classroom teachers committed to the education of all students, we strive to treat boys and girls equally. Indeed, we often think that we are unaffected by the assumptions about gender that are all around us, or we accept differences between girls and boys as natural, normal, and unrelated to achievement, a sense of identity, and future aspirations. After all, we no longer officially assign boys to auto shop and girls to sewing, and Title IX has created a world of sports opportunities for young women. Legal challenges reported in the mainstream press have led to greater awareness of sexual harassment and defamatory slurs. What more is there to be said? The classroom is a place for learning, not social change. As long as everyone has access to educational opportunity, what does gender have to do with curriculum and pedagogy in secondary schools, particularly in the English/language arts classroom or lesson?

That question opens up a door to a process of inquiry we hope to encourage in this chapter on English/language arts. There is a considerable body of current research (American Association of University Women, 1992; Gilligan, 1982; Sadker & Sadker, 1994) that points to both obvious and subtle differences in how boys and girls are treated in classrooms. There are other studies about the need for more gender-inclusive, balanced curricula (McIntosh, 1988; Style, 1988), language (Roy & Schen, 1987; Tannen, 1990), and assessment (American Association of University Women & American Institutes for Research, 1999). How is gender constructed in the literature students are expected to read? Does gender have any effect on writing? What do writing assignments reveal about gendered expectations? Does language in the classroom reflect or create gendered meaning? Do assessment instruments, standardized and homemade, reflect or reinforce assumptions about gender and performance? Although we summarize some of this information and provide a bibliography for additional study, what we hope to emphasize here is the importance of each classroom teacher's role as researcher/inquiring observer while guiding students in their reading, writing, classroom talk, and assessment/evaluation. What better place than the English/language arts classroom to observe, listen, and question not only what students say, read, write, and do, but also how we, their teachers, speak, model, guide, and direct them in their time with us each day?

The following essential equity questions (EEQs) are discussed in this chapter:

- **Essential Equity Question 5.1:** How do assumptions about gender influence the teaching of literature?

- **Essential Equity Question 5.2:** How do assumptions about gender influence the teaching of writing?
- **Essential Equity Question 5.3:** How do assessment instruments, standardized and homemade, reflect or reinforce assumptions about gender and performance?

Each EEQ includes two components: a section titled "What We Know" about teaching language arts and a section of Interactions. Interactions are strategies or approaches that call attention to gender as a critical area of analysis in the language arts classroom.

The role teachers take in their own classrooms opens a niche in the wall of assumptions about equal treatment and opportunity for all students. Lest this subject be construed as applicable only to girls, consider the current studies about boys (Kimmel, 2000; Smith & Wilhelm, 2002). More often than not, researchers conclude that what boys need is what children need. Both boys and girls benefit from inquiry into assumptions and expectations about gender and learning. Both boys and girls need to express their emotions and to be treated with respect. Both boys and girls do well in cooperative settings with constructivist pedagogy.

We have divided this chapter on English/language arts into three sections, each beginning with an EEQ. These categories, reading, writing, and assessment, are not, of course, mutually exclusive. Questions, strategies, and challenges posed in one section are relevant to the other sections. Consider, for example, a question about the choice of reading; what students read leads to classroom talk, writing, and assessment. The goal of this chapter is to offer persuasive evidence, drawn from research and observation, that gender itself and our assumptions about it, both conscious and unconscious, affect classroom teaching, curriculum design, and assessment. What can you do with this evidence? You can refuse to take for granted that all is repaired in the gender equity problem; you can look through the lens of gender analysis at what you see and hear and say in English/language arts classrooms; you can apply the research to your own experience as a teacher in your own classroom; and you can continue the process of inquiry and analysis in conversation with students and colleagues.

We are aware that English/language arts teachers, as well as other teachers, are feeling the pressure of high-stakes testing, and we want to remind readers that attention to gender in the classroom is key to fostering and increasing achievement for both boys and girls. Although, regrettably, the National Council of Teachers of English (NCTE) does not specifically name gender as a category in the standards, they include it in the umbrella definition of diversity: "The multitude of differing viewpoints and perspectives—based at least in part on gender, race, culture, ethnicity or religion—in the United States and the world" (National Council of Teachers of English & International Reading Association, 1996, p. 72).

As we explore the various dimensions of the English/language arts classroom, we reference the particular standard governing literature, writing, speaking, listening, and assessment with the reminder that a gendered lens is mediated by race, class, and, significantly, in these post–September 11 days, religion. Additionally, realizing that many key concepts and terms used in English/language arts classrooms vary in meaning, we want to call attention to our definitions (see the appendix).

ESSENTIAL EQUITY QUESTION 5.1:
HOW DO ASSUMPTIONS ABOUT GENDER INFLUENCE THE TEACHING OF LITERATURE?

> Remember that you are this universe and that this universe is you.
> Remember that all is in motion, is growing, is you.
> Remember that language comes from this.
> Remember the dance that language is, that life is.
> Remember (Harjo, 1983, p. 2548)

> NCTE Standard 2: Students read a wide range of literature from many periods in many genres to build an understanding of the many dimensions (e.g., philosophical, ethical, aesthetic) of human experience. (National Council of Teachers of English & International Reading Association, 1996, p. 3)

WHAT WE KNOW

By now it has become a truism that girls excel in writing and reading with the obverse drawing attention—namely, that boys need to be supported in this area. It is not necessary that the pedagogy employed in the English/language arts classroom create winners and losers. It is possible to practice a pedagogy that supports the development of both girls and boys in the classroom, but it will mean that preservice teachers need to be ready to reflect on their own school experiences and to be close observers in their assigned classrooms. They need to be prepared to take an inquiry stance and make gender one of the critical lenses through which they observe. Research studies on how schools are not girl friendly (American Association of University Women, 1992; Sadker & Sadker, 1994) have alerted classroom practitioners to the way commonly accepted school practices may send both subtle and not-so-subtle messages to girls that they are not as important as the boys in the classroom. For example, the Sadkers powerfully demonstrated that girls frequently get less attention in the classroom and that curricula were not rich in material that focused on women. The American Association of University Women (AAUW) reports continue to monitor both classroom practices, but, increasingly, they have focused on girls and women's participation in math and science fields (AAUW, Gender Gaps, 1999; AAUW, Tech-Savvy, 2000; Kramarae, 2001) as well as on underserved populations such as Latinas in Si Se Puede (Yes, We Can; Ginorio & Huston, 2001). At the same time, developments in feminist pedagogy emphasized how a shift in classroom practices across the curriculum could enhance girls' learning and achievement (Gilligan & Brown, 1993; Maher & Ward, 2002). Researchers began to see that a more cooperative framework for learning as well as an emphasis on personal connections served girls more effectively than a competitive, impersonal environment. What was overlooked in the initial flurry of debate over the validity of these findings was the assertion that a cooperative, stress-free classroom environment is good pedagogy for all members of the classroom and has not been limited to the work of feminist pedagogues (see Sizer, n.d.). Interestingly, there is no credible research to demonstrate that boys do better in impersonal, competitive environments. There are assumptions that, because boys have traditionally done better in those environments they thrive in them. Recently, there has been an outpouring of books and research on boys and the implications for classroom strategies and structures. For some time, research has demonstrated that boys outperform girls in science and math, although that gap is closing, but boys have not kept pace with girls in reading and the language arts in schools as measured by grades and standardized test scores. Yet men still publish more and occupy more of the highest positions in the publishing industry. The research that shows boys lagging behind girls in reading deserves closer analysis. For example, a National Institute of Child Health and Development (NICHD; n.d.) document notes:

> About 10 million children have difficulties learning to read. From 10 to 15 percent eventually drop out of high school; only 2 percent complete a four-year college program. Surveys of adolescents and young adults with criminal records show that about half have reading difficulties. Similarly, about half of youths with a history of substance abuse have reading problems. Even people with a mild reading impairment do not read for fun. For them, reading requires so much effort that they have little energy left for understanding what they have just read. Contrary to what many people believe, NICHD research showed that reading disability affects boys and girls at roughly the same rate. Reading disabled boys, however, are more likely to be referred for treatment because they are more likely to get the teacher's attention by misbehaving. Reading disabled girls may escape the teacher's attention because they may withdraw into quiet daydreaming.

In other words, the popular perception that boys are in greater need of remediation is based on statistics that demonstrate that boys are referred for help more often than girls, not on greater need (Sahywitz, Sahywitz, Fletcher, & Escobar, 1990).

INTERACTION 5.1:
Delving Into the Personal

INTASC Principle 3: Diversity in Learning

Invoking personal experience is an effective way to help challenge conventional assumptions about gender. If you ask most teachers, they think the teaching and study of literature in high school is biased in favor of men. Most teachers will either deny the issue or say that the question is irrelevant; after all, literature is literature, dealing with universals that apply to everyone. If, instead, teachers examine their own experiences and use a participatory exercise and discussion of its results, they may find themselves more willing to consider the topic of gender bias in the study of literature.

1. Begin by completing a stem sheet. (See model or create your own; the idea is to probe your memories of your own experiences of reading in secondary school English classrooms.)
2. Read, initially without comment or discussion, at least one of the responses that you wrote, so there are no interruptions before every voice is heard.
3. Consider what you wrote and heard from peers; use the experiences to discuss the titles that you were asked to read, how ideas about "heroes," important conflicts, the roles of men and women, appropriate behavior for men and women, and so forth are constructed, validated, or interrogated by the reading. Note, too, the intersections of race and class with gender.
4. A useful essay to consider is Emily Style's "Curriculum as Window and Mirror" (1988). A useful poem is Becky Bertha's "In Response to Reading Children's Book Announcements." *Publishers Weekly,* February 12, 1982.

Model Stem Sheet for "Getting Started"

(You may wish to choose from among these suggested stems or create your own.)

As you respond to the following questions, think back to your English/language arts classes in elementary and secondary school.

Women writers I remember reading:

A memorable protagonist from a work read in school:

A female character I remember from a work read in school:

Based on your memories of what you read in English classes in school, complete the following statements either with the name of a character or a descriptive quality.

A hero is:

A "good" woman is:

A "bad" woman is:

My favorite work read for English class is:

because:

What do you remember reading by or about any of the following:

Women of color (Black, Asian, Hispanic, Native American, etc.):

Men of color:

Gays or lesbians:

Do you think the experiences of women and men are validly represented by the literature you read?

INTERACTION 5.2:
Different Ways of Reading

INTASC Principle 7: Instructional Planning Skills

Current research on boys and literacy continues to confirm that feminist pedagogy is really about sound, inclusive pedagogy. It is a pedagogy that emphasizes the importance of knowing students personally and making connections and identifying their interests. It is a pedagogy that builds on the idea that learning is profoundly social. Michael Smith and Jeffrey Wilhelm's (2002) recent study of boys and literacy confirmed those principles. In their study of 49 boys from diverse backgrounds and varied levels of achievement in four very different school settings and three states, they found that generally boys read for information and usually read school materials. Boys who were labeled as struggling readers reported that they became interested in school-based literacy when they had teachers who were attentive and supportive and when they were given choice in their assignments. We can see here the need for personal connections and identification of interests that feminist pedagogy has already stressed. The subject matter may be different, but the principles are the same. Strategies that build on inclusive and personal connections include literature circles, dramatization, visualization, stem sheets, reading logs, and dialogue journals. Undoubtedly, there are others. What follows are some descriptions of these strategies to test and observe in classrooms. Once again, we urge practitioners to become observers of students in the classroom.

Stem sheets are simple writing prompts that give all students the opportunity to reflect quietly before beginning to talk about literature (or a topic). Once all students have spent time reflecting quietly, guided by "stems" devised by the teacher to encourage different ways of thinking about the topic, the teacher can call on a given student; ask students to "read around" in a circle, with each choosing a response; or use the written prompts in other ways. You may wish to give the two following models to your students as examples of strategies for opening up the discussion of reading to everyone in the class.

Sample Stem Sheets

Secondary sample

Title of Work _____

1. When I completed my reading of _____ I felt:

---

2. A particularly moving or affecting scene to me was:

3. A question I'd like to ask the author is:

4. After reading _____, I wonder:

5. Please find and copy here a short passage that affected you or that raises a question or comment for us to discuss.

Elementary sample

Title of Work _____

1. After I finished reading _____, I felt:

2. The character I would choose as a friend is:

3. A question I would like to ask the author is:

4. Something in the story that I would change if I could is:

5. After reading this novel, I wonder:

6. Please write a question that you would like to discuss with your classmates or reading group.

INTERACTION 5.3:
Reading Collaboratively

INTASC Principle 1: Subject-Matter Knowledge

Literature circles are vehicles for supporting independent reading and fostering social connections and learning. They are formed by groups of five students who change roles each time they meet. Students select a book for independent reading, usually with some recommendation from the teacher, and then rotate the following roles (Daniel, 1994):

- Discussion director: thinks up good discussion questions, convenes the meeting, and keeps the discussion on track
- Connector: connects the text to the his or her own experiences in life or with other literature
- Literary luminator/Passage master: selects and reads, or asks someone to read, about four memorable or important sections to the group (these sections should have special meaning for the Luminator)
- Illustrator: makes a graphic representation to represent a selection from the book (this role opens up discussions via multiple intelligences)
- Vocal enricher: selects text from the passage under discussion and provides the page number where they are found, a dictionary definition, and a sentence
- Summarizer: gives a brief overview of the day's assignment.

Literature circles, if used effectively, prevent domination by one person, usually the strong male in the group, and confirm that everyone has a role to play in reading and interpreting texts.

INTERACTION 5.4:
Many Ways to Read

INTASC Principle 4: Variety of Instructional Strategies

A great deal of Jeffrey Wilhelm's (1997) research has been with struggling readers—more often than not, boys. His observations have led him to see that struggling readers frequently decode but do not visualize what they read; thus, Wilhelm employs puppets, skits, and dramatization of scenes from novels to help such readers understand what they are reading. Younger children might be urged to make puppets or use stick figures to enact a scene. The puppets would, of course, represent characters in the book under consideration, and the children would have to demonstrate their understanding of the text by the words and actions of their puppets. Older students also enjoy making and working with puppets, writing and acting out skits, and making audio and videotapes of their work.

INTERACTION 5.5:
Valuing All Voices

INTASC Principle 2: Human Development and Learning

Elaine Amidon of the New York City Writing Project developed the strategy of text rendering a way to give equal weight to what readers think is important in a piece. All too often, teachers ask, "What is the author trying to say here?" Instead, teachers might ask,"What is it that each of us is hearing or seeing in a particular piece? How can I hear, in a nonjudgmental way, what others see and hear in a piece of poetry or prose." This approach works most effectively with a short piece. An excerpt from a longer work, a single page, or, perhaps, a few paragraphs are difficult. Text rendering allows students to stay with a piece and explore it from different angles. The following steps will guide your text rendering:

1. Select a reading that is no more that a single page in length or select a poem. Have students read the passage silently; then aloud.
2. Ask students to choose a sentence that stands out for them and mark it with the numeral 1.
3. Ask students to pick out a phrase (you may have to emphasize the meaning of a phrase) that stands out for them and mark it with the numeral 2.
4. Ask students to select a word that is important in the poem/prose piece and mark it with the numeral 3.

5. Finally, ask students to supply their own word that expresses what they take
from the piece and mark that word with the numeral 4.

The next part of text rendering requires that teachers be very explicit in their instructions, or else the rendering will lose its power. Tell students that they will be responding in four rounds, and they must be prepared to read their choices without
hesitation. Repetition is fine. In fact, it enhances the power of the reading. Ask students to read Selection 1 without comment. After everyone reads Selection 1, go
immediately to Selection 2, then Selection 3, then Selection 4. More than likely
some students will repeat some parts of the piece, and others will pick more obscure
parts. Ask students what they heard. Did the read-arounds open new ways of understanding the piece or seeing new meaning in it? The advantage of text rendering is
that it allows for a variety of readings, with no one right answer. Everyone partici-
pates and adds to the meaning of the piece. The exercise could also be followed by
asking students to write about what new meanings they heard in the piece.

INTERACTION 5.6:
Critical Literary Theory and Some Texts to Consider

INTASC Principle 4: Variety of Instructional Strategies

Critical literary analysis has become important in most high school literature classes,
even as middle school and elementary level books are discussed and interpreted. Although reader response theory still permeates most classrooms, introducing students
to the ways various methods of critical analysis open up literature in new and exciting
ways is also useful for interpreting literature through the lens of gender.

In 1971, Adrienne Rich coined the term *re-vision* to name the challenge of looking at works of literature "with fresh eyes, of entering an old text from a new critical
direction" (p. 35). Since then feminist literary criticism has led the way in opening
up the canon of "great" (and therefore teachable) literature to include more works
by White women and women and men of color. Not without controversy (sometimes referred to as the canon wars), this movement toward greater inclusiveness in
what students read has also raised important questions about how literature is interpreted. Although teachers may take for granted now the presence on book lists of
more works by and about all women and men of color, there is much to be gained by
looking through the lens of gender at all the works taught and discussed in classrooms. Thus the movement toward a more inclusive pedagogy embraces both the
choice of texts (not always the province of the classroom teacher) and the approaches taken to teaching them. Any text may be interrogated in terms of gender as
well as of race, class, and so on. Some questions that teachers might suggest
students ask of a text include the following:

• Who is speaking? Out of what place? What time? What culture?

- Whose voice is absent?
- If the main character changed her or his sex, how would the work be altered? Could the plot develop as in the original work? Why? Why not?
- Are the characters stereotypically gendered? What descriptors or actions lead you to that analysis?
- How do other factors such as race, class, ethnicity, and sexual orientation interact with gender?

These questions and others may be asked about both male and female roles, stereotypes, and characters. They may also be asked about race, class, ethnicity, and sexuality. The boys and girls, young women and men, in our classrooms see themselves through the lens of gender, among others. To be restricted to reading books that claim universality for the experience only of men (usually White men) is to expect a girl or woman to deny or, at least , undervalue her own experience of the world. To be taught to interpret literature without interrogating its many stereotypical assumptions is to deny interesting and exciting opportunities to ask important questions about how gender is constructed and how assumptions about gender permeate expectations, aspirations, and social interactions. Elaine Showalter (1985) noted in her introduction to *The New Feminist Criticism:*

> Whether concerned with the literary representations of sexual difference, with the ways that literary genres have been shaped by masculine or feminine values, or with the exclusion of the female voice from the institutions of literature, criticism, and theory, feminist criticism has established gender as a fundamental category of literary analysis. (p. 3)

Some social critics and educators will argue that such an approach politicizes the teaching of literature; in response, others note that to blind oneself to the ways gender plays out in literature is also a political stance. On a more neutral note, teachers seeking gender equity in their classrooms want to offer students of all ages the opportunity to read literature that offers experiences that are new to them and experiences in which they can see themselves or find role models. Consider the number of mature women who felt the importance of Louisa May Alcott's *Little Women,* one of the few books that offered a variety of female characters and experiences to earlier generations of readers. What Emily Style (1988) named "windows and mirrors" expresses the ideal that curricula should offer all students ways to look without and within their own worlds. For elementary school children, no less than secondary school adolescents, it is interesting to include questions about gender in discussions of reading both classic works and newer titles. How would *Where the Wild Things Are* be different if Max were Maxine? How would *Lord of the Flies* play out if the characters were all girls? Historical stories at all levels offer opportunities to consider how men and women were expected to act in the context of a particular time and place and how some resisted or subverted the stereotypes. Assumptions about courage, violence, the double standard, marriage and family, and many more offer fertile ground for discussions to which all students bring their lived experience of gender.

Strategy: Comparing Critical "Lenses."   Consider the following brief examples of analyzing two works of literature, one a frequently taught "classic" of the high school canon, and the other, a newer addition to many high schools' English curricula.

King Oedipus by Sophocles (1974) is perhaps the most frequently taught Greek tragedy, usually taught as the model for Aristotle's definition of the tragic hero, as the literary inspiration of Freud's concept of the Oedipal complex, and as a representative example of classical Greek philosophy, theology, and justice. Although all of these approaches are mediated by translation over centuries, with its imposition of cultural and social assumptions, the play remains a powerful source of questions about fate and free will, the relationship between human and divine, and the ancient drama of family dynamics and destinies. All of these angles on the play may elicit interest and creative thinking from students and teachers. If the lens of gender is added, the analysis becomes even more interesting and relevant. Consider the following questions and considerations: In what way(s) is Oedipus's "fate" related to his being a man? A son?

Using Carol Gilligan's (1982) ideas about justice and connection, reread the dialogues between Oedipus and Jocasta and consider their different responses to the gradual revelations of the murder and incest that has infected their lives. Consider the fates of the two male and two female children of Oedipus and Jocasta in *Oedipus* by Sophocles (1974). Explore the implications of the distinction based on gender that Oedipus makes when he talks to Creon about his sons and his daughters (pp. 1462–1466). He assumes that his sons will survive, but his daughters will need Creon's help. Later, he bewails the lot of his daughters because they will not be marriageable (pp. 1531–1533).

When a teacher chooses to consider these lines for one day's discussion of the play or as the basis of a journal entry or a written response, when the teacher asks students to compare Oedipus's attitude toward sons and daughters to their lived experience of being sons or daughters, that teacher is looking through what we call the lens of gender. Such an analysis enriches the study without usurping other critical approaches.

Their Eyes Were Watching God, by Zora Neale Hurston, is a more recent addition to the study of literature in many English classes. The novel is very much about gender in the sense that it is the story of a woman's search for identity. As such it fits into a category familiar to and beloved by English teachers, although the most commonly taught titles under this thematic umbrella involve the struggles of male, usually White, protagonists. Thus, it is easy to ask questions about how the search for identity, the Bildungsroman, as it were, looks different when the protagonist is not Holden Caulfield or Huck Finn or Gene and Phineas or Paul Baumer or Stephen Daedelus or Hamlet but instead Janey, a Black girl who is becoming a woman.

Often the introduction of such a woman-centered story leads some students (and critics) to complain about the author being "biased" against men. In fact, in this text, men are not heroic or noble; they are frequently selfish, violent characters who stand between Janey and her dreams. Even her true love, Teacake, is flawed in many ways. Once again, however, such objections can lead to a closer consideration of Hurston's development of character, of how she understands expectations about gender roles as formative influences on both male and female characters.

Joe Starks, Janie's second husband to whom she is married for many years, though self-centered and possessive, is driven by his need to prove his power and success; Hurston makes this clear even as she shows how this drive destroys any chance of tenderness or shared power in their marriage. The discussion of how men are presented in the novel is another example of a gendered lens; it will lead to lively debate and invite comparison with how women are presented in works with male protagonists on a search for identity (see text pairing later in this chapter). This text, of course, also offers opportunities for discussions about race and class, for analysis of Hurston's language, for historical background about time and place, for consideration of structure and form, and for deconstruction, if the teacher so desires. A curriculum is enriched by choosing books by or about women and applying gender as one category of analysis of them.

Text pairing is an interesting approach to a consideration of gender in literature that involves pairing texts that "speak" to one another about stereotypes and assumptions. Here are some possible pairings of texts often taught in high schools:

- *Death of a Salesman,* by Arthur Miller, and *Fences,* by August Williams: Here both gender and race can be interrogated in the closely parallel roles of fathers, mothers, and sons struggling to meet the demands of the "American Dream."
- *A Doll's House,* by Ibsen, and *The Awakening,* by Kate Chopin: Both texts depict the middle-class expectations of female behavior as wife and mother, and different modes of resistance are explored.
- *The Awakening* and *Their Eyes Were Watching God,* by Zora Neale Hurston: This pairing invites a comparison of two women, one White, one Black, searching for a sense of identity and joy. One experienced teacher developed a unit in which students read *Hamlet* and *Their Eyes Were Watching God* and then compared the texts' uses of poetic imagery, themes, and characters, thus embracing several critical approaches with what seem like widely divergent styles and time periods that actually emerge as comparable in many ways.

Strategy: Middle School Reading Lists.   Middle school reading lists have changed considerably over the past years, and while it is still possible to find familiar titles such as *The Red Badge of Courage, Romeo and Juliet, To Kill a Mockingbird,* along with a sprinkling of something by Dickens, one is as likely to encounter some truly wonderful young adult literature that has blossomed over the past 10 or so years.

Many of the works by Mildred Taylor and Christopher Paul Curtis deal with racism in a forthright manner. Lois Lowry explores anti-Semitism and Nazism in The Netherlands in *Number the Stars* and genetic engineering in *The Giver*. Yoshiko Uchida reveals the toll that Executive Order 9066 had on Japanese Americans living on the West Coast. There are many other authors, such as Avi, Gary Paulsen, Gary Soto, and Karen Hesse, who need to be part of a middle school curriculum. However, there are a few titles that are especially useful in generating discussions about issues, and some of them, such as *Speak* by Laurie Halse Anderson, are controversial but address issues faced by girls and are frequently silenced. Anderson's novel deals with the rape of a ninth grader by a school hero. Because the young man is popular, the rape victim is reluctant to talk about the crime; instead, she stops talking altogether. It takes a dangerous situation for her friend to get her talking again. Aside from the literary qualities of the novel, which are impressive, the novel lends itself to discussion of how girls can protect themselves against rape and how to handle it if it does happen. Raising this topic in a coed class can be tricky, but its usefulness outweighs the risks.

Other key texts that lend themselves to gender issues include *The House on Mango Street,* by Sandra Cisneros, a novel that generates discussions of gender construction and provides a gold mine of writing prompts. It can be an interesting contrast to Walter Dean Myers's *Scorpions*. Many teachers use the "My Name" chapter as an invitation for students to write about their name, and, invariably, cultural practices emerge as students compare how they are named. No one can miss that women seldom, if ever, have a junior, senior, or the third, attached to their names. The discussion of such practices involve the rights of women and changing property laws as well as common practices of today where women retain their birth names when they marry. The book is essentially a collection of short pieces describing the girlhood of a working class Latina. *Scorpions* depicts the different pressures that afflict young Black men and the pressure they feel to join gangs. Embedded in the text is the notion of manhood and how it is defined.

Katherine Paterson can be relied on to engage middle school readers in the same way as Walter Dean Myers. Two of her books, *Lyddie* and *Jip, His Story*, can be usefully paired to contrast expectations and restrictions for girls and boys in urban and rural settings. Both books are set in roughly the same time period—1843 for *Lyddie*, 1855 for *Jip, His Story*. With the background of a changing nation, Paterson depicts the different struggles for independence in New England.

At the elementary level, where so many books enter the classroom, the teacher may want to consider the balance of male and female protagonists, be they animals or humans; the roles of women and men in the stories; and the inclusiveness of the pictures. There has been such an explosion of books that emphasize diversity that there is much to choose from, although sometimes diversity does not include gender. The school librarian can be an important resource as well. However, we recommend that Jane Yolen's *Sleeping Ugly,* Robert Munsch's *Paper Bag Princess,* and *Heather Has Two Mommys* be a part of every classroom library.

Strategy: Thematic Inclusion. Many teachers develop language arts units around themes such as war or justice. Gender roles can be developed into a thematic unit, with attention to such subtopics as love and romance, marriage and family, sex, and identity. In developing thematic units, teachers can better ensure gender fairness by including topics that affect women's lives or texts that highlight women's experiences. The sexual double standard, for example, appears often as an accepted norm, with stereotypes emerging unchallenged. For example, undeniable rape occurs or is discussed casually in *Tess of the d'Urbervilles,* by Thomas Hardy; *A Streetcar Named Desire,* by Tennessee Williams; and *One Flew Over the Cuckoo's Nest* by Ken Kesey; however, students seldom see it as such because of the way the text is written. On the other hand, sexual violence is treated very differently in such texts as *Sula* and *Beloved,* by Toni Morrison; *I Know Why the Caged Bird Sings,* by Maya Angelou; and *The Bell Jar,* by Sylvia Plath. Female characters such as Sophocles' Antigone, Shaw's St. Joan, Hurston's Janey (*Their Eyes Were Watching God*), and Hawthorne's Hester Prynne offer complicating challenges to stereotypes about courage, independence, and autonomy.

The examples are endless; any curriculum or text a teacher chooses or is assigned to teach is open to interrogation through the lens of gender. Students bring to that lens a wealth of lived experience and thus respond enthusiastically (sometimes dramatically!) to discussions about how men and women are presented in literature. If we think of film and television as text, using a gendered lens for critical analysis is useful in having students think about the cumulative effect of gendered roles. The following approach opens up the possibility for both a written report and class discussion. In addition, because so many students rely on the Internet for information, the strategy can be adapted for an analysis of Web sites and software programs, especially those aimed at younger children. Although we have included this model under the topic of reading, it certainly applies to writing and classroom discussions.

Secondary Sample

Essay/project incorporating gender as a category of analysis Film, TV, media: Contemporary issues and insights

For this essay/project, we will extend our study of film, television, and media through your research into an area of interest to you. As suggested earlier, posing questions is a good way to begin finding your topic. As always, I expect that this essay/project will be more than a report. The issue you choose should offer room for opinion, argument, speculation, and controversy. Certainly, the general fields of film, TV, and media offer many opportunities for challenging topics. The following questions occur to me as I think about this topic:

What occurs to you?

How are women portrayed in contemporary films (or films of another era)?

Are attitudes toward gender roles shaped by portrayals in film or on television?

Does viewing violence lead to violence?

Are films and TV too violent?

How are older people (particularly older women) portrayed in film or television?

What messages do little girls and boys get from Disney?

How are gay/lesbian people portrayed on film or television?

Do people believe what they hear on talk shows? Should they?

How is sex portrayed on television? In film?

Is news reporting neutral?

What influence do advertisers exert on the content of television shows? Magazines?

What magazines do you read and what are their hidden and not so hidden messages?

Should there be a film rating system? Who should decide and how?

What about children's television? What would you allow your child to watch?

How are Black people (or any group) portrayed on television and in film?

These are just a few ideas. Each of them could easily be reshaped or focused differently. Please make your own list and be prepared to develop a topic idea by _____

Use this space to write some questions of your own or variations on the questions listed above.

ESSENTIAL EQUITY QUESTION 5.2:
HOW DO ASSUMPTIONS ABOUT GENDER INFLUENCE THE TEACHING OF WRITING?

> Here is the great difference between reading and writing. Reading is a voca-
> tion, a skill, at which, with practice you are bound to become more expert.
> What you accumulate as a writer are mostly uncertainties and anxieties.
> (Sontag, 2000, p. 228)

> NCTE Principle 5: Students employ a wide range of spoken, written, and vi-
> sual language (e.g., conventions, style, vocabulary) to communicate effec-
> tively with a variety of audiences for different purposes. (National Council of
> Teachers of English & International Reading Association, 1996, p. 3)

WHAT WE KNOW

Gender Issues in the Teaching of English (McCracken & Appleby, 1992), published 10 years ago, defined issues in the English/language arts classroom that educators are still struggling to identify and remediate. Although teachers are probably
more conscious of surface issues, such as using gender-neutral work titles (e.g.,
mail carrier, chairperson, flight attendant), there is still a need to fully understand
how differences in socialization of girls and boys affect their writing and consequently their grades in school as well as their career choices. Research in the field of
writing has helped educators understand how fluidity may be increased by journal
writing and how gender construction is reified in student pieces. Research into the
academic essay with its assumption of Aristotelian logic as the highest form of
thinking has challenged that assumption and argued for greater variety in the formal essay as a product of different ways of thinking (Sanborn, 1992, p. 144).

Research has also helped us see how writing can be a powerful tool for reform-
ing and constructing gender in the classroom for both girls and boys, if the discourse can be rechanneled to "write against the grain," not an easy task. Pam Gilbert
and Sandra Taylor's *Fashioning the Feminine: Girls, Popular Culture, and Schooling* (1991) demonstrated how difficult it is to shake off popular culture and reposi-
tion women as having agency. They cited a study of a course in which students were
introduced to sexist stereotypes in children's literature. The students became
skilled in identifying how the stereotypes were created, yet they reproduced them
when asked to construct their own children's stories. The authors found that although 82% of the students were female, only 25% of the stories had females as
central characters (pp. 115–116). When they interviewed the students, many felt it
was more natural to write that way. Gilbert and Taylor argued, "The naturalization
of generic convention is a major difficulty in the classroom because it obscures the
discursive and therefore ideological construction of popular genres" (p. 116). In
short, the preponderance of stock qualities ascribed to women and men, a kind of
essentialism, makes it difficult for students to write in a way that challenges con-

ventional notions of gender. Their work makes it incumbent on teachers to raise questions with students when they are involved in creative fiction: Why did you make the main character a male? A female? Could they be the opposite sex? What would you have to change and why? Although Gilbert and Taylor's work centered on creative fiction, their research points to the need for writers of any genre to be aware of how they construct their work.

Gilbert and Taylor (1991) also reviewed studies that point to the resistance that working-class girls bring to school culture and noted that in the studies they considered working-class girls resist middle-class norms of femininity. Their review centered on English schools, but there is growing research to confirm those results in the United States. Tom Newkirk (2000) also wrote about gender differences in writing. His article on the gender gap in writing compared the differences between girls and boys in writing performance and noted that the differential is similar to the differences in achievement between Whites and other racial/ethnic groups. His point is not to minimize the need to reduce the gap between racial groups but to point out that the gender gap is similarly wide. Newkirk made the following points:

> Since Donald Graves' research on gender differences in the early 70's, researchers have documented consistent gender differences in writing:
>
> - When first graders were asked to imagine themselves as an animal in a story they might write, there were clear gender differences in the choices. Girls tended to choose domesticated animals (cat, horse), while boys chose animals that are dangerous and wild (cougar, monster) or comic (monkey), (Ollia, Bullen, & Collis, 1989).
> - Second-grade girls tend to choose "primary territory" (home, school, parents, friends) as topics for writing. Boys consistently choose secondary territory (professions) or extended territory (wars, presidents) (Graves, 1973; McAuliffe, 1994).
> - Second-grade boys write stories which focus on contests, physical and social, in which the protagonists act alone. Success is determined by winning or losing in these combative tests. By contrast, girls' writing tends to focus on joint action and protagonists who struggle to remain connected to the community (McAuliffe, 1994; Trepanier-Street, Momatowski, & McNair, 1990).
> - When boys include females in their stories, they tend to be passive and, not, coincidentally, professionless (Gray-Schlegel & Gray-Schlegel, 1995; Many, 1989). They tend to write about males in traditional roles of authority. When, for example, boys were asked to invert gender roles and write about a male nurse, one had the hospital invaded by aliens to change the terms of the task (Trepanier-Street, Romatowski, & McNair, 1990).
> - Because boys' writing deals so consistently with physical contests, it is far more violent than girls' writing (S. Peterson, 1998), a trend one pair of researchers called "disturbing" (Gray-Schlegel & Gray-Schlegel, p. 167).

- In a study of first-year college students, women wrote autobiographical essays that were judged better than those of their male counterparts (Peterson, 1991). In analyzing the differences, she found that males tended to write about times when they acted individually, often in physical challenges that built confidence. Women tended to write about a crisis in a relationship (boyfriend, family, or an encounter with culturally different persons). In terms of writing qualities, males showed no deficit in rendering detail; their lower scores were due to perceived difficulty in rendering "significance," in the capacity to reflect on the meaning of the experience.

- Boys' preferences in reading and writing narratives are more closely aligned with visually mediated storytelling—film, TV, video games, computer graphics. They also rank humor higher than girls do. Millard (1997) suggested that the traditional literature-based curriculum may ignore the more visually-mediated narratives that boys prefer. (p. 295)

Newkirks's (2000) summary of some of the outstanding research on gender and writing throughout the grades raises very complex questions: Is it the role of the English/language arts teacher to give boys' writing a lower grade because its subject matter may tend toward the individualistic or violent? Is there a way to use the kinds of writing content that students gravitate toward as a point of discussion in writing conferences? How can teachers construct effective assignments that ask students to invert the roles they normally assign to the sexes? How do English/language arts teachers separate content from form and should they? Isn't education about striving for a better, less violent world?

Curiously enough, the kinds of writing in which girls seem to excel in school does not seem to matter in the larger world (the increased use of computers has changed the nature of secretarial work, but computer use for women has still largely remained in the keyboarding realm, not in programming):

[I]t is men who are generally regarded as being the writers of philosophy, psychology, science, history, poetry and drama. Control of the more powerful discourses lies with men; the lower status forms—the service industry of writing such as secretarial work, family letter-writing, diary entries, genealogical records, novel writing—are the ones dominated by women workers. (Gilbert & Taylor, 1991, p. 105)

The research demonstrates how complicated writing issues are, but teacher inquiry/research offers an opportunity for teachers to test how consistent the patterns are in their own classrooms. Teacher inquiry can also provide a way of observing how and when gendered writing resists the expected. There are no easy answers, but the data we have alert us to the ways that students exercise choice in their writing and give us a key to understanding how they think about gender.

The current emphasis on writing process is exactly what it is called. Writing process is concerned with the process that helps writers move from early drafts to more polished pieces. However, teachers need to consider product as well. A polished piece of sexist writing is no more desirable than an unpolished one. Although there are style manuals that provide guidance in editorial questions, there are no manuals to avoid recreating stereotypes (for a brief history of the development of nonsexist use of language with examples, see http://www.stetson.edu/departments/history/nongenderlang.html). The author provides suggestions on how to alternate gendered pronouns and includes suitable synonyms for words such as *mankind* (use *humanity* or *human kind* and avoid *manning* a table; *staff* it instead). We would argue that the research on writing is evidence of the need for teachers to be keen observers in their own classrooms and to use student writing to raise critical questions about gendered preferences with the students.

INTERACTION 5.7:
Switching Genders

INTASC Principle 4: Variety of Instructional Strategies

K. M., a first-year teacher in a large urban high school, asked her students to write a response to the following question: If you woke up tomorrow and discovered that you were the opposite sex from the one you are now, how would your life be different? Although some of the responses dwelled on the physical changes, many focused on the expectations for girls and boys. One girl wrote:

> If I woke up as a boy, I wouldn't have to clean the whole house by myself all the time. I wouldn't have to cook for myself all the time either. My mom would probably spoil me more, give me anything I wanted. I would have the same amount of freedom. But my mom wouldn't ask me as many questions. I probably wouldn't be all stressed out about succeeding in life and my family probably wouldn't expect much of me. I really wouldn't have to care about my outside appearance, nope, I would have to care more than I do now. I wouldn't be as close to my mom as I am now. I would probably be more outspoken and not so reserved. I would have more of a social life, more buddies.

The following response is more or less typical from a boy:

> If I woke up as a girl, I would feel the same. I would be angry at myself because I like being a boy because you have so many advantages. My mom said being a girl is hard work. You have to go through pregnancy, being ladylike and keep your hair done, etc. There is nothing wrong with girls but I would hate to wake up and become one. I can't even think to put myself in the situation. It is too many responsibilities.

This assignment served to open a sustained critical analysis throughout the semester of how literature constructs gender expectations. It was not a standalone assignment but became part of a thread that was a part of the teacher's curriculum. However, the assignment itself purposefully invited the students to think about the privileges and disadvantages accrued to each sex. As a starting point for asking students to think about gender roles, it was effective, but only because it became a point of reference. The teacher continued to use writing assignments that required the students to think about what traits/qualities authors attribute to women and men.

INTERACTION 5.8:
The Importance of Choice

INTASC Principle 5: Motivation and Management

There are hundreds of strategies that English/language arts teachers use to analyze literature, promote improved writing skills, and support literacy in K–12 classrooms. The writing strategies that are emphasized here have the following characteristics:

- They support and honor independent thought and choice.
- They encourage cooperative learning
- They use literature prompts that raise questions about gender roles and expectations.
- They build on authentic experiences and writing assignments.

Across the grade levels, it is critical that students be given opportunities to write for authentic purposes. They can create posters, write letters to the editors, construct surveys, keep class meeting minutes, and author school handbooks. With sexual harassment still a largely unaddressed topic, students in middle and senior high schools can develop and write a sexual harassment policy. Not only would that involve careful technical writing, but students would also have the opportunity to see and understand how the careful choice of words is both important and difficult in a first draft.

With service learning rapidly becoming a part of many students' lives, the opportunity to suggest projects that affect the lives of students in schools is obvious. Aside from projects that may affect lunch menus or subject selection, service learning can be connected to investigations of such topics as bullying, harassment, and teasing; street violence; and other topics that affect the lives of students on a daily basis. Bullying and teasing go across grade levels, and students can be encouraged to research the topic in their school to affect changes in school handbooks, for example. The critical point here is that students identify a topic that is important to them.

INTERACTION 5.9:
Literacy Autobiography

INTASC Principle 2: Human Development and Learning

Asking students to write literacy autobiographies is not only a useful assignment allowing the instructor to know her or his students in a different way but is also an opportunity for students to reflect on how their socialization has affected their self-concept. The assignment, however, needs to clearly indicate that the essay is not a chronology but an investigation of the forces that shaped them. Where and how did they learn to doubt themselves? Feel confident? How did they learn about gender? What have been some of the critical incidents in their lives? More pointedly, asking students to write about their history as writers is useful in surfacing gender issues as students think about their experiences and have an opportunity to share them. They should be asked to think about the following questions:

- What are some of your earliest recollections of writing? Did you keep a diary? Did you keep a log of your trading cards?
- When did you start using a computer? How do you use it? Do you use it primarily for e-mail or for other purposes?
- What do you recall about teacher responses to your earliest assignments? What were you encouraged to do? Not do?
- Did you write about what you read? What are your memories of some of the things you read in elementary school? High school?

These questions are just a sample of the kinds of issues students might consider. It is far more effective to have the class brainstorm possible questions that would help surface how students are socialized into gendered writing. However, the assignment will lose its impact if the teacher is the only audience. It is important for the students to share their essays and analyze them for differences that could be attributed to gender.

As students share their essays, it is useful to chart them so that students can see similarities and differences. For example, how many boys and how many girls kept diaries? What are the different ways boys and girls use the Internet? What kinds of writing are favored by whom? How do people use e-mail—to stay in touch or for information? Students will soon discover that the writing they like and the writing they reject are by no means universal, and the process of analyzing writing preferences will sensitize them to gender and other equity issues.

INTERACTION 5.10:
Turf Map

INTASC Principle 4: Human Development and Learning

A turf map activity can be as simple as a rough freehand drawing of the route a child takes to school or a representation of his or her world (i.e., the area where the child is allowed to travel alone). Or a turf map can made precisely and involve scale. Geographic accuracy may be more important in the social studies classroom if cartography is the subject at hand. For the purposes of an English/language arts classroom, the turf map is used as a vehicle to demonstrate how students view the range of their world, safety issues, and their histories.

Ask students to draw a freehand map of how they traveled from their home to their school in their elementary school years. Students' experiences will usually range from taking a bus to walking with someone. After they complete their drawings, ask the class to do some categorizing and classification: How many walked? With whom? Were they bused? Were there gender differences? Did girls walk in groups? With an adult or one other person? The map can also include information about places they were forbidden to go and why.

After a class discussion of the differences in the way they explored the world as youngsters, ask the students to write an autobiographical account based on the turf map. Students might consider the following experiences before they write: fond memories of a nearby relative whose house was always open to them, games they played with neighbors, and memories of the house they left. Then have the students form small groups to share their work. Ask them to notice correspondences and differences. It is highly likely that students will discover that boys were permitted to explore larger areas than were girls, more frequently traveled in larger groups, and were outdoors more often. Students can then discuss what those differences mean in terms of gender construction.

INTERACTION 5.11:
Body Biography

INTASC Principle 5: Motivation and Management

Opportunities for collaborative writing experiences in secondary schools provide opportunities for students to engage in dialogic rather than dialectic conversations. Unlike the discussions that are frequently held in classrooms in an attempt to discover and articulate the one "right" answer, a dialogic conversation honors the exchange and perspectives of all involved in the conversation. One strategy for providing a framework for such discussions is to assign a body biography of a character in a novel or play.

Working in small groups of four or five peers, students pick a character from the literature being read in class. They draw the outline of the character, probably using one person in the group as a template (elementary students are comfortable with drawing the outline of their bodies and filling in clothing, accessories, and so forth; this is the same type of drawing). Students then determine how, through color, lines from the novel or play would best represent the character. It is through the discussion that students have about which lines, for example, capture or define a character that the students have an opportunity to understand how their classmates read and interpret. The assignment involves a good deal of discussion and negotiation. Additionally, it involves a visual representation as well as a written one.

After the body is complete and presented to the class, students can write about either the process of deciding how to represent the character or they can write an analytical paper about the character. The body biography draws on reading, speaking, and writing skills. It is highly adaptable to any grade level and might range in subject matter. For example, in elementary classrooms, students can trace each other's body outline. The students can draw the body parts and provide a sentence or a few words about themselves. The same assignment in secondary school lends itself to more sophisticated analysis of characters in fiction (adapted from O'Donnell-Allen, & Smagorinsky, 1999).

INTERACTION 5.12:
A World of Journals

INTASC Principle 4: Variety of Instructional Strategies

Writer's Notebook.   To address the different preferences that girls and boys have in writing, English classes need to offer and value a wide range of writing activities. Although journal writing has become almost a standard in English classrooms, it may not be the most effective vehicle for promoting fluidity for boys. Girls, for a variety of reasons, are associated with a preference for writing about feelings, and journals satisfy that predilection. Boys may prefer a more informational approach to support their comfort with and fluidity in writing. This is not to say that all girls favor one approach and boys another; we simply suggest offering different options for the range of students in a typical classroom. Instead of a journal, a writer's notebook provides wider latitude in what counts. Students can write an entry about how they feel, but they can also record an overheard conversation, information about something they noticed, an idea for writing a science report, a poem, and so on. For many students, the writer's notebook will have the aura of something that is useful and objective. Because many students are not comfortable writing about their feelings, a writer's notebook provides a different kind of vehicle for daily writing that also values personal observations but not necessarily those of the writer. Notebooks can be used across grades, starting when students can draw and associate a few words or invented spellings with the drawing. As they proceed through the grades, students can use notebooks as the source of writing ideas, as a record for scientific experiments, and to record favorite sections from books.

Reader's Log.   Students can be encouraged to keep a log of what they read and their reactions to the texts. The log may contain a straightforward summary, or it can be structured as a double-entry journal (see later section). A reader's log is also an excellent source of information for teachers: Are students reading both male and female authors? Do they tend to notice only male or female actions? Teachers can use the logs to support students in developing critical analysis skills. Furthermore, when logs, journals, and notebooks are used consistently, fluidity and confidence increase, a first step in developing competent writers.

Double-Entry Journals.   Double-entry journals are useful in satisfying both an objective report of something as well as a reflective stance. The double-entry journal has a page divided roughly in half. On the left side of the page is a summary of a film, a lesson, a report (i.e., whatever is being studied). On the right side is a reflection (i.e., what the writer thinks about the material or a personal reaction to it). The left side is informational; the right hand side can be emotional.

Dialogue Journals.   Dialogue journals are effective tools for engaging students in conversation with the teacher. It provides the teacher with a window into the life of the student. These journals are highly effective in forging personal connections between students and teachers, but they are sometimes avoided because they seem to be a huge undertaking if there are more than 30 students in a classroom. With a little planning they are quite manageable. Teachers can rotate through the class, perhaps responding to only five students every night or every other night. The dialogue journals support fluidity, are authentic, and provide insights into the lives of students.

INTERACTION 5.13:
Writing Prompts

INTASC Principle 1: Knowledge of Subject Matter

Writing prompts provide many opportunities to invite students to investigate how gender is constructed in subtle ways. Many teachers already use "My Name" from Sandra Cisneros's *House on Mango Street* as a writing prompt. Students should read the short piece and then write their own "My Name" piece. After the students write their pieces, they might discuss them in small groups and then report what they notice. Undoubtedly, they will uncover cultural differences, family stories, and naming practices. They should also be challenged to stretch, to think about why men frequently add a junior or a second (II) or third (III) to their name. Other questions that they might discuss include why do women have a birth name and a married name and why do so many names end in *son* (e.g., Johnson, Henderson)? Another piece that is effective in raising gender awareness is Jamaica Kincaid's "Girl." After reading the text aloud or silently, students should be asked to write about the messages they heard as they were growing up. Student writing should be shared in small groups. There should then be a general reporting from the small groups, and the teacher should ask the students to note the messages they got from their parents: Were they the same for boys and girls? More often than not, girls receive messages about not being sexual, and there is a noticeable lack of such messages for boys. However, this may vary and should be discussed.

INTERACTION 5.14:
Take a Line for a Walk

INTASC Principle 4: Variety of Instructional Strategies

At times, a piece of prose or a poem may excite the imagination or stump the reader. One way to use a piece of writing without insisting on one correct answer is to "take a line for a walk." What follows is an example of how the strategy might work:

> I am not a scholar of English or literature. I cannot give you much more than personal opinions on the English language and its variations in this country or others.
>
> I am a writer. And by that definition, I am someone who has always loved language. I am fascinated by language in daily life. I spend a great deal of my time thinking about the power of language—the way it can evoke an emotion, a visual image, a complex idea, or a simple truth. Language is the tool of my trade. And I use them all—all the Englishes I grew up with. (Tan, 2000, p. 112)

Ask students to choose one line and copy it onto their paper. After they've copied the line, they need to keep writing in a free-form way. There's no need for them to censor their thoughts. They should continue writing for about 10 minutes. If the students say that they don't know what else to write after copying the line, ask them to keep writing the same line until they want to add to it. After 10 minutes, ask the students to stop and read what they've written. They can also share it with a partner. As they read their pieces, ask what stands out for them and what they would like to revisit and expand. Such an exercise is almost akin to the prewriting that many teachers who follow the steps of the writing process employ. For younger children, a less sophisticated piece can be employed:

> As they walked, Willie stole a look back over his shoulder. A man Willie had never seen before was sitting on a red plastic milk crate near the curb. His matted, streaky gray hair hung like a ragged curtain over a dirty face. His shoes were torn. Rough hands lay upon his knee. One hand was palm up. (Avi, 2000, p. 367)

Such a selection lends itself to both nonfiction and fiction writing. Students might want to discuss the issue of homelessness or create a short story from the line they choose. In any case, the selection will encourage a variety of writing that will appeal to both boys and girls.

INTERACTION 5.15:
I-Search Papers

INTASC Principle 4: Variety of Instructional Strategies

I-search papers are research papers written in the first person that tell the story of the author's interest in and research into a topic that is important to him or her. Unlike traditional research papers that demand an objective third-person stance, the I-search paper encourages the researcher to share why he or she is interested in a particular subject. For girls, especially, this kind of assignment gives them the freedom to incorporate their personal feelings and thoughts into the project. Boys may choose not to highlight that part of the assignment but, in fact, may welcome the opportunity to express themselves in the first person and to investigate topics of their own choice. According to Michael Smith and Jeffrey Wilhelm (2002) in their study of boys and literacy, one of the most frequently voiced suggestions boys had for English teachers was that they should provide choice (p. 111). In addition, the boys in their study who took an inquiry-based class reported the class to be a favorite (p. 11). Incorporating an I-search paper into an inquiry-based classroom is easily adaptable, but it is equally at home in even more traditional classrooms. This assignment offers opportunities for students to explore, among other things, topics in the "the evaded curriculum" (American Association of University Women, 1992).

During the brainstorming stage of the process, when students are probing for topics of interest, the teacher can indicate that subjects such as eating disorders, violence against women, dating violence, body image for men and women, single-sex versus coed schools, and gay/lesbian issues may be legitimate material to explore. (We are aware that some school climates may forbid discussion of topics such as gay/lesbian issues.) Once the door is opened, students will think of many topics that are directly related to their own lives as well as important social, health, and political issues on which much has been written. Students can be encouraged to interview, survey, and observe peers and other adults as a complement to more traditional library research. Issues of gender are interesting and important to young people; validating these issues as legitimate topics of inquiry is a powerful inducement not only for self-expression but also for authentic writing and research/ I-search. The rough format of an I-search follows:

1. A narrative describing:
    Where did the idea come from?
    Why is it interesting to the researcher?
    What is the researcher curious about?
    What questions does the researcher have?
2. What does the researcher already know and still not know about the topic? (This section needs to be fully developed.)

3. What did you do to learn new things? Answer your questions? Figure something out?
4. The report about what you learned should include the following:
   Information, facts, data, and knowledge of the subject
   The ways to answer the original question
   Revisions of ideas that were present at the beginning (I used to do this, but now I ....)
   Description of new things the search has made you curious about
   What you thought about the research (this part also includes new questions raised by the research/report)
5. A title page and an alphabetized bibliography

Journals, writers' notebooks, and logs are equally appropriate for the elementary grades and should include drawings. However, many teachers worry about their students absorbing rules of grammar. We believe that as students learn to write and want to make their thoughts clear to others, they will master rules of grammar and punctuation, but they should be exposed to frequent but brief minilessons. Constant drill has not worked in the past, and there is no reason to think it will work in the future.

Consider having students participate in the Monster Exchange Project (http://www.monsterexchange.org/index.asp), a very creative Internet site that inspires student writing and fun. Although not every classroom is well equipped with computers, the idea behind the Monster Exchange is simple enough to recreate. The added benefit for students to participate online is that more girls would have the opportunity to use computers. Ask students to draw a monster. They should be encouraged to use as much color and detail as they like, but they should not let anyone see their monster. They might need to spread out around the room. Next, ask them to describe their monster verbally. They need to pay attention to all the details in their drawing. Then have them exchange the verbal descriptions of their monsters with one other student, who recreates the monster from the description. The students then compare the original monster to the recreated one and discuss how and why they are the same or different. What may be of particular interest is to note the differences in the monsters that the boys and girls draw and the evidence of the research on the drawings. In general, boys tend to include violent acts in their drawings, whereas girls tend include flowers and hearts. The activity might also be modified by having students draw and describe a scientist, a mathematician, a writer, and so on, and note the gender of the person. A discussion and a writing assignment about stereotypes is a logical follow-up. Robert Munsch, the author of *The Paper Bag Princess* and other nontraditional stories, maintains a Web page that is interactive. Youngsters send him drawings and captions, and he writes a story, but he also encourages the students to write their own stories. Encourage students to visit it and have children submit work at http://www.robertmunsch.com.special.cfm.

ESSENTIAL EQUITY QUESTION 5.3:
HOW DO ASSESSMENT INSTRUMENTS, STANDARDIZED AND HOMEMADE, REFLECT OR REINFORCE ASSUMPTIONS ABOUT GENDER AND PERFORMANCE?

At the outset, we need to differentiate between *evaluation* and *assessment* as we use the terms here. Evaluation is usually synonymous with grading. Although assessment might include grading, it is more commonly associated with determining the strengths and weaknesses of students' learning. Assessment is a starting point for weighing what students know and understand to develop a plan for deeper and richer learning.

Standardized and homemade instruments that are used to determine a mastery of content knowledge, such as multiple-choice tests, are about limited knowledge. Although students may learn about women inventors and artists, for example, and be able to recite their names, dates of birth, and accomplishments, they may not grasp why women had limited access to registering patents or attending art schools. There is no doubt that ensuring that students have knowledge of common cultural references is important, but our history has been notably centered on White men's accomplishments. Standardized tests tend to reify the importance and inevitability of that history. Furthermore, homemade tests that emphasize a "who did what" approach in lieu of a "why did who do what she or he did" approach merely mimic standardized tests.

Standardized tests, because they are written for a national audience rather than a local one, by definition measure an agreed-on body of knowledge and skills. Because gender equity is not present in most school curricula and instructional approaches, it is less likely to appear or to be evaluated in those tests. They serve a different purpose.

Open-ended assessments that get closer to observing how students internalize a gender equity stance and analysis are what is needed, because achieving gender equity is as much about the long-term process involving the internalization of equity values and heightening of critical analyses as it is about being familiar with literature by women. Single assessments will not determine if gender equity as a core value is part of what students are learning. Teachers need to have assessment tools that permit them to observe students' work over time, and they should be readily available in English/language arts classes.

INTERACTION 5.16:
A Double-Entry Journal (Authentic Assessment)

INTASC Principle 8: Assessment

Assessments that are more authentic involve the strategies noted in the writing section of this chapter. The double-entry journal is an especially effective means of assessing student growth. The left side of the journal is for what is read or done. The right side is for reflection. With these journals, teachers can see what students are working on and see what questions arise for the students and what sense the students are making of the work.

Example: Double-Entry Journal for *Romeo and Juliet*

Date	What Happened	Reflection
9/17/04	Juliet swallowed a potion to make it appear that she had died.	Did Juliet have any other way to marry Romeo? What rights did women have at that time? Do women need similar ruses in some countries?

The questions signal an awareness of gender equity. If the reflection side of a double-entry journal never raises questions nor provides comments about gender differences, teachers need to assess whether students are aware of gender. If it appears that the students aren't, then the double-entry journal can be modified to have students reflect on a specific question attached to an event in what they are reading.

Example: Double-Entry Journal for *Romeo and Juliet*

Date	What Happened	Reflection
9/17/04	Juliet swallowed a potion to make it appear that she had died.	Why didn't Juliet simply run away and elope with Romeo?

The teacher can then assess whether the students base a reflection on money concerns or gender limitations. They do not need to be exclusive of one another. The point is to have students demonstrate an awareness of gender implications.

Such an assessment tool captures what the students are doing and learning as well as the analysis they bring to bear on an event. In other words, authentic assessment is primarily about close teacher observation and assignments that permit students to make connections to the world around them as well as to their own personal experiences. In the previous examples, it is possible that students might cite an example of a relative or friend who eloped and suffered exclusion by friends or family. Such examples open up discussions about how or whether gender is a factor, and they help link the play to modern times.

An authentic assessment for this chapter is to initiate your own double-entry journal, to record how you feel about the topics and strategies raised. Look over your reflections and assess your own insights and developments for this chapter or for your teaching year. If you are maintaining a professional portfolio, your double-entry journal can become a valuable part of this effort. Reflection offers the opportunity for growth, in gender equity or, more generally, in all your teaching skills.

INTERACTION 5.17:
Listening to Students and Equalizing the Curriculum

INTASC Principle 8: Assessment

Depending on age and grade level, teachers might employ other assessment strategies. For very young children, teachers may want to pay closer attention to a child's language. Does the child always say "he" as an inclusive pronoun? Does the child vary language? Does the child read a variety of books that feature both female and male protagonists? In middle school, are students offered books that deal with relationships and action-related plots, and how do the boys and girls relate to them? It is the reaction to a variety of books that the teacher needs to note.

INTERACTION 5.17:
Keeping a Teacher Journal

INTASC Principle 8: Assessment

Keeping a teacher journal is consistent with the inquiry stance we have emphasized in this chapter, but it is daunting and seems to add even more work to an already oversized workload. However, few would deny its usefulness. The key to keeping one successfully is to make it fit in with daily and long-time planning. The following tips will help you keep a teacher journal:

- Have a question that interests you—for example, what kinds of books do the boys like? What do the girls like? What happens when I ask students to switch roles in plays? These are just a few possible questions that warrant close observation. That's the first step. Trying out different strategies is part of the on-going observation.

 • Keep the journal open and convenient in the classroom. Make quick nota-tions as you notice something that pertains to your question. These quick notes will serve to jog your memory.

 • Look over your journal and reflect on it periodically. Of course, the more frequently you do so, the better.

 • Share your journal with a group of interested colleagues. Getting other per-spectives is important.

 • Use your journal to make instructional decisions.

The teacher journal informs the work of the classroom and provides a record of student growth through observation. It's not easy, but it is valuable as a way of find-ing out what students know and can do.

RESOURCES

Literature

Anderson, M., & Hassler, D. (Eds.). (1999). Learning by heart: Contemporary American poetry about school. Iowa City: University of Iowa Press.

Bauer, M. D. (Ed.). (1994). *Am I blue: Coming out from the silence.* New York: HarperCollins.

Cisneros, S. (1983). *The house on Mango Street.* Houston, TX: Arte Publico Press.

Cisneros, S. (1991). *Women hollering creek and other stories.* New York: Random House.

Dorris, M. (1987). *Yellow raft in blue water.* New York: Henry Holt.

Gibbons, K. (1987). *Ellen Foster.* New York: Random House.

Gilbert, S., & Gubar, S. (1985). *The Norton anthology of literature by women: The tradition in English.* New York: W.W. Norton.

Heron, A. (Ed.). (1983). *Two teenagers in twenty: Writings by gay and lesbian youth.* Boston: Alyson Publications.

Homes, A. M. (1989). *Jack.* New York: Macmillan.

Hong, M. (Ed.). (1993). *Growing up Asian American: Stories of childhood and ad-olescence.* New York: Avon Books.

Katz, J. (Ed.). (1995). *Messengers of the wind: Native American women tell their life stories.* New York: Ballantine.

Kincaid, J. (1985). *Annie John.* New York: Farrar, Straus, Giroux.

Misiroglu, G. (Ed.). (1999). *Girls like us: 40 extraordinary women celebrate girl-hood in story, poetry, and song.* Novato, CA: New World Library.

Newman, L. (1988). *"A letter to Harvey Milk": Short stories about being lesbian and Jewish in high school.* Ithaca, NY: Firebrand Books.

Paterson, K. (1992). *Lyddie.* New York: Puffin Books.

Ryan, P. M. (2000). *Esperanza rising*. New York: Scholastic Press.
Woolf, V. (1929). *A room of one's own*. New York: Harcourt, Brace.

Films

Billy Elliott
Ma Vie En Rose
La Vida Loca
Just Another Girl on the IRT
Ruby in Paradise

Web Resources

The National Research Center for English Language and Achievement: http://
cela.albany.edu
Full text reports are available on curriculum issues in English/language arts class-
rooms
International Reading Association: http:// www.reading.org
Standards and professional materials for literacy educators from preschool to adult
education
National Council of Teachers of English: http://www.ncte.org
Standards, strategies, and resources for the English/language arts council
WSSLINKS—Women, Girls, and Education: http://www.library.wisc.edu/libraries/
WomensStudies/womened.htm
Developed and maintained by the Women's Studies Section of the Association of
College and Research Libraries
Boys, Girls and Literacy: http://www.literacytrust.org.uk/Database/boys/
Based in England, consciously developing approaches/programs that support liter-
acy achievement
American Association of University Women: http://www.aauw.org

Ongoing research on women and girls and education

MS Foundation: http://www.ms.foundation.org/publications.html
Funding numerous projects of defining girls' leadership
Yell-Oh Girls: http://www.yellohgirls.com/main.html
A site based on the book and much more
Middle School Girls Selected Reading List and Resources: http://www.utexas.edu/
depts/wstudies/publications/msrl/
A rich site maintained by the University of Texas, Austin
A girlsworld.com: http://www.agirlsworld.com/amy/new-voices/

Girls sharing their writing online

The Center for Gender Equity: http://www.wri-edu.org/equity/

Gender Equity in Western Massachusetts: http://www.genderequity.org/
Equity Online (WEEA): http://www.edc.org/WomensEquity/
Myra Sadker Advocates for Gender Equity: http://www.sadker.org/
Teacher Education and Gender Equity: http://www.ericfacility.net/ericdigests/ed408277.html
Beyond Title IX: Gender Equity Issues In Schools: http://www.maec.org/beyond.html
Gender Equity: http://www.genderequity.org/book/contents.html
Jo Sanders's Workshop Guidelines: http://www.josanders.com/resources.html
Writing for Change: http://www.tolerance.org/teach/expand/wfc/wfc_sctn1_4.html

APPENDIX: KEY CONCEPTS

Action research/practitioner inquiry: Teachers identify an issue that puzzles them or presents a problem. It may be the need for livelier discussion or how to engage a very quiet child. The teacher sets aside time to systematically collect and look at data that will help her or him understand what is going on in a classroom. The teacher may keep a teacher journal, collect student work, or chart classroom interactions. The investigation is intentional, systematic, and carried out over time. Throughout the time, the teacher continues to reflect on the data to ascertain how the data address the salient question. Not infrequently, such research leads to other questions and supports the ideal of the reflective teacher. It is an ideal approach to ensuring that the classroom is gender fair. Example questions include the following: Do boys talk as much as girls about character development in a novel? What kinds of topics do girls gravitate toward when they do an I-search? Do I want to encourage a broader range for girls and boys? The following graphic is a way of presenting action research:

Problem/question ➔ Collect data ➔ Analyze/reflect ➔ New problem/question

Authentic/alternative/performance assessment: Often used interchangeably, these labels have different shades of meaning. All refer to assessments that give students opportunities to demonstrate understanding and apply knowledge and skills in contexts other than conventional paper-and-pencil tests. Such assessments often occur as a process, over a period of time, and result in student-created performances or products. They often involve self-evaluation, revision over time, complex scoring, evaluation beyond "right" and "wrong" answers, rubrics that outline degrees of proficiency based on published criteria, an audience that may include peers or other community members in evaluating, and collaboration with others. For example, instead of multiple-choice or even essay tests, students can write plays, create poems, or assume the role of a character to demonstrate understanding. Authentic assessment should reveal a student's deep grasp of literature.

Balanced literacy: Many districts have adopted a balanced literacy approach in their elementary schools. Such an approach involves providing for shared, guided, and independent reading and writing times throughout the week (e.g., Fountas & Pinnell, 1996). Balanced literacy builds on the best research on the use of phonics, the writing process, and whole language. In many ways it addresses the need for different learning approaches by providing for more social settings for learning as well as independent settings.

Canon: Despite the rhetoric surrounding the culture wars, the canon, or authorized body, of literature considered critical for every educated person to know has always been in flux. Many readers know it as the collection of works called "the classics." The more recent debate on what the K–12 canon should include has focused more pointedly on a balance of male and female authors from a diversity of cultures. It is not enough to have the same number of male and female authors; for example, they must, in addition, represent Black, Asian American, Native American, Hispanic, and Anglo cultures as well as different classes. The danger of establishing a canon is that the selection resists change.

Feminist critical theory: In the 1970s, writers such as Adrienne Rich, Ellen Moers, Elaine Showalter, Barbara Smith, Susan Gubar, Sandra Gilbert, and many others developed critical theory that placed women's experience at the center of literary analysis. They worked to recover a female tradition in literature, to interpret literature by men and women from a female perspective, to uncover stereotypes and assumptions about women in texts, to challenge the accepted canon of classic works, and to become more aware of the politics of language and style. As feminist theory developed, it posed a challenge to consider the absence of works by and perspectives of women of color, lesbians, elderly women, and others.

Feminist pedagogy: Gilligan (1982) and Belenky, Goldberger, Clinchy, and Tarule (1996) laid the groundwork for a different kind of pedagogy. Their work asked teachers to consider that not everyone learns best in a competitive, one-right-answer, "objective" environment. They noted that many women, and some men, thrive in classrooms that make connections to people's personal lives, that honor a variety of perspectives, and that support the social aspects of learning by implementing cooperative/collaborative classroom strategies. This approach to teaching has become known as feminist pedagogy, but, in fact, it is good pedagogy. Both girls and boys thrive with this approach.

Gendered lens: A term used often in this chapter, it refers to literary analysis and classroom observation that focus on gender. That is, when choosing or interpreting texts and considering classroom interactions, one takes gender seriously as a category of analysis because one is committed to gender equity in the classroom.

Writing process: In too many instances, the writing process has been reduced to a five step formula. Although it does encompass five stages—prewriting, draft, revision, editing, publication—these stages are not discreet. They are recursive and ongoing. Writing process classrooms very often also use writing and reading workshops to allow for more freedom of choice and experimentation with different genres in writing. Choice has figured strongly in the research that looks at what encourages males to write more extensively in school-based assignments (Smith & Wilhelm, 2002). We remind our readers that attention to gender in the classroom is key to fostering and increasing achievement for both girls and boys. Our approach is centered in a pedagogy that attends to developing everyone's capacity to learn and succeed in the English/language arts classroom and is reflective of the *Standards for the English Language Arts* developed by the National Council of Teachers of English and the International Reading Association (1996).

REFERENCES

American Association of University Women. (1992). *How schools shortchange girls: A study of major findings on girls and education*. Washington, DC: Education Foundation and National Educational Association.

American Association of University Women and the American Institutes for Research. (1999). *Gender gaps: Where schools still fail our children*. New York: Marlowe and Company.

American Association of University Women. (2000). *Tech-savvy: Educational girls in the new computer age*. Washington, DC: American Association of University Women Educational Foundation.

Avi. (2000). What do fish have to do with anything? In *Elements of Literature*. Austin, TX: Hold, Reinhart and Winston.

Belenky, M., Goldberger, N. R., Clinchy, B. M., & Tarule, J. M. (1996). *Women's ways of knowing*. New York: Basic Books.

Daniel, H. (1994). *Literature circles: Voice and choice in the student-centered classroom*. New York: Stenhouse Publishers.

Fountas, I. C., & Pinell, G. S. (1996). *Guided reading: Good first teaching for all children*. Portsmouth, NH: Heinemann.

Gilbert, P., & Taylor, S. (1991). *Fashioning the feminine: Girls, popular culture, and schooling*. North Sydney, Australia: Allen & Unwin.

Gilligan, C. (1982). *In a different voice: Psychological theory and women's development*. Cambridge, MA: Harvard University Press.

Gilligan, C., & Brown, L. M. (1993). *Meeting at the crossroads*. New York: Ballantine.

Ginorio, A., & Huston, M. (2001). *Si, se puede! Yes, we can: Latinas in school*. Washington, DC: American Association of University Women Educational Foundation.

Harjo, J. (1983). Remember. *The Heath Anthology of American Literature* (Vol. 2). Lexington, MA: D. C. Heath and Company.

Hurston, Z. (1998). *Their eyes were watching God*. NY: Harper Perennial, a division of Harper Collins.

Kimmel, M. (2000, October/November). What about the boys? *WEEA Digest* (pp. 88–91).

Kramarae, C. (2001). *The third shift: Women learning online*. Washington, DC: American Association of University Women Educational Foundation.

Maher, F. A., & Tetreault, M. K. T. (2001). *The feminist classroom: Expanded edition*. Boulder, CO: Rowan Littlefield.

Maher, F. A., & Ward, J. W. (2002). *Gender and teaching.* Mahwah, NJ: Lawrence Erlbaum Associates.

McCracken, N. M., & Appleby, B. C. (Eds.). (1992). *Gender issues in the teaching of English.* Portsmouth, NH: Boynton/Cook.

McIntosh, P. (1988). *White privilege and male privilege: A personal account of coming to see correspondence through work in women's studies* (Working Paper No. 189). Wellesley, MA: Wellesley College Center for Research on Women.

National Council of Teachers of English & International Reading Association. (1996). *Standards for the English language arts.* Urbana, IL: National Council of Teachers of English.

National Institute of Child Health and Development. (n.d.). *Why children succeed or fail at reading.* Washington, DC: Author.

Newkirk, T. (2000). Misreading masculinity: Speculations on the great gender gaps in writing. *Language Arts, 77*(8), 294–300.

O'Donnell-Allen, C., & Smagorinsky, P. (1999). Revising Ophelia: Rethinking questions of gender and power in school. *English Journal, 88*(3), 35–42.

Rich, A. (1971). When we dead awaken: Writing as re-vision. In *On lies, secrets, and silences: Selected Prose 1966–1978* (pp. 33–50). New York: W.W. Norton & Company. (Norton reissue 1995)

Rich, A. (1984) Invisibility in academe. In *Blood, bread, and poetry* (pp. 198–201). New York: W.W. Norton.

Roy, P., & Schen, M. (1987). Feminist pedagogy: Transforming the high school classroom. *Women's Studies Quarterly, 15,* 110–115.

Sadker, M., & Sadker, D. (1994). *Failing at fairness: How America's schools cheat girls.* New York: Charles Scribner's Sons.

Sahywitz, S. E., Sahywitz, B. A., Fletcher, J. M., & Escobar, M. D. (1990). Prevalence of reading disability in boys and girls. *Journal of the American Medical Association, 265*(8), 998–1002.

Sanborn, J. (1992). The academic essay, a feminist view of student voices. In N. M. McCracken & B. C. Appleby (Eds.), *Gender issues in the teaching of English* (pp. 142–160). Portsmouth, NH: Boynton-Cook.

Showalter, E. (1985). *The new feminist criticism.* New York: Pantheon.

Sizer, T. (n.d.). *Coalition of essential schools 10 principles.* Retrieved March 29, 2006, from http://www.essentialschools.org/pub/ces_docs/about/phil/10cps/10cps.html

Smith, M., & Wilhelm, J. (2002). *"Reading don't fix no Chevys": Literacy in the lives of young men.* Portsmouth, NH: Heinemann.

Sontag, S. (2000). Directions: Write, read, rewrite. Repeat steps 2 & 3 as needed. NY: The New York Times. Retrieved June 13, 2006 from http:/www.rnm.edu/~gmartin/sontag.htm

Sophocles. (1974). King Oedipus. In E. F. Watling (Trans.), *The Theban plays* (pp. 25–70). London: Penguin.

Style, E. (1988). Curriculum as window and mirror. In M. Crocco (Ed.), *Listening for all voices: Gender balancing the school curriculum.* Summit, NJ: Oak Knoll School.

Tan, A. (2000) Mother tongue. In J. Loughery (Ed.), *The eloquent essay* (p. 112). NY: Persea.

Tannen, D. (1990). *You just don't understand: Women and men in conversation.* New York: William Morrow.

Wilhelm, J. D. (1997). *You gotta BE the book: Teaching engaged and reflective reading with adolescents.* New York: Teachers College Press.

6

A Gender Inclusive Approach
to Science Education

Janice Koch
Hofstra University

Science teaching needs to encourage, invite, engage, excite, interrogate, challenge and shine like a beacon, signaling that science is truly for everyone. Seeing the light, girls would flock toward the science classroom, feeling connected, competent, and anxious to engage in scientific experiences. (Koch, 1998a, p. 474)

What comes to mind when you think of a scientist? Many teachers think of a stereotyped image not that different from the images their students consider. Usually the stereotype is male, White, and crazy looking (Barman, 1997). Science has become one of the subjects more often associated with males than females. Thus, it is necessary to help teachers see all their students as capable and competent in science, regardless of gender.

When teachers are asked what comes to mind when they think of gender equity, they respond to the term as meaning "treating boys and girls equally." That notion of equality addresses most teachers' strong desires not to show favoritism. What research shows, however, is that girls and boys come to school with very different sets of needs due to the ways in which they are socialized in their families and in contemporary culture. Hence, meeting those needs in different ways can ensure equality of outcomes, even if treatment differs.

Consider a recent cartoon in a newspaper that shows Cinderella talking to her fairy godmother. The caption reads, "Forget the royal ball; can you send me to Harvard?" The message is that the Cinderella social stereotype for females probably does not ring as true today as it may have some decades ago. Girls and boys envision achievement in the public sphere as a means of preparation for the broader adult world of earning a living and caring for oneself. This chapter responds to the question, "How can teachers be assisted to see themselves as pivotal in the decisions females and males make about their potential to be successful in science?"

The chapter is designed to help you to integrate gender equity issues in science methods courses at the elementary, middle, and secondary levels. Whereas science education has typically been represented as a field of study that elementary school teachers avoid, this discussion invites elementary school teachers to study their own "scientific selves" (Koch, 2005) and consider the possibilities for engaging their students and themselves in inquiry. Some of this work builds on the rich history of women in science and creates science experiences from the study of science in women's daily lives. Drawing a scientist and nature journaling are two examples of science education assignments that help teachers to see themselves as potentially part of the scientific enterprise. The checks lab experience described later engages students in a kind of science activity that reminds teachers that science is collaborative and highly personal and requires repetition and consensus. Middle school and secondary school science teachers can benefit from the Interactions described in this chapter as they seek to represent science as a human activity that spurs their desire to increase their understanding of how the natural world works.

The following essential equity questions (EEQs) are addressed in this chapter:

- **Essential Equity Question 6.1:** How does the stereotype of the scientist affect students' abilities to see themselves as competent in scientific inquiry?
- **Essential Equity Question 6.2:** How does understanding the nature of science encourage greater participation in scientific activities?
- **Essential Equity Question 6.3:** How does engaging students in locally relevant scientific issues foster greater enthusiasm for science by all students?

Each EEQ includes two components: What We Know contains a brief summary of the issues surrounding science education and gender equity. Interactions are based on the research and suggest ways for you to engage teachers in examining gender and science issues.

ESSENTIAL EQUITY QUESTION 6.1:
HOW DOES THE STEREOTYPE OF THE SCIENTIST AFFECT STUDENTS' ABILITIES TO SEE THEMSELVES AS COMPETENT IN SCIENTIFIC INQUIRY?

WHAT WE KNOW

Research on science and gender reveals numerous variables affecting who succeeds and who becomes discouraged in pursuing science as a lifelong endeavor. Parental attitudes, the media, stereotyping, textbooks, clothing, peers, toys, teacher bias, societal influences, discrimination, curricula, and classroom dynamics are some of the variables that influence attitudes toward science. In the last decade, there have been many reports and studies published on the gap between male and female students' performance in science (American Association of University Women, 1998; Kahle & Meece, 1994; National Center for Educational Statistics, n.d.). The influences on both boys' and girls' knowledge, behavior, and attitudes toward science are so enormous that it is easy for teachers and researchers to become overwhelmed. However, there are researchers and teachers throughout the nation who are actively working on solutions to solving the science inequity between genders.

Researchers are experimenting with different types of science programs, some that focus on gaining active participation of parents and highlighting role models in science (Hammrich, Richardson, & Livingston, 2000). Teachers are receiving in-service training to reevaluate how they relate to both boys and girls when teaching science. Teachers are beginning to hold high expectations for all students, to restructure groups so that girls can play active roles, and to showcase women who have chosen careers in science. Unfortunately, the quality programs and teacher training efforts reach only a small audience and are needed on a larger scale than what is currently being produced. Teacher training in creating gender equitable classrooms needs to begin with preservice teachers before their teacher behaviors become ingrained (Levine & Orenstein, 1994).

Research indicates that at every grade, cultural norms inhibit the identification of girls with scientific study. When visiting an after-school science club in the Northeast, I was struck by the way in which the boys outnumbered the girls as early as fifth grade. What was wrong with the science education at this school that more girls were not clamoring to join? Many cultural norms are at work. For example, the assumed squeamishness of girls in the science lab is one example of cultural stereotyping that limits the science potential of many females. Although these girlhood stereotypes tell girls not to get messy, the women they become are often getting messy as they maintain the daily fabric of life: They get messy with diapers, chickens, turkeys, and toilets; as young girls, they could certainly get messy in the science lab. A former student explained in a familiar story that she loved to dissect frogs in seventh grade, but she screamed the entire time so that the boys would think she was acting like a girl. Herein lies the challenge—to present how acting like a girl means acting scientific (Koch, 1998b).

When teachers are asked to name a woman scientist other than Marie Curie, few know any responses. The stereotypes of scientists can discourage individuals who are other than White and male from seeing themselves as truly scientific. The hidden history of women in science, when revealed, exposes that women have always done science and among them are Nobel Laureates and world-class scientists whose lives and work inspire others to follow (Mozans, 1991).

When, for example, teachers explore the double bind that American women in the late 1800s faced when trying to pursue careers in natural science, they are surprised to learn that women were denied higher education until the 1850s and that, for women, majoring in natural science was unladylike. As women, those studying science were thought of as not fitting into the cultural stereotype of what it meant to be female; as scientists these women were largely ignored by the White male professionals emerging in the field of professional science. In fact, when women at Vassar College wanted to hear some of the astronomy lectures at Harvard in the 1880s, they were allowed to attend provided they sat behind a screen (Abir-Am & Outram, 1987). Who were these women and what compelled them to pursue science despite the difficulties? How does learning about them inspire students to consider scientific work for their own lives? Exploring the hidden history of women in science empowers all students to see themselves as potentially connected to a scientific future.

INTERACTION 6.1:
Who Were These Women in Science?

INTASC Principle 4: Variety of Instructional Strategies

This interaction requires that you become familiar with historical and contemporary women in science in a way that engages you in a design challenge. A design challenge is an instructional strategy that helps you to solve problems by meeting certain designated specifications and constraints. The design challenge for this activity is the following:

> This historical project is an exploration of the life and work of a woman scientist. Working collaboratively with at least one partner, select a person to research and a mode of presentation with which you are comfortable. Your design challenge is to design and construct an artifact that relates to this scientist's life and work. The artifact must provide information about the person to your audience. Be prepared to distribute to the class a one-page abstract about the scientific contributions that this historical or contemporary figure

has made. An example of an artifact for a group studying the life and work of Barbara McClintock, a geneticist who studied the maize plant, would be to design and construct a model ear of corn with removable felt husks. Inside each husk would be data about Barbara McClintock, the Nobel-winning scientist who discovered that when genes "jumped" their positions on a chromosomal strand, a mutation occurred. Think about a woman whose work and life you want to explore and then plan to design and construct an artifact that would have a meaningful connection to her work. Remember, the artifact needs to provide data about the scientist's life. Try to explain the nature of the scientific discovery made by your woman scientist.

INTERACTION 6.2:
The Draw a Scientist Project

INTASC Principle 5: Motivation and Management

Close this book. On a piece of paper, using a pencil, sketch a picture of what you think a scientist might look like. When you have completed the drawing, open the book again to this spot. If you are like most people, your drawing will show a White male with one or more of the following characteristics: wild hair, eyeglasses, a white lab coat, a pocket protector, and some bubbling flasks.

Not long ago, two third-grade teachers in a local elementary school were interested in exploring their students' beliefs about scientists. Distributing crayons and drawing paper, they asked each student to draw a picture of a scientist and describe what the scientist was doing. The 39 students' drawings contained 31 men and 8 women. Further, of the 31 male scientists, 25 had beards and messy hairstyles.

One boy added a bubble quote for his scientist that said, "I'm crazy." Another third-grade boy described his scientist as follows: "He is inventing a monster. He painted his face green." Still another boy wrote, "My scientist makes all kinds of poisons. He is a weird person." Another caption on the bottom of a drawing said, "Dr. Strangemind," and on the back the student explained, "He does strange things like blow up things and other crazy stuff." Many of the children described their scientists as "blowing things up," "acting crazy" or "goofy," or working with "a lot of potions."

You can see that most of these third graders, young as they were, had already internalized the stereotyped image of the scientist. To understand why this is important, ask yourself the following questions:

- Who is omitted in this stereotype?
- Does the type of person represented in the stereotype reflect the makeup of any class you have recently seen?
- If the students in a typical classroom were omitted by the stereotype, how would that make them feel about science?

You may suppose that stereotypes about scientists diminish as children mature. In fact, however, a study of more than 1,500 students in grades K–8 revealed that students' drawings of scientists become more stereotypical as students age. These students drew mostly White male scientists, suggesting that the stereotype persists despite recent changes in curriculum materials (Barman, 1997).

The scientist stereotype can discourage individuals who are not White and male from seeing themselves as truly scientific. Some of the consequences are obvious. For example, substantially fewer females enroll in high school advanced placement computer science courses or advanced placement physics courses than do males. This leads to the underenrollment of females in computer science and engineering courses in college (National Science Foundation, n.d.). This gender gap persists despite many types of interventions designed to encourage the participation of girls and young women in physics and computer science. A significant, consistent finding in the gender-equity research is the understanding that, for example, the lack of participation of females in the computer sciences and physics is a response to teaching environments, not to girls' lack of abilities to do well in these areas. The deficit model that infers that we need to "fix" the girls to make them better achievers in science, is simply not accurate (Boaler, 2002).

It is a complex issue, but the way in which teachers conceptualize "who does science" certainly contributes to the problem. One primary school teacher holds a gigantic mirror up to her students when the question of who can be a scientist emerges. This helps the students envisage themselves in the role of the scientist, ensuring that they will feel entitled to be scientists as they explore natural phenomena in their own classrooms (excerpted from Koch, 2005, p. 41).

This activity is designed for teachers (and students) to examine how they see scientists. Teachers teach who they are, and if they believe that only certain types of people can be scientists then they will communicate that to their students in ways they are not always conscious of. Are your images of a scientist influenced by the stereotypes of the White male wearing a lab coat and eyeglasses? Do you view science as a part of your life, or do you perceive it as something that is done only in the classroom and the laboratory (Barman, 1997)? Consider these questions:

- What is the gender of your scientist?
- What activity is your scientists engaged in?
- What is your scientist wearing?
- How old is your scientist?
- Do you relate to your scientist? If yes, in what way?

You may also evaluate your drawing or your partner's drawing with the following checklist.

Once you know what the drawing is showing, use the checklist to record any stereotypic images represented. Examine the checklist and see how many stereotype attributes you included. Then switch with a friend who did the same activity and

---

Draw-a-Scientist Test (DAST) Checklist

Gender (circle):   M / F   Age _____

Yes___ No___   1. Lab coat (usually but not necessarily white)

Yes___ No___   2. Eyeglasses

Yes___ No___   3. Facial hair (beard, mustache, abnormally long sideburns)

Yes___ No___   4. Symbols of research (scientific instruments, lab equipment of any kind)

Yes___ No___   5. Types of scientific instruments/equipment; symbols of knowledge (books, filing cabinets, clipboards, pens in pockets, and so on)

Yes___ No___   6. Technology (the "products" of science); types of technology (televisions, telephones, missiles, computers, etc.)

Yes___ No___   7. Relevant captions (formulae, taxonomic classification, the "eureka!" syndrome)

Yes___ No___   8. Male gender only

Yes___ No___   9. White only

Yes___ No___   10. Middle-aged or elderly scientist

Yes___ No___   11. Mythic stereotypes (Frankenstein creatures, Jekyll/Hyde figures, etc.)

Yes___ No___   12. Indications of secrecy (signs or warnings that read "Private," "Keep Out," "Do Not Enter," "Go Away," "Top Secret," and so on)

Yes___ No___   13. Scientist working indoors

Yes___ No___   14. Indications of danger *Note:* Several images of the same type in a single drawing count as one image (e.g., two scientists each with eyeglasses receive only one check, not two)

---

discuss why you have this image. Where does it come from? Do you think scientists like the image? Why or why not? How many checks would indicate that you have drawn a stereotype?

INTERACTION 6.3:
Faces on Mt. Rushmore

INTASC Principle 4: Variety of Instructional Strategies

The default mode for thinking about who does science is often a White, bearded or bald male as revealed by these interactions. Asking students to explore the issue of who does science and why is often an excellent way to begin to deconstruct this pervasive stereotype. Teachers need to know that participation of all students in science rests on the understanding that the greater the engagement of diverse groups in science, the greater the possibility for accurate representations of observations and inferences: "We do not see things as they are; we see things as we are" (The Talmud).

This exercise helps you to focus on heroes and heroines and to share those images in a group setting. It helps you to see the gender issues implicit in who gets remembered in history and makes you aware that *greatness* is a term loaded with political and social implications. The idea of who defines *greatness* and who is served by that definition is at the heart of this experience. You and your colleagues are encouraged to think of greatness in terms of those currently contributing to further the social welfare of humanity, in a public or private way.

You may want to work in groups of four, if possible. Your task is as follows: Currently the four faces on Mt. Rushmore are Thomas Jefferson, Abraham Lincoln, Theodore Roosevelt, and George Washington. Ask this question of your colleagues: Are you familiar with the faces on Mt. Rushmore? Your first task is to recarve the faces of Mt. Rushmore so that all of the images are female scientists. Which scientists would you select? You may select a public or private figure (i.e., one known only to you); however, each selection requires an explicit, written rationale. Write your selection on poster board and tape the posters to walls in the room. Then have your group share its poster, discussing the choices and rationale. Then, redo the activity over time, recarving Mt. Rushmore with the faces of only women scientists. The same procedure applies. Who gets included? Who has done "great" scientific work? How has their work affected people's lives? Some important women who come to mind are Marie Curie, Rosalyn Yalow, Barbara McClintock, and Gertrude Elion.

The following list below represents female Nobel prize-winners in science and medicine over the past 100 years. More information about these remarkable women may be found at http://almaz.com/nobel/women.html.

Marie Curie	1903 Nobel Prize for Physics
	1911 Novel Prize for Chemistry
Irene Joliot-Curie	1935 Nobel Prize for Chemistry
Gerty Radnitz-Cory	1947 Nobel Prize in Physiology & Medicine
Maria Goeppert Mayer	1963 Nobel Prize for Physics
Dorothy Crowfoot Hodgkin	1964 Nobel Prize for Chemistry

Rosalyn Yalow	1977 Nobel Prize in Physiology & Medicine
Barbara McClintock	1983 Nobel Prize in Physiology & Medicine
Rita Levi Montalcini	1986 Nobel Prize in Physiology & Medicine
Gertrude Elion	1988 Nobel Prize in Physiology & Medicine
Christianne Nusslein-Volhard	1995 Nobel Prize in Physiology & Medicine

Exploring the lives and work of women scientists, past and present, is one way to dispel the weird, White male stereotype. As well, having a history enables women to see themselves as potential scientists. Black women scientists have made extraordinary contributions in the past century, and their stories have the power to influence our long-held stereotypes. Consider the following scientists, two of whom went on to become college presidents and one to become president of the General Mills Foundation:

Dr. Reatha Clark King—chemist: http://www.hill.af.mil/fwp/kingbio.html

Dr. Jewel Plummer Cobb—biologist: http://www.princeton.edu/~mcbrown/display/cobb.html

Dr. Shirley Ann Jackson—physicist: http://www.princeton.edu/~mcbrown/display/jackson.html

Dr. Mae Jemison—astronaut: http://starchild.gsfc.nasa.gov/docs/StarChild/whos_who_level2/jemison.html

Madame C. J. Walker—inventor (1867–1919): http://www.princeton.edu/~mcbrown/display/walker.html

ESSENTIAL EQUITY QUESTION 6.2:
HOW DOES UNDERSTANDING THE NATURE OF SCIENCE ENCOURAGE GREATER PARTICIPATION IN SCIENTIFIC ACTIVITIES?

WHAT WE KNOW

There are many ways to think about science. For example, you can think of it as a way to explore nature. Some people think of science as a subject that holds the key to understanding the secrets of the universe. That sounds exciting—and a bit mysterious. Many people think about a long list of facts to be memorized, a common notion of school science.

Whatever your associations, remember that science is basically an area of knowledge created by people—men and women—who devote much of their energies to exploring a part of nature and trying to make sense of it. In this sense, human societies have a long tradition of scientific exploration. Ever since the dawn of civilization, people have studied nature and tried to understand it. The best definition for science takes account of its three different facets, describing science as a process, a set of ideas, and a set of attitudes.

The middle part of that definition, the "set of ideas," is familiar because the mention of science typically conjures up images of biology, chemistry, physics, geology, and earth science, the subjects that commonly fall under the rubric of science in schools. As they explore nature, scientists go through a series of steps that help them learn more about their area of study. This process is sometimes called the scientific method. In fact, there are many scientific methods, but all of them have some principles in common. *Science as process* refers to the ways in which scientists go about their work. They usually begin by exploring the questions about nature that engage them. A question is considered scientific when, to find the answer, people (usually) go through these steps:

1. Make careful observations.
2. Set up an experiment and explore the results.
3. Test their ideas through further experimentation.
4. Ask others to repeat the experiments.

These steps comprise the process of science. Scientists collect information through careful observation of nature and natural phenomena. Their ideas are explored and tested through experiments. Their experiments are repeated by others in the search for consistent outcomes. To help make one set of results comparable to another set, different scientists follow similar procedures in their investigations.

This process is what sets science apart from other ways of knowing the world. Using the process involves a particular set of skills that are often called process skills. Observing is an example of a process skill, as are predicting and making inferences, classifying, and planning an experiment, to name a few. Through the process of observation, experimentation, exploration, and repetition, scientists gather concepts about the natural world. Science also includes a set of attitudes or dispositions that encourage people to engage in scientific study. Scientific attitudes evolve when people are engaged in the processes of science. These attitudes include a curiosity and wonder about how the natural world works, as well as an excitement about the journey of discovery. Science is actually much more about trying to find things out than it is about knowing answers. Scientific attitudes, therefore, include persistence and a desire for evidence to support statements, an open-mindedness and willingness to change one's mind when confronted with new evidence, and a willingness to cooperate and collaborate with others.

Many science teachers believe that the nature of scientific activity is revealed simply by engaging their students in science investigations in the classroom. Research indicates (Lederman, 1992) that teachers need to directly teach the nature of science for students to understand that scientific activity is pursued within a culture of biases and beliefs based on who the scientist is and what has been her or his life experiences. To highlight the personal nature of science and to stress that scientific activity requires concrete evidence before conclusions are drawn, the following interaction is very important. Because of the collaborative nature of scientific processes, the more diverse the group of scientists, the more varied the types of observations. This diversity is essential to having a more accurate representation of nature.

INTERACTION 6.4:
The Checks Lab

INTASC Principle 5: Motivation and Management

This activity is a way to create a metaphor for the type of group collaboration required for scientific discovery. The importance of sharing ideas and hearing everyone's voice is crucial to the outcome of the activity. Go the Web site http://www.indiana.edu/~ensiweb/lessons/cheks.a.html and print the cancelled bank checks. You will receive 16 cancelled checks from a specific family. Working in groups of four, select four checks at a time, randomly, from the envelope and examine them. Everyone's input is extremely important in making meaning of the final story that you will construct. The operative question for this activity is "What kinds of data do cancelled checks give us?" Think about dates, names, addresses, check numbers, and specific creditors or vendors to which this family owed money. You can see that the checks are evidence for something. You can document the activities of this family and begin to create a story.

As each new set of checks is analyzed, do your group members revise and change their existing ideas? Do you notice that each group has had access to different sequences of information? Do you think that this may affect group members' final conclusions? On large poster paper, summarize your group's conclusions based on the inferences they made from examining 16 checks and present your summary to the class. After all groups have presented, look for the conclusions that the entire class (all groups) agrees on. These become the basis for the class's theories about the family. Science works in a black box, where predetermined answers are never available and testing and retesting are a necessary part of the work. Your final conclusions are based on the order in which the checks were received, the importance of the evidence not received, and the significance of the personal bias within each group.

The activity is jarring for many because it has no right answer and is a stark reminder that the nature of science is a relentless search for data and new evidence that builds on prior data and constructs new knowledge. Such is the nature of science: a quest for new knowledge based on repeated efforts to explore the evidence and draw conclusions in a social community of workers. This activity is important for gender equity because it highlights the necessity for a diverse community of scientists to examine the same sets of data. This activity also reminds teachers that science is a social activity dispelling the "lone White male" stereotype that often alienates females from science.

ESSENTIAL EQUITY QUESTION 6.3:
HOW DOES ENGAGING IN LOCALLY RELEVANT SCIENTIFIC ISSUES AND PROBLEMS FOSTER GREATER ENTHUSIASM FOR SCIENCE?

WHAT WE KNOW

Wherever a school may be located, there is enormous diversity in nature. Whether amid the rich deciduous forests of the suburban or rural Northeast or close by the vast cornfields of the Midwest or near the rocky shores of a coastal community, opportunities to study nature abound. In the South, one is surrounded by the dramatic flora and fauna of arid or tropical regions. Even at an inner city school, you may find trees in planting squares in the sidewalks or at least a dandelion breaking through the cracks.

There may be a great deal of diversity among students as well. People notice different things in nature and respond to them in different ways. Consider the little dandelion in the sidewalk, for example. One person may see it as a sign of the stubborn persistence of plant life; a student with relatives in the suburbs may see it as a weed that ought to be exterminated. One student may come from a family that serves dandelion greens at a meal; others probably have no idea that people would eat such a thing. One person may think the dandelion flower is beautiful; another may think it ugly or not even recognize it as a flower. By taking advantage of diversity inside and outside of a group—seizing opportunities to make interesting connections between students' lives and the natural world around them—the classroom can become a more dynamic, vital place. Building these links stimulates learning in two major ways: It helps students see the larger picture, and it counteracts the traditional alienation of many people from science (Koch, 2005).

Research has shown that many girls and women and many males, as well, are disenfranchised by science when it makes few connections to their daily, lived experiences (Meyer, 1998). The informal science curriculum should be ongoing in classrooms where changes in nature, the seasons, and phases of the moon are routine science topics. Even daylight savings time becomes an opportunity to explore the Earth's rotation on its axis and its revolution around the Sun and the length of day and night at differing times of the year. This is a strong gender issue when we consider the proportionally higher number of women in the life sciences as compared to the physical sciences. Research indicates that female participation in the life sciences shows their desire to be connected to their objects of study. That connection can happen in the physical sciences as well; however, it is not as obvious at first. Context is everything! For example, visiting the school playground introduces young students to simple machines. One university professor takes her class ice-skating to help them learn more about the relationship between force, mass, and acceleration and the dynamics involved with friction and resistance. In a local elementary school, fifth-grade students take samples of water from the school fountains and test the water for acidity and contaminants. Studying science gives students a unique lens through which they can study their local environment, both inside and outside of the classroom.

The rigor of natural science is not seen as a deterrent to female participation; rather, the method of teaching emphasizes a false dichotomy between studying the sciences and understanding their contributions to society. In a recent study (Linn, 2000), researchers and teachers created important curricular contexts for making science relevant to students' lives. By integrating scientific controversies into the secondary science curriculum, students gained the opportunity to connect to a contemporary scientific controversy and began to see that scientists regularly revisit their ideas and rethink their views, empowering students to do the same. "I challenge all concerned about science education to remedy the serious declines in science interest, the disparities in male and female persistence in science, and the public resistance to scientific understandings by forming partnerships to bring to life the excitement and controversy in scientific research" (Linn, 2000, p. 16).

In Linn's (2000) study, students were engaged in exploring a contemporary controversy about deformed frogs. By using selected Internet materials to construct their own arguments, students prepared for a classroom debate around two main hypotheses: the parasite hypothesis, stating that the trematode parasite explains the increase in frog deformities, or the environmental hypothesis, suggesting that an increase in specific chemicals used to spray fields adjacent to the frog pond caused the frog deformities. To construct an argument, students examined evidence from research laboratories, discussed their ideas with peers, and searched for additional information. Using a Web-based environment, middle school students partnered with graduate students working in a laboratory at the University of California at Berkeley as well as with technology and assessment experts (see http:// wise.berkeley.edu).

In their study of this project, researchers interviewed and surveyed teachers and students prior to their participation in the partnership. They designed pre- and posttests, inquiry activities, and curriculum materials that ensured curriculum and assessment were aligned. The classroom research continued to help teachers refine the materials used for instruction. Prior to this scientific controversy unit, the students often reported that science had no relevance to their lives and that science was best learned by memorizing. In the deformed frogs study, pre- and posttest assessments revealed that more than two thirds of the students were able to use the mechanism they learned from the Internet evidence for the parasite hypothesis. Their answers often revealed the complex use of language learned from reviewing and integrating Web resources. On all assessment measures for content, females and males were equally successful.

This scientific controversy unit about deformed frogs was carried out with diverse middle school students: Half of the students qualified for free or reduced-price lunches and one out of four students spoke English at home. As a result of this unit of study, more students participated in science, gained scientific understanding, and became more aware of the excitement that motivates scientists to pursue careers in science (Linn, 2000, p. 25). The skills that students acquired by working in these partnerships and their critical evaluations and interpretations of scientific data were contextualized within the real world of science, ponds, and frogs.

Think about this question: Have you had an opportunity to conduct an investigation in the real world? If you are a collector, a gardener, a cook, or a daily observer of nature, you are connecting to scientific study. Documenting that connection is what the next section is all about.

INTERACTION 6.5:
Keeping a Science Journal

INTASC Principle 4: Variety of Instructional Strategies

Exploring the real world, posing questions, and carrying out investigations are activities that people frequently do in daily life. Often, people do not code these behaviors as working scientifically. Understanding locally relevant and real-life science issues is important for encouraging lifelong participation in science. To begin to explore nature, many people keep their own science journal and share their findings with their peers. A science journal is a personal diary in which the focus of the writer's attention is nature and natural events in daily experiences. Science can be thought of simply as a way of knowing the natural world. Therefore, a science journal contains observations of and questions about nature. Often, as people charge through life in this fast-paced world, they are oblivious to the ways in which nature presents itself. Keeping a science journal forces people to take notice of nature. For this reason, science journals are a way of contacting the scientific self. Science journals can also contain items about a science show on television or a newspaper story about a recent scientific breakthrough.

Keep your science journal in a separate notebook and make entries in it on a regular basis—about two or three times a week. Remember that a science journal can encourage you to ask your own questions and seek answers. If you observe something that you do not understand, write about it. A science journal may contain scientific wonderings and can be a log, recording the natural events that capture your curiosity and take you by surprise.

Keeping a science journal means taking notice of your natural surroundings. It also invites you to develop a keen ear and eye for news stories that involve scientific matters. Anything can be grist for the mill. Keep these reminders handy as you begin your journal:

- All of your observations are important. No observation is silly or too simple.
- All of your questions have value; collect them in your journal.

• Note the date and time of all your entries. This information can be helpful later if you want to go back and look for a pattern or connections.
• Entries in your journal can be of any length.
• Watch for interesting science shows on television.
• Make use of any opportunities to find out what other people are thinking about natural events.
• Have fun and write freely. (Koch, 2005)

INTERACTION 6.6:
Science in the News

INTASC Principle 6: Communication Skills

Select a local newspaper or science weekly magazine that regularly explores scientific topics of interest. Look through the publication until you see an article that interests you. Read the article with respect to the following questions:

• Who is doing the research?
• Who is funding the research?
• How many people are in the study?
• Who will be served by the results of this investigation?
• How will it affect your life?
• Why does this article interest you?

In teacher education classes, participants are surprised to learn that, given a specific context, like the "Science Times" section of *The New York Times* in a particular week, many people select the same article for review and discussion.

This activity further explores the human side of science and the understanding that scientific activity is a human construction. It also helps teachers understand that the more diverse a group of scientists who engage in investigations, the more diverse the observations and inferences about a given phenomenon. What articles interest you? How do you feel about scientific discoveries?

RESOURCES

Abir-Am, P., & Outram, D. (1987). *Uneasy careers and intimate lives: Women in science 1789–1979.* Piscataway, NJ: Rutgers University Press.

Alic, M. (1986). *Hypatia's heritage: A history of women in science from antiquity through the nineteenth century.* Boston: Beacon Press.

American Association of University Women Educational Foundation. (1994). *School Girls: Young women, self-esteem, and the confidence gap.* Washington, DC: Author.

American Association of University Women Educational Foundation. (1995). *Growing Smart: What's working for girls in school-executive summary and action guide.* Washington, DC: Author.

American Association of University Women Educational Foundation. (1995). *How schools shortchange girls: The AAUW report.* Washington, DC: Author.

American Association of University Women Educational Foundation. (1996). *Girls in the middle: Working to succeed in school.* Washington, DC: Author.

American Association of University Women Educational Foundation. (1998). *Gender gaps executive summary.* Washington, DC: Author.

American Association of University Women Educational Foundation. (1998). *Gender gaps: Where schools still fail on children.* Washington, DC: Author.

American Association of University Women Educational Foundation. (1999). *Voices of generations: Teenage girls on sex, school, and self.* Washington, DC: Author.

American Association of University Women Educational Foundation. (2001). *Beyond the "gender wars": A conversation about girls, boys, and education.* Washington, DC: Author.

American Association of University Women Educational Foundation. (2001). *Hostile hallways: Bullying, teasing, and sexual harassment in schools.* Washington, DC: Author.

Bleier, R. (Ed.). (1986). *Feminist approaches to science.* New York: Pergamon Press.

Campbell, P., & Storo, J. (1994). *Why me? Why my classroom? The need for equity in coed math and science classes.* Groton, MA: Campbell-Kibler Associates.

Chapman, A. (1997). *A great balancing act: Equitable education for girls and boys.* Washington, DC: National Association of Independent Schools.

Clewell, B., Anderson, B., & Thorpe, M. (1992). *Breaking the barriers: Helping female and minority students succeed in mathematics and science.* San Francisco: Jossey-Bass.

Ehrhart, J. K., & Sandler, B. (1987). *Looking for more than a few good women in traditionally male fields.* Washington, DC: Association of American Colleges.

Fort, D., & Varney, H. (1989). How students see scientists: Mostly male, mostly White, and mostly benevolent. *Science and Children, 26,* 8–13.

Frederick, J., & Nicholson, H. J. (1991). *Explorer's pass: A report on the study of girls and math, science and technology.* Indianapolis, IN: Girls, Inc.

Gallas, K. (1995). *Talking their way into science.* New York: Teachers College Press.

Gallas, K. (1998). *"Sometimes I can be anything": Power, gender, and identity in a primary classroom. The practitioner inquiry series.* New York: Teachers College Press.

Gornick, V. (1983). *Women in science: Portraits of a world in transition.* New York: Simon & Schuster.

Green, K. C. (1989). A profile of undergraduates in the sciences. *American Scientist, 77,* 476.

Hubbard, R. (1990). *The politics of women's biology.* New Brunswick, NJ: Rutgers University Press.

Kahle, J. B., & Lakes, M. K. (1983). The myth of equality in science classrooms. *Journal of Research in Science Teaching, 20*(2), 131–140.

Kahle, J. B., & Meece, J. (1994). Research on gender issues in the classroom. In D. Gabel (Ed.), *Handbook of research on science teaching and learning* (pp. 542–557). New York: Macmillan.

Keller, E. (1983). *A feeling for the organism: The life and work of Barbara McClintock* (pp. 15–17). New York: W.H. Freeman.

Keller, E. (1985). *Reflections on gender and science.* New Haven, CT: Yale University Press.

Keller, E. (1989). The gender/science system. In N. Tuana (Ed.), *Feminism and science* (pp. 33–44). Bloomington, IN: Indiana University Press.

Keller, E. (1990, October 15). Long live the differences between men and women scientists. *The Scientist.*

Koch, J. (1998). Response to Karen Meyer: Reflections on being female in school science. *Journal of Research in Teaching Science, 35*(4), 473–474.

Krockover, G., & Shepardson, D. (1995). The missing links in gender equity research: Editorial. *Journal of Research in Science Teaching, 32*(3), 223–224.

Larson, J. O. (1996). *"I'm just not interested": Gender-related responses in a high school chemistry curriculum.* (Eric Document Reproduction No. ED 393705)

Lyman, K. (2000, Spring). Girls, worms, and body image: A teacher deals with gender stereotypes among her second- and third-graders. *Rethinking Schools,* 1–6.

Manis, J., Thomas, N., Sloat, B., & Davis, C. (1989). An analysis of factors affecting choices of majors in science, mathematics and engineering at the University of Michigan (Center for the Education of Women: Research Report, No. 23). Ann Arbor, MI: University of Michigan.

Martinez, M. E. (1989). *Gender differences in science interest.* Princeton, NJ: Educational Testing Service.

McIlwee, J., & Robinson, J. G. (1992). *Women in engineering: Gender, power and workplace culture.* Albany: State University of New York Press.

McIntosh, P. (1983). *Interactive phases of curricular re-vision: A feminist perspective* (Working Paper No. 124). Wellesley, MA: Wellesley College Center for Research on Women.

Marshall, C. S., & Reinhartz, J. (1997). Gender issues in the classroom. *Clearing House, 70*(6), 333–337.

Martin, M. V. (1996). *Inside a gender-sensitive classroom: An all girls' physics class.* (Eric Document Reproduction No. ED398053)

Nelkin, D. (1987). *Selling science.* New York: W.H. Freeman.

Quinn, S. (1995). *Marie Curie: A life.* New York: Simon & Schuster.

Reynolds, T. H. (1995). *Addressing gender and cognitive issues in the mathematics classroom: A constructivist approach.* (Eric Document Reproduction No. ED404183)

Rop, C. (1998). Breaking the gender barrier in the physical sciences. *Educational Leadership, 56*(4), 58–60.

Rosendale, L. (1990). *Thoughts of a research scientist: A conversation with Dr. Barbara McClintock.* Unpublished manuscript.

Rosser, S. V. (1990). *Female friendly science.* New York: Pergamon Press.

Rosser, S. V. (1992). *Biology and feminism: A dynamic interaction.* New York: Twayne.

Rossiter, M. (1982). *Women scientists in America: Struggles and strategies to 1940.* Baltimore: Johns Hopkins University Press.

Sadker, M., & Sadker, D. (1994). *Failing at fairness: How America's schools cheat girls.* New York: Charles Scribner's Sons.

Sanders, J., Koch, J., & Urso, J. (1997). *Right from the Start: Instructional activities for teacher educators in mathematics, science and technology.* Mahwah, NJ: Lawrence Erlbaum Associates.

Sandler, B. (1984). *The classroom climate: A chilly one for women?* Washington, DC: Association of American Colleges.

Shepherd, L. (1993). *The feminine face of science.* Boston: Shambhala Publications.

Shiels, B. (1985). *Women and the Nobel prize.* Minneapolis, MN: Dillon Press.

Smith, I. (1981). *The stone lady: A memoir of Florence Bascom.* Bryn Mawr, PA: Bryn Mawr College.

Streitmatter, J. (1997). An exploratory study of risk-taking and attitudes in a girls-only middle school math class. *Elementary School Journal, 98*(1), 15–26.

REFERENCES

Abir-Am, P., & Outram, D. (1987). *Uneasy careers and intimate lives: Women in science, 1789–1979.* New Brunswick, NJ: Rutgers University Press.

American Association of University Women. (1998). *Gender gaps: Where schools still fail on children.* Washington, DC: Author.

Barman, C. (1997). Students' views of scientists and science: Results from a national study. *Science and Children, 35*(1), 18–24.

Boaler, J. (2002). Paying the price for sugar and spice: Shifting the analytical lens in equity research. *Mathematical Thinking and Learning, 4,* 127–144.

Hammerich, P., Richardson, G., & Livingston, B. (2000). *Sisters in science confronting equity in science and mathematics education.* Paper presented at the annual American Educational Research Association conference, Seattle, WA.

Kahle, J. B., & Meece, J. (1994). Research on gender issues in the classroom. In D. Gabel (Ed.), *Handbook of research on science teaching and learning* (pp. 542–557). New York: Macmillan.

Koch, J. (1998a). Response to Karen Meyer: Reflections on being female in school science. *Journal of Research in Teaching Science, 35*(4), 473–474.

Koch, J. (1998b). Science education: An invitation. In C. Nelson & K. Wilson (Eds.), *Seeding the process of multicultural education* (pp. 262–272). Minneapolis: Minnesota Inclusiveness Program.

Koch, J. (2005). *Science stories: Science methods for elementary and middle school teachers.* Boston: Houghton Mifflin.

Lederman, N. G. (1992). Students' and teachers' conceptions of the nature of science: A review of the research. *Journal of Research in Teaching Science, 29*(4), 331–359.

Levine, E. Z., & Orenstein, F. M. (1994). *Sugar and spice and puppy dog tails: Gender equity among middle school children.* (Eric Document Reproduction No. ED389457)

Linn, M. C. (2000). Controversy, the Internet, and deformed frogs: Making science accessible. *Who Will do the Science of the Future?* (pp. 16–27). Washington, DC: National Academy Press.

Meyer, K. (1998). Reflections on being female in school science. *Journal of Research in Teaching Science, 35*(4), 473–474.

Mozans, J. J. (1991). *Women in science.* South Bend, IN: University of Notre Dame Press.

National Center for Education Statistics. (n.d.). *Digest of education statistics, tables and figures.* Retrieved October 15, 2004, from http://nces.ed.gov/programs/digest/d02/dt129.asp

National Science Foundation. (n.d.). *Women, minorities, and persons with disabilities in science and engineering: Undergraduate degrees in science and engineering.* Retrieved November 30, 2004, from http://www.nsf.gov/sbe/srs/wmpd/sex.htm

7

Gender Equity Intersects With Mathematics and Technology: Problem-Solving Education for Changing Times

Karen N. Bell
State University of New York at New Paltz

Karen Norwood
North Carolina State University

T his chapter's focus is to provide a lens through which to view mathematics, technology, and their instruction. It is our intention to demonstrate that mathematics and technology are important to everyone, that the disciplines have intrinsic beauty, and that they provide an excellent mode for the communication of complex ideas. We also explore how cultural factors have shaped attitudes toward mathematics, and we suggest a variety of instructional practices that can be implemented to foster more equitable learning and greater appreciation of mathematics and technology.

In this chapter we explore four Essential Equity Questions (EEQs) for use with preservice teachers who are working to develop their repertoire of instructional tools at the elementary or middle school levels, with in-service teachers through ongoing professional development, as well as with modifications for use with elementary and middle school pupils themselves.

The EEQs addressed in the chapter are as follows:

- **Essential Equity Question 7.1:** Why is mathematics important?
- **Essential Equity Question 7.2:** Are there gender differences in cognitive ability or learning style in mathematics and technology?
- **Essential Equity Question 7.3:** What kinds of social and cultural factors influence gender differences in cognitive abilities or in academic performance pertaining to mathematics and technology?
- **Essential Equity Question 7.4:** What kinds of instructional and assessment strategies foster mathematics and technology achievement for all students in the classroom?

A section titled What We Know, which is a brief overview of gender-related research that focuses on mathematics and technology, follows each EEQ. Scattered throughout the chapter are Interactions, which are tested classroom activities that assist individuals in discovering and understanding their relationship to mathematics and technology. These activities are designed to challenge assumptions and break down barriers that may stand in the way of fully knowing and appreciating the value and beauty of mathematics and the technological world. They also provide a new lens from which to view the disciplines of mathematics and technology, so their value and approaches to problem solving can be used in all arenas of life.

ESSENTIAL EQUITY QUESTION 7.1:
WHY IS MATHEMATICS IMPORTANT?

Mathematics has been described as a science, an art, and a language. The more teachers teach and learn mathematics, the more this statement holds true. The Mathematical Sciences Education Board describes *mathematics* "as the science of pattern and order" (p. 31). Using this definition, teachers become focused on the rhythmic and repetitive nature of the description through patterns as well as the idea of quantification or magnitude. As a science, mathematics contains an element of exactness in calculations and procedure, while at the same time engages one in inquiry, problem solving, and systematic investigating to explain phenomena. Mathematics, as a science, is a vehicle to measure characteristics, quantify amounts, express relationships, and ultimately make decisions or look for explanations.

Mathematics as an art is the expression of its patterns in an aesthetic form. This can take on many variations so often found in nature, from simple shapes to complex tiling patterns. It can also take a musical form with sound patterns. In considering the visual aspects of mathematics, we associate Gardner's (1993) spatial intelligence as one that is important in understanding geometry and its structures, both two- and three-dimensional. Spatial intelligence is used in translating mathematical ideas and processes into graphical representations, such as graphs, charts, and tables. In the auditory realm, music is inherently mathematical with its rhythms, patterns, and notation as well as the connection between vibration frequencies and sounds or tones. Mathematics is thus expressed aesthetically, both visually and auditory.

Mathematics as a language is a way of communicating. First it has its own symbols, rules, and procedures by which people express mathematical ideas. Examples include the basic operations of addition, subtraction, multiplication, and division. Second, people use the symbols of mathematics to describe mathematical situations, such as equality and inequality. In the language of mathematics, the words *equality* and *inequality* have very specific meanings. Many words used in a mathematics context are homonyms of everyday words with specialized meanings. To be mathematically literate, individuals need to develop a strong working mathematics vocabulary. Third, mathematical language has developed across all cultures worldwide, independent of religion, race, and other divisive lines. The mathematics educators teach and the symbolism they use is globally recognized. In this way, mathematics can be thought of as a universal language, not tied to any one location or people. Music, too, can be thought of as this kind of language, available to all regardless of culture or spoken language. The National Council of Teachers of Mathematics (2000), in its *Principles and Standards for School Mathematics*, includes "Mathematics as Communication" as one of its major principles for mathematics education.

If you start from the premise that mathematics is a science, an art, and a language, then you can explore how mathematics is intricately part of people's lives, both directly and indirectly. Mathematics directly affects corporal selves through the measurement of bodily functioning. These include pulse, blood pressure, and cholesterol level. Each day you wake and go through your daily routine where mathematics indirectly intersects with your life. You tell and measure time; drive or take public transportation and figure cost, time, and convenience; and exchange currency for goods and services that are calculated into a monthly budget. Mathematics is involved when you buy and cook food, whether you are calculating cost, tax, and change or measuring cups, teaspoons, and pints. You work for an hourly or annual wage and calculate the real cost of buying a product on time. Mathematics is everywhere, and the more you recognize this, the more relevant its study becomes.

WHAT WE KNOW

The world we live in today is increasingly information and technology driven. Citizens are presented with a vast amount of information, much of it reported as statistics. When researching, you are faced with many options and opinions, some fact, some fiction. It is your job to decide what information is worthwhile and use it most beneficially given the situation at hand. A considerable amount of summary information is displayed pictorially, in the form of graphs and tables. Each of these pictures tells a specific mathematical story that is to be deciphered. To fully understand that picture, analytical skills are necessary. Further, graphs and visual representations of numerical relationships can be slanted. Higher order thinking is necessary to determine if the information reported is accurate, decide what is worthwhile, and synthesize the pieces.

Individuals who possess these skills won't be taken, will be able to assess a "good deal," and will understand how numbers can be used, both informatively and deceptively. Being mathematically and technologically literate is a requirement for today's world. Many of the problems people face in their backyards—development in environmentally sensitive areas, drinking water protection, air quality, cell tower and high voltage transformer and wire placement, mining in previously protected areas—will affect people, their children, and their children's children. Teachers need to prepare students to be the citizens of tomorrow who will be able to face such issues as global warming, toxic waste management, and natural disaster detection. Society needs individuals who can consider many different aspects of an issue simultaneously and see how they connect and diverge. These skills are developed in the learning and doing of mathematics. Mathematics provides tools to explain and understand the world through analytical thinking and logical decision making.

In tomorrow's employment market, there will be fewer jobs that require physical labor. Karadimos (2004), a Michigan math teacher, stated why it is important to study mathematics and what employers are looking for in future workers:

> Machines and robots are replacing labor-intensive jobs and even when those jobs are available, the pay is usually substandard. In order to gain successful employment, technical skills must be learned. Someone has to fix all of those machines and robots. … Employers are looking for three basic traits. They want their employees to be able to reason, work with technical equipment, and communicate their thoughts with other employees. (p. 3)

At this time, perhaps more so than at any other time in history, people need to be able to use mathematics in the workplace to perform their everyday tasks. Individuals who possess these skills will be more employable in the future. It is critical, as more women are entering the workforce worldwide, that they are prepared for the skilled jobs that will be available. The highest paying professions often require significant training in the areas of mathematics and technology. It is vitally important that women develop their skills in these areas, if they have any hope of achieving equity in employment opportunities. According to the recent report, *Global Employment Trends for Women 2004* (International Labour Office, 2001), society is far from achieving equity in employment. It is our view that equity can only happen when women exercise their mathematical power effectively. The report paints the following picture of the state of women's employment at this time:

> More women work today than ever before: in 2003 out of the 2.8 billion people that had work, 1.1 billion were women. The share of women with work in total employment has risen slightly in the past ten years to just above 40 percent.

However, improved equality in terms of quantity of male and female workers has yet to result in real socioeconomic empowerment for women, an equitable distribution of household responsibilities, equal pay for work of equal value, and gender balance across all occupations. In short, true equality in the world of work is still out of reach. (p. 1)

The report (International Labour Office, 2001) explains how women are partially responsible for undermining equality and equity in pay:

Can wage equality be achieved? The evidence is not favorable in the short term. Women everywhere typically receive less pay than men. This is in part because women often hold low-level, low-paying positions in female-dominated occupations. A review of data available for six diverse occupation groups shows that in most economies, women still earn 90 percent or less of what their male co-workers earn. ... One might expect to find near wage equality in high-skill occupations where the education and training level of applicants would presumably be comparable (accountant in the banking sector or computer programmer in the insurance sector, for example). This is not the case. Even in these occupations the average female wage is still only 88 percent of the male wage. One of the reasons identified for the wage differential is women's lack of negotiating capability as well as bargaining power. (p. 13)

Not only are women's wage negotiating skills less powerful, but there is also a tendency for male wages to surpass women's, even in traditionally female jobs as described further in the report:

In the United States in 1990 the earnings of female nurses were almost equivalent to that of male nurses. By 2000, however, female nurses were earning less than 90 percent of their male counterparts. There was a similar decrease in the earnings gap by gender for accountants in the banking sector. (p. 15)

Statistics abound concerning the wages of women and men for various professions. The Department of Labor Bureau of Labor Statistics reports many of these statistics on its Web site (http://www.bls.gov/). Hanna (2003) summed it up as follows:

In 1998, women held 53 percent of all U.S. professional jobs, including teaching and nursing, but only 28 percent of the jobs in the six better-paying professions (engineering, law, medicine, natural science, computer science, and college and university teaching). In addition, those women who did have jobs in these professions were paid less. (p. 212)

This disparity is even more evident in the area of technology:

Similar to advanced mathematics, a working familiarity with information technology is fast becoming a filter for screening subsequent career options.

Such knowledge *is* now a strong asset in an increasingly competitive job market. Yet females are underrepresented in computer-learning environments, from computer camps to enrollments in secondary school classes and continuing into college and graduate school. The data confirm this reluctance and ambivalence. (Salomone, 2003, p. 91)

Salomone (2003) goes on to comment that this is a great departure from the past because some of the greatest early contributions to the field of computer science came from women:

In the nascent days of the industry, 65 percent of computer operators were women. Fast-forward to the present and the contrast is striking. Female students who enroll in computer classes in high school or in community colleges are significantly more likely than boys to be found in clerical and data-entry classes. Yet at the same time, high school coursework is a critical factor for girls in their career choice at the more advanced levels. ... According to a 1999 survey, there is a 4:1 male-to-female ratio in the information technology profession, where women's earnings are 85 percent that of men. (pp. 91–92)

Given that this is the state of affairs at the beginning of the 21st century, it is an appropriate time to reflect on what research has discovered over the past to assess where teachers should be headed in the mathematical education of children and young adults.

For the purpose of this chapter, we first need to discuss the differences between the terms *sex* and *gender*. Research published before 1970 used the term *sex differences* when referring to differences that were believed to be biological or genetic. This allowed schools to attribute the differences between boys and girls in mathematics to genetics and, as a result, could not be changed. Therefore, the differences were accepted, even expected. From the 1970s to 1980s, the term *sex-related* was introduced. This term implied "that while the behavior of concern was clearly related to the sex of the subjects, it was not necessarily genetically determined" (Fennema, 2000, p. 2). Recently, researchers have used the term *gender differences*, which encompasses biological as well as social and environmental factors, all of which affect the achievement differences between boys and girls in mathematics.

Researchers have shown that many of the causes that keep minorities from going into mathematics, science, and engineering also act as barriers for females: negative attitudes about mathematics and science, lower performance levels than those of White males in mathematics and science coursework as well as on standardized tests, limited exposure to extracurricular mathematics and science activities and failure to enroll in advanced mathematics and science courses, and lack of information about mathematics and science related careers (Clewell, Anderson, & Thorpe, 1992).

As a starting point for those individuals who are planning to be teachers, who must all either use or teach mathematics, it is important to have an understanding of their own relationship to mathematics. Interaction 7.1 is designed to help preservice and in-service teachers to focus on their own experiences with mathematics and to investigate how these experiences shape their current attitudes and beliefs about mathematics and technology.

INTERACTION 7.1:
What Is Your Confidence Level in Mathematics and Technology?

INTASC Principle 2: Human Development and Learning

Concentric Circle Exercise. Have participants stand and form two circles, one inside the other. The people of the inner circle face out and the people of the outer circle face in so each person is opposite another and has a partner. Participants are directed to consider a particular incident in life and to share it with their partner. Each person shares for 2 minutes. The facilitator directs the outer circle to move clockwise one person, so each individual has a new partner. Another question or directive is posed until each person has met with about four or five others in the group. Consider these directives:

- Remember a time in school when you had a negative experience in mathematics.
- Remember a time in school when you had a positive experience in mathematics.
- Consider a time when your gender had an impact on your experience of mathematics. How did that make you feel?
- Consider a time when your gender had an impact on your experience of something technical. How did that make you feel?
- Describe your confidence level in mathematics and technology.

Debriefing and Discussion. Ask participants to respond to the following questions:

- By a show of hands, how many people shared a positive experience when speaking about gender affecting you in a mathematical context? Negative experience? Comments?
- By a show of hands, how many people shared a positive experience when speaking about gender affecting you in a technological context? Negative experience? Comments?
- Would anyone like to share an experience or reflect on this exercise?

The results of Interaction 7.1 may initiate a conversation that leads to the real question teachers should be asking: "Why are there fewer women than men in math-related fields, when the gender differences are so small?" An American Association of University Women (AAUW; 1992) study found that, from elementary school to high school, there is a large drop in the number of girls who perceive themselves as good in math. The following causes might result in girls' lack of interest or poor performance in math:

- Math anxiety
- Perceived usefulness of math
- Math as a male domain
- Teachers' differential treatment
- Autonomous learning behavior of males and females
- Perception of self as learner

During a keynote address at the American Association of University Women (AAUW) conference "Girls Succeeding in Science, Math, and Technology: Who Works and What Works," Shirley M. Malcom, of the American Association for the Advancement of Science (AAAS), stated

> The effort to equalize educational opportunities is far from complete. [She notes], unlike some other nations, female students in the United States are legally guaranteed access to math and science courses. While our legal barriers to this education have been removed, there are often still barriers we face; these are "barriers of the mind." (as cited in Hammrich, Richardson, & Livingston, 2000, p. 44)

One barrier that prevents girls from studying mathematics is mathematics anxiety. *Mathematics anxiety* is defined as "involving feelings of tension and anxiety that interfere with the manipulation of numbers and the solving of mathematical problems in a wide variety of ordinary life and academic situations" (Richardson & Suinn, 1972). There is not one specific cause for mathematics anxiety but a combination of several factors (Norwood, 2004).

Tobias (1980) discussed the types of math games others play on math-anxious individuals. These games include a list of statements or beliefs that are said to math-anxious students that can cause or increase their anxiety:

- "You did it the wrong way."
- "You should know that."
- "You'll never be able to do math."
- "I don't know why you can't get it; everyone else did."
- "It's obvious."
- "That's an easy problem."
- "Mathematics is not feminine."
- "All you have to do to learn mathematics is to work hard."
- "Let me do it for you."
- "Women are nonmathematical."
- "Boys are better at math than girls."

INTERACTION 7.2:
Empowering People to Investigate Mathematics Anxiety

INTASC Principle 2: Human Development and Learning

For the first part of this activity, remember a time when one of the previous statements was said to you. Describe in writing what you said or did at the time. Rewrite the response you would make now if those words were said to you. Then, rewrite the statements in such a way so that they would alleviate mathematics anxiety and increase student confidence in the classroom when working in mathematics.

There is no single cure for mathematics anxiety. Just as there is no one cause of mathematics anxiety, there is no one strategy to cure mathematics anxiety. According to Norwood (2004), there may not be a cure for mathematics anxiety, but there are prescriptions for alleviating mathematics anxiety:

- Creating a positive, supportive atmosphere in the classroom
- Encouraging interesting approaches and ideas
- Using concrete materials to teach concepts
- Using cooperative learning
- Giving positive, written feedback on tests
- Helping students wean themselves from time-consuming algorithms and rely on their ability to reason
- Helping students develop and use alternative algorithms, especially those arising from the creation and manipulation of models
- Finding out why wrong answers make sense to students and helping them determine why the reasoning is faulty (error analysis) and introducing new, non-remedial, relevant mathematics courses into the curriculum
- Requiring 4 years of high school mathematics for all students
- Being sensitive but determined
- Dispelling the "math mind" myth

These strategies are discussed in more detail later in this chapter.

ESSENTIAL EQUITY QUESTION 7.2:
ARE THERE GENDER DIFFERENCES IN COGNITIVE ABILITY OR LEARNING STYLE IN MATHEMATICS AND TECHNOLOGY?

Through EEQ 7.1, we explored the importance of studying mathematics and how it plays important roles in people's lives and acts as a critical filter for educational and employment opportunities. From what is known, a distinct pattern emerges as to women's participation in mathematics and technology. To what can you attribute these patterns? Are there specific differences between males and females that can be identified that cause a difference in mathematics achievement? What other factors influence mathematics learning?

WHAT WE KNOW

Over the past three decades, a significant amount of attention has been paid to the differences in mathematics achievement of males and females. Researchers have worked to explain why women's mathematics SAT scores have consistently been lower than men's. Why is it that there are still fewer women earning degrees in mathematics, engineering, and computer science? Why is it that girls and women seem to be less confident and less interested in studying mathematics?

These questions arise, in part, because the majority of students in school are female and they earn more grades of A and B (male students earn more grades of D and F). Further, male students are at greater risk of dropping out and being referred for special education services than female students are, and males are more frequently written up for behavioral problems in the classroom. Why is it, then, that girls' performance on the SAT seems to be at odds with their perceived performance in school?

The SAT, though accepted as one standard by which precollege students are measured, is not without its critics. Many individuals have claimed that the exams are biased against women and minorities because these groups have consistently scored lower, particularly on the mathematics section. To further explain why the SAT, like any single measure, does not present the complete picture of a student, Shmurak (1998) explained why SAT scores do not always correlate with grades: "For example, a girl with low math ability (as indicated by a low SAT-M score) may take a low level math or science course and do quite well, whereas a girl with high ability (and a high SAT-M score) may take calculus or an AP science course and do less well" (p. 146).

As of March 2005, the test format of the SAT was changed. It now includes a section on 3rd-year high school mathematics and a written component, and the Quantitative Comparisons section has been eliminated. The changes to the SAT mean that an even higher level of mathematics achievement is necessary to score well. Although it is thought that the written section will improve women's scores overall, it may actually create a larger disparity in the mathematics section. The question then becomes "Does mathematical achievement mean that women are less mathematically able than men?"

In the field of gender differences and mathematics, Elizabeth Fennema (2000) is one of the most widely published and extensively quoted experts on the subject. She summarized what she knows about gender differences in the learning of mathematics:

- The issue is very complex and seems more so than previously thought.
- Children are not being taught mathematics equitably because for mathematics equity to exist, it may be necessary to teach girls differently from boys.

- In a research study, it was found that boys used more invented strategies to solve mathematics problems and were more able to extend their thinking to non-routine problems.
- Girls tended to use more concrete strategies such as modeling and counting, while boys used more abstract strategies even as early as grades 1–3 (pp. 12–15).

At this point in history, just after the turn of the 21st century, there is a movement toward looking longitudinally or at many studies over time to see where there are similarities or conflicting results. These meta-analyses look to identify patterns, replications, and places of deviation. Critically looking through new eyes in light of other similar studies, researchers can offer reinterpretations and often question basic assumptions or research designs.

Rogers (2001) discussed the research of Alan Feingold of Yale University who looked at sex differences in performance in scholastic aptitude tests over time. Rogers made the following report after looking at studies between 1947–1983:

The usual sex differences were found—girls did better than boys in verbal abilities, and boys better than girls in spatial and mathematical tasks—but these differences, to quote the researchers, "declined precipitously" over the years surveyed, "That is, the recorded sex differences were greater in the early studies than in the later ones. Another study by Janet Hyde and colleagues at the University of Wisconsin found the same result as Feingold. They reviewed a hundred published reports of studies on sex differences (they used the term "gender differences") in mathematics and compared the size of the difference in studies published before 1974 with that found in studies done after that date. The sex difference after 1974 was half what it was before. This is probably due to the changing attitudes about which careers are more appropriate for girls and which are more appropriate for boys. (p. 33)

Hanna (2003) who analyzed international data from three studies done by the International Association for the Evaluation of Educational Achievement (IEA) and the three International Mathematics Studies (FIMS, SIMS, and TIMSS) asserted the answer to the question whether mathematical achievement directly relates to mathematical ability is no. She summed it up as follows:

The IEA studies provided convincing evidence that gender differences in achievement vary widely from country to country, with the degree and direction of variation depending greatly on topic and grade level. ... These findings are potentially of major importance. They indicate, first of all, that some educational systems do provide, wittingly or unwittingly, educational conditions that work to prevent an achievement gap between males and females in mathematics. Second, in showing that gender differences in mathematics achievement vary in magnitude and direction from country to country, the IEA findings call into question the validity of the claim made by a number of researchers that there are innate differences between males and females in mathematical ability. (p. 206)

Salomone (2003) also pointed to how declining differences in the performance of girls and boys, due to intervention strategies and changing attitudes, "indicate that ability in these areas is changeable and not carved in biological stone" (p. 106). These arguments taken together make a convincing case that the differences of mathematics achievement found in the scores on standardized tests do not reflect the innate ability of girls and women in mathematics but are more bound by the social and cultural climate of the time. Hanna (2003) would certainly agree and offered growing evidence that the views once held by educational researchers about gender differences in mathematical achievement are not due to physical differences:

Most modern educational research on gender similarities and differences suggests no physical or intellectual barrier to the participation of women in mathematics, science, or technology. Indeed, it is now generally accepted that women have been and continue to be underrepresented in these fields mainly because of social and cultural barriers that did not and still may not accord them equal opportunities. (p. 205)

On the other hand, Gurian and Henley (2001) discussed the considerable research done by Camilla Benbow:

Benbow, and most researchers like her, started doing their research twenty years ago, when searching for sociological reasons for male-female difference was the accepted practice. Benbow ended up with this result: "After 15 years of looking for an environmental explanation and getting zero results, I gave up." The differences, she discovered, were in the brain, with culture playing an important part but not the defining role that many people have wished to believe. (p. 17)

Rogers (2001) and Gurian and Henley (2001) reported on researchers who are using sophisticated medical imagery technology, such as magnetic resonance imaging (MRI) and positron emission tomography (PET) scans, to look for physiological and functional differences in the brains of males and females. They reported on considerable research being done to determine how male and female brains are physically different, how hormones affect male and female brains, and how this information is helpful in designing curricula for girls and boys.

One such study by Haier and Benbow, with results published in 1995, administered a dye to participants who were assigned to one of four groups, average- or high-performing men and women. After they received the dye, participants were asked to solve mathematics tasks for 30 minutes. At the end of the half hour, a PET scan was performed to see where the brain was metabolizing the dye, thus indicating brain activity. The results showed that high-performing men had a statistically significant difference in how they used their brains. Their temporal lobes, on the sides of each hemisphere, were used more while solving mathematics problems (p. 15). Although Haier and Benbow consider this to indicate a difference in how the male and female brains function, Rogers is not so quick to accept these results. Rogers (2001) questioned whether other possible influences might be confounding the experiment, such as level of interest of participants, stress, or the desire to do well. Such things as heart rate monitors to measure stress levels or exit interviews asking participants about their other thoughts could have been used to account for these variables, but were not (p. 16).

Gurian and Henley (2001) further reported on other researchers, Laurie Allen at University of California at Los Angeles and Ruben Gur at the University of Pennsylvania, who found that there were structural and functional differences between male and female brains. Some of these differences are directly related to how hormones affect brain development and the functional roles that males and females played early in our history. These physical and functional differences in male and female brains have been corroborated worldwide (p. 17). For an excellent chart that details the results of the aforementioned studies, consult Gurian and Henley's book, *Boys and Girls Learn Differently!* What the authors suggest is that we acknowledge that male and female brains are different, each having its advantages and disadvantages. Knowing this, educational curricula that address these differences and use them to best meet the needs of all students should be the goal.

The current thinking is that though male and female brains function differently and though male brains may be more predisposed to mathematical thinking and spatial reasoning, these differences can be overcome with targeted intervention strategies to support girls' development in these areas. One response to this has been to design programs that focus on single-sex classrooms for males and females, especially in mathematics and science during the middle school and high school years.

In the hopes of not overgeneralizing, it has been our experience that female students tend to prefer cooperative or group learning in mathematics over silent, independent work. This conversational style supports group consensus and the development of concepts using ideas that build on each other. On the other hand, many males seem to prefer to learn through individualized activities and will often seek to work alone rather than with others when given a choice. Although this is not true in all circumstances, it is important to offer a selection of instructional techniques in the classroom to support all learning styles. Most classroom structures, however, are organized for independent rather than collaborative thinking, which limits the learning opportunities (Pearson & West, 1991). Discussions and verbalizations assist all learners as they work to articulate their thoughts and understandings. Some single-sex classrooms focus their attention on girls' preferred learning style, offering learning activities that require teamwork and collaboration, whereas others offer the same old chalk-and-talk method though all the students are the same sex. Obviously, results vary, and critics cite that single-sex classrooms do not mirror the outside world and therefore question the approach as a viable way to prepare women for the workplace. "Coeducation has successfully reduced gender gaps in math and science achievement and course participation but not in interest in the subjects or continuation into related careers. However, it is not clear that single-sex education would do any better" (Campbell & Sanders, 2002, p. 38).

ESSENTIAL EQUITY QUESTION 7.3:
WHAT KINDS OF SOCIAL AND CULTURAL FACTORS INFLUENCE GENDER DIFFERENCES IN COGNITIVE ABILITIES OR IN ACADEMIC PERFORMANCE PERTAINING TO MATHEMATICS AND TECHNOLOGY?

From our examination of Essential Equity Question 7.2, we saw how females and males have traditionally been engaged in mathematics. Through sophisticated technology, there have been specific structural and functional differences recorded between male and female brains. It has also been shown that there is considerable debate about how biology affects achievement in mathematics and technology. In this section, we explore how social and cultural factors influence women's participation in mathematics and technology.

WHAT WE KNOW

In looking at women's roles in mathematics historically, Bossé and Hurd (2002) stated that women's greatest contributions have been in the areas of mathematics communication and mathematics education. They suggest that women have been kept subservient within this male-dominated discipline and present autobiographical and biographical data that show how women have been consistently discouraged from pursuing higher learning in mathematics. Some family members of these women went to great lengths to prevent them from pursuing mathematics by "depriving young women of creature comforts (even heat and light) in order to curtail their impassioned study of mathematics. In many families, even when the head of the home was a noted mathematician, adolescent girls were directed away from mathematics and toward more culturally acceptable pursuits" (p. 220). Hannah (2003) stated:

> What seems to have made the difference, in particular over the two decades, is the attention paid to social and political factors. This attention owed much to the extensive research carried out on barriers to the equal participation of girls in school mathematics, such as inadequate parental support, inequitable treatment in the classroom (in particular inequitable interaction between teacher and student), and the preconceptions that mathematics is a male domain and in any case is useful in later life only to men. (p. 212)

Streitmatter (1999) stated:

> The concept of equity as the basis for remedy of gender inequities in schools suggests that what is fair is not necessarily equal. Simply removing barriers of access to females does not address the issue of inequitable treatment once they are admitted, nor does it constitute a means of restructuring the existing culture of schools and classrooms which would be required in order to make schools truly inclusive. Public coeducational schools are Euro-male centric cultures, and until this is no longer the case, females as a group represent a sub-culture and continue to be marginalized. (p. 121)

Research has found that confidence and self-esteem are keys to the success of girls in mathematics. Fennema (1974) felt that the worst hidden behavior that teachers unconsciously displayed was the overnurturing of female learners, especially by males. Fennema believes that the success of girls in mathematics is based on their self-esteem. Girls who do well in mathematics tend to credit their ability to luck. However, when girls do poorly in mathematics, they attribute their failure to lack of ability. This was not found to be true with males. When boys did well in mathematics, they attributed it to their ability and blamed lack of effort to their poor performance in mathematics. Fennema found that 6th-grade girls' level of confidence could be used to predict their 12th grade achievement in mathematics. It is in the sixth and seventh grades when the decision is made as to whether or not to take algebra in the eighth grade. This is an important decision in the mathematical future for not only female students but for all students.

Other research published by the AAUW (1992) discussed factors that lead girls to be successful in mathematics. The AAUW in their report "How Schools Shortchange Girls" made the following conclusions:

- Girls are more successful in classes in which there is fairness and equitable treatment.
- Girls who see mathematics as what girls and boys do are more apt to go on in mathematics and do better in it than are girls who see math as a "boy" thing.
- Getting more girls into advanced mathematics and science classes makes a difference. When there are only a small number of girls in the class, they said that they felt more intimidated and uncomfortable.

In addition, research has also shown that teacher beliefs and attitudes greatly influence the attitudes and beliefs of female students toward mathematics. The findings by Clewell, Anderson, and Thorpe (1992) reported that females more so than males are influenced by what they believe their teachers think of them. Therefore, the actions of the teachers have a great effect on female students. The AAUW (1992) report found that although teachers believe that they treat all students equally, they are mistaken:

- Teachers initiated more interactions (positive and negative) with boys than with girls. Teachers have been found to give boys more praise, more criticism, and more remediation and are more apt to accept boys' responses.
- Boys initiated more interactions with teachers than did girls. As a result, the teachers responded more to the boys than to the girls.
- Boys almost always dominated the classroom.
- Teachers tended to respond to boys and girls differently when asked for help. Teachers coached the boys to get them to answer themselves, whereas they simply gave the girls the answers. Teachers also responded more frequently to boys' requests for help and talked to boys more about ideas and concepts.
- Teachers focused on boys' academic work and criticized boys for unsatisfactory academic quality. At the same time, girls were complimented on the appearance and neatness of their work and not the academic quality of their work.

Societal messages often reflect a society's beliefs and attitudes about mathematics and mathematicians. These beliefs are spread throughout culture through television, books, parents, teachers, and school administrators. Interestingly, societal messages about mathematics can substantially influence students' views about mathematics and their mathematical ability.

Television, movies, comic strips, and toys add to the stereotypical idea that girls are not mathematically inclined. For example, Teen Talk Barbie, an electronic talking version of the Mattel top-selling doll, manufactured in 1992, was programmed to say, "Math class is hard," one of four phrases randomly selected from a total of 270. This is definitely not a statement young girls need to hear. At a press conference, a spokesperson for Mattel denied the allegations that the doll reinforced stereotypes that girls are not as adept as boys at mathematics. Reading from a prepared statement, Mattel's spokesperson added, "We at Mattel, Inc. are shocked and chagrined by the irresponsible statements made by members of the so-called 'public' regarding Teen Talk Barbie. We feel that Teen Talk Barbie serves as a wonderful role model for today's girls, as she is even smaller than Camille Paglia and has no reproductive organs—the perfect 90s Kind of Girl." Mattel first offered to exchange Teen Talk Barbie for another doll after complaints from math teachers, women's organizations, parents, and the media, but this did not satisfy the opposition. Finally, Mattel withdrew the phrase from the list of phrases for Teen Talk Barbie. In a letter to the AAUW, Mattel responded by saying that they did not fully consider the potentially negative implications of this phrase and that they (Mattel) were not aware of the findings in the AAUW's report.

Another example of girls being stereotypically portrayed as nonmathematical can be found in the *Luann* comic strip. Two math professors at Marymount College wrote to the Gannett newspaper to protest Greg Evans's stereotypes about women and mathematics in his daily comic strip for the week of April 8, 1991. The comic strip showed the class nerd offering to help Luann with her math homework, while she confesses to feeling "stupid, frustrated, and sick to my stomach." Luann makes a remark about her purse holding the coins in the algebra problem and then gives up completely on the problem. In the last strip, she gives the nerd credit for her correct solution.

The letter of protest concluded: "We have been striving hard to make our female students realize that they are just as good as men in subjects requiring mathematical reasoning, and at least some of their anxiety has been caused by the popular stereotype that math is not suitable for women" (Greg Evans, 1991).

Other comic strips such as *Peanuts* and *Foxtrot* also portray girls as nonmathematical and unable to understand mathematical concepts. It's no wonder that girls feel justified in their fear and dislike of mathematics.

In the United States, the study of math carries a stigma, and people who are talented at math or enjoy it are often treated as though they are not quite normal and must be nerds. It comes as a surprise to many Americans that this attitude is not shared by other societies. In Japanese, Chinese, African, Russian, and German cultures, for example, mathematics is viewed as an essential part of literacy. Educated persons would be considered ignorant to reveal their ignorance of basic mathematics.

This attitude toward mathematics in the United States has been exacerbated by the way in which it has been taught in the past century. Teaching methods have relied on the behaviorist theory of learning, focused on rote memorization of facts and algorithms. Students are encouraged to memorize mathematics, without any real understanding of the concepts. Skills are only the surface of mathematics and are only marginally useful without the underlying concepts. Reform efforts have challenged the behaviorist theory and advocate that it be replaced with constructivist and more progressive models of learning. There is still much controversy surrounding the use of reform mathematics curricula in the schools.

Even in the year 2004, some people in our society still hold beliefs that interfere with equity in mathematics education. Tobias (1980) and Kogelman and Warren (1979) organized a list of some common beliefs or myths that perpetuate mathematics anxiety, particularly in girls:

- Men have "math minds" and therefore are naturally better in mathematics than women.
- Math requires logic, not intuition.
- You must always know immediately how you got the right answer.
- Mathematics is not creative.
- There is a best way to do a math problem.
- It's always important to get the answer exactly right.
- It's bad to count on your fingers or to use a calculator.

- Mathematicians do problems quickly in their heads.
- Mathematics requires a good memory.
- There is a trick to doing mathematics.

These myths are detrimental to students' self-esteem, can increase their level of mathematics anxiety, can lead to poor mathematics achievement, and can create a dislike of mathematics. According to Lockhead, Thorpe, Brooks-Gunn, Casserly, and McAloon (1985), students tend to succeed at subjects they like. The dislike of mathematics by many girls can contribute to their decision to stop taking advanced mathematics classes. This vicious cycle can cause mathematics avoidance, resulting in students electing to stop taking mathematics classes.

Recommendations for Encouraging Mathematics Achievement.   National Assessment of Educational Progress (NAEP) data reveal and other studies report (Campbell & Meece, 1994; Kahle, 1991) that as girls age, their confidence in their mathematical ability declines, their successful participation in mathematics and science activities decreases, and they are less likely than boys to enroll in upper level mathematics classes. Sadker and Sadker (1993) reported that boys are eight times more likely to call out during a discussion than are girls. In addition, Sadker found that teachers were more willing to accept this type of behavior from boys than from girls and that girls were discouraged and even disciplined for this type of behavior.

Classroom attitudes also affect the attitude and achievement of girls in mathematics. Following are some recommendations about classroom climate that help encourage girls to continue their study of mathematics:

- Encourage a "can do" attitude; teach students to give themselves credit.
- Encourage all students to take additional math and science courses (teacher encouragement has been shown to be a major factor in students' decision-making processes).
- Encourage girls to take risks.
- Judge *what* girls say, not *how* they say it (don't assume that if they hesitate or apologize, they don't know the answer).
- Help female students value themselves (girls often have a severe drop in self-esteem during the middle school years. Women teachers need to model healthy self-respect, and male teachers need to have respect for both girl students and female colleagues).

There are other key influential persons in girls' lives that can affect their feelings and beliefs about mathematics. Parents can also support their preadolescent girls in many ways, as in the following recommendations made by the Australian Association of Mathematics Teacher (AAMT, 1990; Clewell, Anderson, & Thorpe, 1992):

- Give girls toys that develop premath and science skills, including puzzles, board games, and manipulatives, like building toys.

- Find television programs, books, movies, and other materials that show positive role models for women and discuss with girls the roles of women in society.
- Visit school and ask questions about classroom participation and academic progress.
- Attend school information and parent-teacher sessions and talk with girls about what is happening in mathematics.
- Hold high expectations and instill positive beliefs about daughters' capabilities in mathematics. Assume they will do well in mathematics.
- Be positive about mathematics. Avoid recounting personal negative experiences.
- Encourage girls to continue mathematics studies.
- Build girls' confidence in their mathematical ability.
- Encourage girls to talk about what they are doing in mathematics.
- Discuss how mathematics is used in everyday life, in paid and unpaid work and in leisure activities.
- Discuss the many roles women play in society and the changing view of femininity.
- Discuss girls' personal and career goals often and express support and interest in their choices.
- Take girls into the workplace and point out the value of the work and contributions of women.

ESSENTIAL EQUITY QUESTION 7.4:
WHAT KINDS OF INSTRUCTIONAL AND ASSESSMENT STRATEGIES FOSTER MATHEMATICS AND TECHNOLOGY ACHIEVEMENT FOR ALL STUDENTS IN THE CLASSROOM?

To foster mathematics and technology achievement for all students, one must create a safe, communal learning environment that develops mathematical confidence. One of the important learning outcomes of gender equitable practices is for each person to develop his or her own voice. The vision is one of a classroom filled with active participants, not quiet, passive learners. Environments in which wrong answers are seen as learning opportunities and students are not ridiculed for incorrect responses go far to promote learners' willingness to take risks and speak up in class.

WHAT WE KNOW

In mathematics, development of one's own voice is related to one's confidence in learning and doing mathematics. Typically, preservice and in-service elementary and secondary teachers of subjects other than mathematics, science, and technology have a low level of confidence in mathematics. Teachers at the elementary level, who feel this way, spend less time teaching mathematics and tend to teach in a traditional, abstract manner with little relation to the real world. The next two inter-actions are designed to assist individuals in developing their own voice in a mathe-matical context and to begin to feel comfortable speaking up.

INTERACTION 7.3:
Developing One's Mathematical Voice and Defining a Broad, Hard-to-Grasp Concept

INTASC Principle 4: Variety of Instructional Strategies

Joyce and Weil's concept formation model in mathematics, as well as other sub-jects, can be a tool for the development of student voice in the classroom. The con-cept development model focuses on the attributes or characteristics of a concept, which participants identify, categorize, label, and define or generalize. This induc-tive method increases student participation through the use of open-ended ques-tions and grouping and labeling, along with synthesis activities. It has been shown that females prefer an inductive approach, based on experiences that build up a gen-eral idea or concept.

The basic model follows these four phases or steps:

1. *Data collection:* A concept word is placed in the center of the chalkboard or on an overhead projector. Using open-ended questions, the facilitator aims to access participants' prior knowledge of the concept word. Words, phrases, and pictures of items related to the concept in question are generated by the students and recorded by the facilitator in a random fashion. This is done for a specified period of time or until a certain number of items is produced.
2. *Grouping:* Participants are asked to group items into categories based on a common attribute, characteristic, or property. All generated items are grouped into approximately four to eight categories.
3. *Labeling:* After or in conjunction with the grouping of items into categories, each category is given a title or name.
4. *Generalization statement:* Using the names of all the categories developed in the grouping and labeling phases, a definition of the concept in question is constructed.

The following interaction is designed to show how a good and true mathemat-ics problem and the launch, explore, summarize (LES) lesson plan format can foster the development of valuing multiple perspectives and diverse ways of thinking. This interaction is also intended to develop mathematical confidence in problem solving.

INTERACTION 7.4:
Valuing Multiple Perspectives When Solving Mathematics Problems

INTASC Principle 4: Variety of Instructional Strategies

The LES lesson plan format is based on problem solving. In the launch phase, one presents the problem to be solved. This is often in the form of a story, not simply a verbal problem that is an arithmetic problem in words and requires simple calculation for an answer, but a good and true problem. What is a good and true problem? A good problem is one that can be accessed at many levels of understanding. This allows students to come to the problem from whatever prior knowledge base they have and address it. A good problem has a context that is of interest to students, a context that can motivate them to want to learn a particular type of mathematics because of a perceived need. In this case, the problem is engaging enough that the students want to solve it. A true problem is one that students need to think about because they do not immediately recognize a direct solution. What may be a true problem for one student may not be true for another. The general format of the LES method of instruction follows:

1. *Launch:* The lesson begins with a problem posed within a story. The problem should be one that is challenging to the group but not so difficult that it stifles students' willingness to try. The launch phase sets the stage for the activity. It is a time when students may ask questions about the problem to make sure they are clear about what is being asked, to learn any mathematical vocabulary they don't know, and to consider the mathematics that one might need to solve the problem. The teacher sets the expectations and responds to any questions posed by the students. If there is a specific kind of mathematical calculation that students have not yet mastered, but recognize as something necessary to solve the problem, the teacher may use this opportunity to teach the algorithm as necessary.

2. *Explore:* The students go to work investigating the problem at hand, and the teacher is available to redirect students when they are off-task or off-track by asking probing questions to assess student understanding. The teacher may offer additional challenges to those who are moving at a faster pace and modify the problem for those who are experiencing difficulty. During this phase, the teacher is the observer and remains in the background.

3. *Summarize:* This final phase is when the teaching actually takes place. This phase allows the teacher to lift out the important mathematics exemplified in the problem as different students present their solutions and explanations. It provides the teacher an opportunity to assess student learning and to plan instruction based on that learning.

Single-Sex Math Classes.   There has been a long history of schooling designed specifically for girls and women. According to Streitmatter (1999), "The original consequence of single- sex schooling was that of isolation, social reproduction, and oppression of women, while the current goal is to provide females with learning environments that provide every opportunity for future success in a competitive and heterogeneous world" (p. 25). Just about all single-sex schools in the United States are religious or private schools. Much of the research on public single-sex education comes from countries such as Australia, England, Ireland, and Jamaica. Streitmatter (1999) reported on a study conducted by Riordan in the early 1980s where "Girls in the single-sex schools demonstrated the highest scores of all groups, outperforming their female and male peers in coeducational schools on nearly all measures. When comparing girls who attended coeducational Catholic schools to those in single-sex Catholic schools, girls in single-sex schools demonstrated the higher math scores" (p. 37).

In a study conducted in Britain by Steedman in the mid-1980s comparing the achievement of boys and girls in single-sex and coeducational high schools, Streitmatter (1999) wrote:

> The results suggested that, in general, boys outperformed girls on the educational outcome measures in chemistry, physics, and math, while the girls did better than the boys in English, French, and biological sciences. However, the results also indicated that both girls and boys in single-sex settings did better in most subjects than their peers in coeducational schools. (p. 40)

So, overall, it may be beneficial for students to learn in a single-sex environment. Streitmatter (1999) discussed enrollment of girls in girls-only schools, as follows: "One point is clear: Being in classes with only girls holds benefits for them. This study found that they encountered fewer distractions to learning, they had all of the teacher's attention, and they did not need to make a space in a different culture. The culture was theirs" (p. 87). Whereas Streitmatter believed that single-sex schools are beneficial for girls, Shmurak (1998) wasn't completely convinced based on her own research results. She described both the single-sex and coeducational institutions where she conducted her studies as examples of the following organizational structure that may mean more than whether they are single-sex or coeducational:

> [T]he organizational features that enhance both school effectiveness and equity include: small school size, a curriculum that emphasizes academics, expectations for high student involvement in their own learning, teachers' willingness to take responsibility for students' learning, and a feeling of community to the social relations within the school. (Lee, 1997, as quoted in Shmurak, 1998, p. 171)

These are worthwhile goals in any school. According to Zittleman (2004), there are many strategies that can be used in the classroom to support gender equity. One of these is increased wait time—the time a teacher waits before calling on a student for a response. Zittleman recommends being deliberate about waiting longer for students to raise their hands, allowing for a wider level of participation. Although this is an excellent strategy, we suggest that teachers spend more time asking students to write their responses to questions before calling on an individual. The result this activity has on participation is significant. When students write what they are thinking, they become more focused on and clearer about their ideas. Further, when they respond to the teacher's question before the other students in the room, the answer is not lost and the their confidence is increased.

Children's Literature.   A second strategy suggested by Zittleman (2004) is to balance one's curriculum with "books and stories that show girls and women in strong, non-stereotyped roles" (p. 6). Although it may be difficult to find books and stories that meet this criterion in every area for which you want to include children's literature, existing books with stereotypical figures can still be used. Challenge your students to be critical observers and ask them to find the stereotypical characters and roles that may appear in books. Children's trade books containing mathematics are many with more being published regularly. Some of these books have gender bias and mathematical mistakes. Instead of removing them from the reading list, use them to your best advantage. The use of mathematical literary criticism and editing[1] can be employed to help students find mathematics problems that exist in stories, edit stories to make the mathematics more explicit, and extend mathematical thinking beyond the story. Have students rewrite the stories to better fit with their personal experiences and to address the roles that girls and women may play in those stories.

Exposing Bias and Stereotyping at Every Opportunity.   Exposing bias and stereotyping at every opportunity sensitizes individuals to this phenomenon. After being sensitized, people choose how they view and behave. Exposing bias and stereotyping shows people how these qualities are insidiously created and perpetuated within U.S. culture. Only when people recognize these characteristics and expose them can patterns of behavior be changed. Being a mathematician often requires showing why something is not true through a counterexample. There have been many documentations of bias in textbooks, children's literature, advertising, and statistical reports. Use activities within these contexts to assist students in recognizing bias when they see it. Allow them to explore how being mathematically literate can dispel incorrect notions about people.

Using *The Doorbell Rang,* by Pat Hutchins, teachers and their students can explore an important mathematics concept as well as reveal some underlying social stereotyping. In his book *Integrating Children's Literature and Mathematics in*

---

[1]The term *mathematical literary criticism and editing* is taken from Michael Schiro's text and refers to a deeper examination of children's trade books to include revisions and mathematical enhancements.

the Classroom, Michael Schiro offered an evaluation instrument to analyze children's trade books from a mathematical perspective as well as from a literary perspective. Although the use of children's literature has been advocated for the instruction of mathematics for some time, literature is often used solely to introduce a topic, rather than as a full-scale, in-depth investigation. Schiro's (1996) evaluation instrument and suggestion of trade book use for mathematical literary criticism and editing provides a far richer option for learning mathematics as well as for finding bias and stereotyping in the process. The mathematical literary criticism and editing aspect allows teachers and their students to enhance and revise books, become editors, make the mathematics more explicit, correct incorrect drawings, add greater engagement and interaction opportunities, and remove stereotypes when they are present.

In *The Doorbell Rang,* two children continually divide a dozen cookies as new arrivals come into the room. The big-picture mathematics that comes across in this book is, when using the division (sharing cookies), as the divisor (the number of children who share cookies) gets larger, the quotient (the number of cookies each child gets) becomes smaller. From a mathematical point of view, this book presents an important concept in an easy to understand context to which children can easily relate. There are some underlying concerns, however, when this book is investigated through the lens of gender and multicultural equity.

The following questions should be considered before using this and other mathematically inspired children's trade books:

- Are stereotypical characters in the illustrations?
- Who is doing the mathematics?
- How empowered is the reader of the book to become engaged in the story's mathematics?
- Are there stereotypical characters in the book? Who are they? How are they portrayed?
- What words or pictures support these ideas?

Textbook Analyses.   Have students ask the following questions to compare textbooks to see how the authors and publishers portray mathematics:

- Is the book context oriented or does it merely contain abstract lessons focused on procedures?
- Is there a diversity of children actively doing mathematics in the pictures?
- Are roles for females and males traditional and stereotypical? Cite examples and explain why or why not.
- How does the book offer a variety of approaches to meet students' different needs?

Some interesting facts about gender equity related to mathematics education follow:

- Women make up 52% of the U.S. population and 45% of the workforce.
- In 1988, only 16% of scientists, 6% of engineers, and 4% of computer scientists in the United States were women.
- There are no gender differences in mathematical problem solving until high school, at which time the differences favoring males begin.
- During the middle grades (6–8), young girls begin to make selections that limit their opportunities in mathematics and other technical fields.
- Girls consistently equal or exceed boys' achievements in mathematics and science as measured by scholastic aptitude, achievements tests, and classroom grades.
- Girls and boys are taking approximately the same number of math courses; however, girls are less likely to take trigonometry or calculus.
- In mathematics classes, boys tend to receive more teacher time and attention than do girls. (Sanders, 1994)

For these reasons, gender and equity in mathematics have become critical issues leading to another important question: "At what age do we need to intervene to prevent girls from turning away from studying mathematics?" Research has shown (Berryman, 1983) that the middle school years are the critical intervention point to address the decrease of girls and their pursuit of mathematics. Clewell et al. (1992) believed that "to be effective, intervention approaches must be grounded in an understanding of the growth and developmental needs of students in grades 4 through 8, as well as a sound knowledge of educational experiences and instructional strategies that promote learning and enjoyment of mathematics and science" (p. 18). Clewell et al. further recommend the following interventions that focus on females in middle school:

- Increase the number of female-focused programs in middle schools that offer activities and experiences to enhance the achievement and participation of girls and mathematics, both in and out of school.
- Increase the number of female-focused programs offering role models, career awareness, and counseling activities. Provide abundant opportunities to interact with people from industry, universities, and professional societies.
- Add test preparation to programs offering awareness and motivational activities as well as substantive achievement activities. Emphasize that females can excel in mathematics.
- Establish more programs in the southeast United States and in states where there are none.
- Expand the services of existing programs to fourth and fifth graders.

The research community has found many successful strategies that encourage girls to take more mathematics and science and to consider careers in mathematics and science. Here are some of the strategies that have proven effective (Campbell, 1991; Campbell & Metz, 1987; Campbell & Shackford, 1990; Fenema & Leder, 1990; Hyde, Fennema, & Lamon, 1990):

- Intervene in seventh and eighth grades. At this age students decide if they will take algebra, an important first step to continued math involvement.
- Intervene in ninth and tenth grades. Sophomore year is another key decision-making time. Students decide if they will take geometry, another critical step to continued math involvement.
- Design programs and math classes that incorporate what girls feel they are currently missing in much school math. Include math sessions that are more fun and more relaxed, with less pressure and less competition, and are more cooperative, with more hands-on work and problem solving and with teachers who explain more and answer questions.
- Get girls beyond the "nerd factor." Informal social sessions with female mathematics educators and mathematicians and in careers that involve mathematics have been shown to change high school girls' views of people who are good in math and science from nerdy and strange to likeable and fun.
- Emphasize career exposure, not career choice, and involve girls in activities that reflect the work of people in different scientific and mathematics careers.
- Reduce the isolation frequently felt by girls who are already interested in mathematics and science by making sure that they are in classes with other girls and by scheduling time for them to just get together and talk.

The following recommendations from Clewell (1987) will help teachers improve the performance of females in mathematics:

- Offer hands-on activities
- Allow for sufficient time on tasks
- Provide adequate precollegiate training
- Establish contacts with role models in scientific and technical careers
- Require laboratory work
- Use cooperative learning activities
- Provide manipulative instructional materials
- Provide for nonthreatening competition
- Allow for independent projects
- Include test preparation
- Provide support from parents, teachers, counselors, administrators, and peers
- Provide positive academic and personal counseling

You can take the following 10 actions to combat gender bias in the classroom:

1. Encourage your female students to strive in mathematics and to participate in advanced courses.

2. Have an introduction or pep talk with the girls in your class expressing your expectations of them.
3. Create (with your students) a prominent bulletin board or monthly display showcasing the contributions women have made to mathematics, science, or computers.
4. Organize computer time and calculator usage to allows girls access and usage independent of boys.
5. Invite women in mathematics, science careers, or business to speak to the class about how they use mathematics.
6. Arrange for successful girls in your school at all levels to interact with each other and build a support network.
7. Communicate with parents of girls in your class about the importance of mathematics courses for their daughter's future.
8. Strive to offer equal amounts of attention to all students, with modifications to meet students' needs and learning styles.
9. Analyze textbooks for forms of gender bias and modify appropriately.
10. Look for opportunities to tell each girl in your class how much you appreciate her work and thinking and that you believe that she can do mathematics (http://www.pbs.org/teachersource/whats_new/math/tips398.shtm)

According to Campbell (1991), the following strategies should be employed by teachers and administrators to work toward the elimination of gender inequities in mathematics classrooms. It is important not only for teachers but for administrators and counselors to support this effort and monitor their progress in creating a more equitable climate in the school and the classroom:

- Be aware of your voice, gestures, and body language and the attitudes that such communications may convey about gender.
- Do not talk down to girls.
- Use questions and comments to encourage girls' thinking skills; talk with girls about ideas and concepts.
- Be attentive to girls' requests for help; arrange for math tutoring clubs, if appropriate.
- Be aware of your own math anxieties and convey positive attitudes and behavior toward mathematics.
- Find out more about students' attitudes by using mathematics journals and attitude assessments.
- Discuss math anxiety and learned helplessness with girls who are having problems.
- Increase your knowledge of mathematics and share new knowledge enthusiastically with students.
- Make independent and small-group mathematics experiences available to all and encourage girls to participate in such experiences.

- Design mathematics activities that are fun, relaxed, and collaborative and include hands-on work and problem solving, which often are missing from school math.
- Start teaching high-level mathematics in primary grades; use specific terms, such as *geometry* and *probability*.
- Avoid perpetuating gender bias in your treatment of academic subjects, skills, daily living tasks, careers, ethnic groups, and so forth.
- Provide activities that parallel those of careers in mathematics.

Teachers can unconsciously use strategies that foster gender inequities. The following techniques are a result of the Woodrow Wilson GEMS Congress (Hanson, 1992; Jacobs, 1992; Sandler, 1992) and are suggested to improve the classroom climate to make it a more equitable environment.

Awareness

- Call on girls as often as you do boys and be sure to ask girls some of the higher level cognitive questions (research shows that both male and female teachers initiate more interaction with boys and on higher cognitive levels).
- Encourage girls to use manipulatives and to participate in hands-on experiences (without encouragement, girls tend to be passive learners).
- Balance cooperative and competitive activities (most girls learn more readily in cooperative situations).
- Use gender-free language in classroom discourse (avoid the use of male terms for generic concepts; e.g., use *synthetic* instead of *manmade*).
- Make eye contact with all students and call them by name.
- Don't interrupt girls or let other students do so. This sends a message that what girls say is less important.
- Don't stop talking to a girl when a boy approaches. This too sends a message that what the girl is saying is less important and that you would rather interact with the boy.

Classroom Strategies

- Mentally divide your room into quadrants. If students in all quadrants don't participate, you can say, "Let's hear from someone in the back right corner."
- Ask students to state concepts aloud (this helps students learn the vocabulary of the subject).
- Cultivate bonding around an intellectual challenge (this provides students with an opportunity to feel like a team).
- Use the human body as a vehicle for interesting girls in physics and other sciences (girls often find the human body fascinating and will identify with phenomena related to the body).

- Encourage girls to participate in extracurricular math and science activities.
- Stress safety precautions instead of dangers (girls will sometimes be reluctant to participate in lab activities if they seem too dangerous).
- Use computer and lab partners (most girls work better in teams).
- Introduce lessons with an overview (girls learn more readily from the big picture, rather than from disconnected details).
- Incorporate students' comments into lectures (this technique validates the students' understanding of concepts).
- Acknowledge the contributions of both men and women to mathematics and science via posters, reports, examples, story problems, guest speakers, and so on.
- Use cooperative activities and some single-sex small groups.
- Provide opportunities for girls to develop spatial visualization skills.
- Use writing to help students express and clarify their feelings and thoughts (e.g., math autobiographies, science journals).
- Encourage girls to develop skills in risk taking through guessing, estimating, attempting partial solutions, and using trial-and-error methods.
- Create an attractive classroom environment (research shows that girls learn better in an aesthetically pleasing environment).
- Wait 4 or 5 seconds before calling on a student to answer the question (girls often wait until they have formulated an answer before they raise their hands; boys often raise their hands immediately and then formulate an answer).
- Don't grade on a curve (encourage all students to realize their potential rather than to compete against one another).
- Solve problems by multiple methods (this appeals to students with different learning styles).
- Cater to a variety of approaches to learning by using various pedagogical methods.

Higher Level Mathematics Enrollment

- Identify key faculty, counselors, and administrators who are concerned about the importance of increasing young women's participation in mathematics. Encourage them to meet to share strategies and experiences.
- Collect baseline enrollment data in your school or district to assess the current participation of young women in mathematics, science, and technical education and to monitor progress in increased enrollments.
- Use the baseline enrollment data in a brainstorming session with parents, students, teachers, counselors, administrators, and school board members to develop solutions that will work for your school or district.
- Raise awareness of the importance of math in high school and college with materials such as startling statements about mathematics and employment.

• Encourage career centers to acquire up-to-date information on opportunities, salaries, and entry-level requirements in scientific, technical, and apprentice fields. Share that information with students, parents, and teachers.

• Help career centers develop and disseminate to teachers a resource list of films, videotapes, activities, and materials that raise awareness of the importance of career preparation.

• Develop in-school programs using the Expanding Your Horizons Conferences model, for 6th through 10th-grade students. Encourage students to keep their options open by taking the maximum possible number of math and science courses in high school.

• Arrange for classroom visits by women role models in science, engineering, technology, and the skilled trades.

• Provide release time for teachers to develop appropriate methods for teaching needed skills.

(Strategies to Increase the Participation of Young Women in Mathematics Math/Science Resource Center, Mills College. Oakland, California 94613)

The Australian Association of Mathematics Teachers (AAMT, 1992) stated that a mathematics curriculum should meet the following criteria to encourage girls to continue taking higher-level mathematics courses:

• Focuses on the development of mathematical thinking rather than rote learning
• Presents mathematics as a human endeavor
• Includes and values achievements of women and girls
• Emphasizes the creative and imaginative appeal of mathematics
• Develops creative and diverse problem-solving skills and strategies for groups and individuals
• Includes open-ended investigative problems where there is no single correct method or answer
• Encourages and develops verbal and visual communication skills
• Ensures that the contexts in which mathematical ideas are introduced and developed are familiar to both girls and boys
• Incorporates applications of mathematics to important social issues

In the teaching and learning of mathematics, consider it a science, an art, and a language. Look to see how you use it in your life, how mathematics intersects with your body and your daily routine. Look to see the visual patterns, the geometry of form. Listen for the rhythms in music and poetry. Learn to communicate ideas using numbers, symbols, relationships, graphs, charts, and models. Look to see how you can use inquiry skills and problem-solving processes to find answers to questions and offer explanations. When the beauty that is mathematics becomes revealed, then its importance is recognized.

When teachers present mathematics enthusiastically as a science, an art, and a language, more students find mathematics interesting and want to explore its beauty. When women develop and use their mathematical power effectively, they begin to achieve true equity in the workplace and beyond.

RESOURCES

Web Sites

Women of NASA: http://quest.arc.nasa.gov/women/resources/annbib.html: This site includes many online games and other activities designed by Cynthia Lanius. http://math.rice.edu/~lanius/Lessons

GirlTech: http://math.rice.edu/~lanius/club/girls.html: This site is devoted to getting girls more interested in computer science.

Virtual manipulatives: http://matti.usu.edu/nlvm/nav/vlibrary.html

http://arcytech.org/java/: This site includes interactive mathematics games and learning experiences using a variety of virtual manipulatives.

Base 10 applet: http://www.arcytech.org/java/b10blocks/b10blocks.html

Pattern block applet: http://www.arcytech.org/java/patterns/patterns_j.shtml

Integer blocks: http://www.arcytech.org/java/integers/integers.html

Make your own manipulatives and graph paper: http://mason.gmu.edu/~mmankus/Handson/manipulatives.htm

http://www.galaxy.gmu.edu/~drsuper/: This site allows you to explore transformation geometry (turns, flips, and slides) using triangles of three sizes (for younger students).

http://www.bls.gov/opub/rtaw/stattab2.htm: Visit this site for detailed information on American workers, specifically the number of working people, their characteristics, and the types of jobs they hold.

http://www.bls.gov/oes/2003/may/oes_ny.htm: This site has state employment and wage information.

http://www.bls.gov/k12/html/edu_over.htm: This site lists various curriculum areas and professions that focus on these subjects. It provides an overview of educational requirements, what a job entails, growth for the future, and the salary range for each profession listed along with similar professions. This is a kid-friendly site that offers considerable information about careers and the career planning. This site also has links to many other sites with additional information about careers in specific areas of interest.

http://www.bls.gov/oco/images/ocotjc07.gif: This site provides a chart that outlines the majority of increases in jobs between 2002–2012.

http://math.about.com/library/blmath.htm: This site provides information about math grade by grade.

http://www.geocities.com/karadimosmd/whymath.html: This site contains an article by Mark Karadimos that discusses why math is important.

www.nctm.org: This is the official website for the National Council of Teachers of Mathematics. The organization offers many resources for the improvement of mathematics education at all levels.

http://www.ncrel.org/sdrs/areas/issues/content/cntareas/math/ma100.htm: This is a position paper called "Critical Issue: Ensuring Equity and Excellence in Mathematics" and presents useful suggestions on how to achieve these goals.

http://camel.math.ca/Women/EDU/Education.html: This site contains several essays about gender and practices in mathematics education.

Women's Career Resources: http://jobsearchtech.about.com/cs/womencareer/index_2.htm: This site provides a list of professional organizations that focus on women's involvement.

http://www-instruct.wccnet.org/~kstrnad/career/nontrad.html: This site offers calculations of the earnings of traditional and nontraditional jobs for women and makes a strong case for the continued study of mathematics and science as a way to achieve financial success.

National Council of Teachers of Mathematics Principles and Standards for School Mathematics: www http://standards.nctm.org/

International Society for Technology in Education: http://www.iste.org/

REFERENCES

American Association of University Women. (1992). Agenda for action (Publication No. 90-13S). Washington, DC: Author.

American Association of University Women. (1992). *How schools shortchange girls: A study of major findings on girls and education.* Washington, DC: AAUW Educational Foundation, The Wellesley College Center for Research on Women.

Australian Association of Mathematics Teachers. (1990). *School mathematics and your daughter.* Author.

Bailey, S., Burbridge, L., Campbell, P., Jackson, B., Marx, F., McIntosh, P. (1993). *Girls, gender, and schools: Excerpts from the AAUW report: How schools shortchange girls. American Women in the nineties: Today's critical issues,* S. Matteo (Ed.). Boston, MA: Northeastern University Press.

Berryman, S. F. (1983). *Who will do science? Trends and their causes in minority and female representation among holders of advanced degrees in science and mathematics.* New York: Rockefeller Foundation.

Boaler, J. (2002). Paying the price for "sugar and spice": Shifting the analytical lens in equity research. *Mathematical Thinking and Learning, 4*(2/3), 127–144.

Bossé, M. J., & Hurd, D. A. C. (2002). Women communicating mathematics: The historic role of women. *Mathematics and Computer Education, 36*(3), 218–216.

Campbell, P. B. (1991). *Douglass Science Institute: Three years of encouraging young women in math, science and engineering.* Groton, MA: Campbell-Kibler Associates.

Campbell, P. B. (1992). Math, science, and your daughter: What can parents do? In Women's Equity Act Program (Ed.), Encouraging girls in math and science. Washington, DC:

Campbell, P. B., & Metz, S. S. (1987). *What does it take to incease the number of women majoring in engineering?* In ASEE Annual conference proceedings, Washington, DC: American Society of Engineering Education, 1987. Reprinted in The Stevens Indicator 104, no. 4.

Campbell, P. B., & Sanders, J. (2002). Challenging the system: Assumptions and data behind the push for single-sex schooling. In A. Datnow & L. Hubbard (Eds.), *Gender in policy and practice: Perspectives on single-sex and coeducational schooling* (pp. 31–46). New York: Routledge.

Campbell, P. B., & Shackford, C. (1990). *EUREKA! Program evaluation.* Groton, MA: Campbell-Kibler Associates.

Clewell, B. C. (1987). What works and why: Research and theoretical bases of intervention programs in math and science for minority and female middle school students. In A. B. Champagne & L. E. Hornig (Eds.), *Students and science learning.* Washington, DC: American Association of Advancement of Science.

Clewell, B. C., Anderson, B. T., & Thorpe, M. E. (1988). *Integrating theory, research, and practice: A continuing challenge for intervention programs.* Princeton, NJ: Educational Testing Services.

Clewell, B. C., Anderson, B. T., & Thorpe, M. E. (1992). *Breaking the barrier: Helping female and minority students succeed in mathematics and science.* San Francisco: Jossey-Bass.

Fennema, E. (1974). Sex differences in mathematics-learning: Why? *Elementary School Journal, 75*(3), 183–190.

Fennema, E. (2000, May). *Gender and mathematics: What is known and what do I wish was known?* Paper presented at the fifth annual Forum of the National Institute for Science Education, Detroit, MI.

Fennema, E., & Leder, G. C. (Eds.). (1990). *Mathematics and gender.* New York: Teachers College Press.

Gilson, J. (2002). Single-gender or coeducation for middle-school girls: Does it make a difference in math? In A. Datnow & L. Hubbard (Eds.), *Gender in policy and practice: Perspectives on single-sex and coeducational schooling* (pp. 227–242). New York: Routledge.

Hammerich, P. L., Richardson, G. M., & Livingston, B. (2000). Sisters in science: Teachers reflective dialogue on confronting the gender gap. *Journal of Elementary Science Education, 12*(2), 39–52.

Hanna, G. (2003). Reaching gender equity in mathematics education. *Educational Forum, 67,* 204–214.

Hanson, K. (1992). Teaching mathematics effectively and equitably to females. In *Trends and issues* (Vol. 17). New York: Teachers College Press.

Hyde, J., Fennema, E., & Lamon, S. (1990). Gender differences in mathematical performance: A meta-analysis. *Psychological Bulletin, 107*(2), 139–155.

International Labour Office. (2004). *Global employment trends for women, 2004.* Retrieved April 20, 2006, from http://www.ilo.org/public/english/employment/strat/download/trendsw.pdf

Jacobs, J. (1992). Women's learning styles and the teaching of mathematics. In *Math and science for girls: A symposium sponsored by the National Coalition of Girls' Schools.* Concord, MA: National Coalition of Girls' Schools.

Kahle, J. B., & Meece, J. (1994). Research on gender issues in the classroom. In A. B. Champagne (Ed.), *Handbook of research on science teaching and learning.* New York: MacMillan.

Kogelman, S., & Warren, J. (1979). *Mind over math.* New York: McGraw-Hill.

Lockhead, M., Thorpe, M., Brooks-Gunn, J., Casserly, P., & McAloon, A. (1985). *Understanding sex-ethnic differences in mathematics, science, and computer science for students in grades four through eight.* Princeton, NJ: Educational Testing Service.

Malcom, S. M. (1997). *Girls succeeding in science, mathematics, and technology: Who works and what works.* Paper presented at the American Association of University Women Conference, Philadelphia, PA.

Norwood, K. S. (2004, April). *New research on mathematics anxiety.* Paper presented at the annual meeting of the National Council of Teachers of Mathematics, Philadelphia, PA.

Pearson, J. C., & West, R. (1991). An initial investigation of the effects of gender on student questions in the classroom: Developing a descriptive base. *Communication Education, 40,* 20–32.

Richardson, F. C., & Suinn, R. M. (1972). The mathematics anxiety rating scale: Psychometric data. *Journal of Counseling Psychology, 19*(6), 551–554.

Rogers, L. (2001). *Sexing the brain.* New York: Columbia University Press.

Sadker, M., & Sadker, D. (1994). *Failing at fairness.* NY: Simon & Schuster.

Salomone, R. C. (2003). *Same, different, equal: Rethinking single-sex schooling.* New Haven: Yale University Press.

Sanders, J. (1994). *Lifting the barriers: 600 strategies that really work to increase girls' participation in science, mathematics and computers.* Seattle, WA: Jo Sanders Press.

Sandler, B. R. (1992). Warming up the chilly climate. In *Math and science for girls: A symposium sponsored by the National Coalition of Girls' Schools.*

Sandler, B. R., & Hoffman, E. (1992). *Teaching faculty members to be better teachers: A guide to equitable and effective classroom techniques.* Washington, DC: Association of American Colleges.

Shmurak, C. B. (1998). *Voices of hope: Adolescent girls at single sex and coeducational schools.* New York: Peter Lang.

Single-sex schooling. (1993). Washington, DC: U.S. Department of Education, Office of Educational Research and Improvement.

Stallings, J. (1985). School classroom and home influences on women's decisions to enroll in advanced mathematics courses. In S. Chipman, L. Brush, & D. Wilson (Eds.), *Women and mathematics: Balancing the equation.* Hillsdale, NJ: Lawrence Erlbaum Associates.

Streitmatter, J. L. (1999). *For girls only: Making a case for single-sex schooling.* Albany: State University of New York Press.

The task force reports: Math and science for girls: A symposium sponsored by the National Coalition of Girls' Schools. (1992).

Tobias, S. (1980). *Overcoming math anxiety.* Boston: Houghton Mifflin.

Werner, E. (1989, April). Children of the Garden Island. *Scientific American* (pp. 106–108).

Wilson, J. S., & Milson, J. L. (1993). Factors which contribute to shaping females' attitudes toward the study of science and strategies which may attract females to the study of science. *Journal of Instructional Psychology, 20,* 78–86.

Zittleman, K. (2004). *Making public schools great for every girl and boy: Gender equity in the mathematics and science classroom: Confronting the barriers that remain.* Washington, DC: National Education Association.

8

Practical Strategies for Detecting and Correcting Gender Bias in Your Classroom*

David M. Sadker and Karen Zittleman
American University

L et's face it: All the skills you learned in this book are valuable only if they are used. Have you acquired the skills, and, more important, are you integrating them into classroom life and instruction? During your student teaching and related classroom experiences you can begin this self-examination. Are your classroom interactions equitable or biased toward one group or another? Are your curricular materials teaching fairness or subtle bias? Is there an objective way to sort all this out? You bet!

This last chapter is intended to help you see if the skills you learned in this book are actually being used in the classroom. We want to teach you how to carefully and clearly observe instruction. We also want you to consider the curriculum that you are using. We believe that this will make you a more reflective teacher—and a more valuable colleague. In this sense, the chapter goes beyond teaching skills or an evaluation of the curriculum to a broader vision of the classroom.

Detecting bias in a classroom is no casual affair. Subtle biases often characterize teaching styles and curricular materials, and careful attention is needed to redress these challenges (Babad, 1998). Careful observation requires an astute observer us-

---

*This guide is adapted in part from *Teachers, Schools, and Society* by Myra and David Sadker (McGraw-Hill, 2005).

259

ing objective approaches to measure the levels of equity (or bias) present in the classroom. Once this observation is done, a thoughtful analysis is needed so that the teacher can focus on specific skills needed to become both more equitable and more effective.

Although you have spent many hours (let's face it, many years) working in classrooms as a student, effective observation still can be quite challenging. Thousands of hours spent behind students' desks inure us to many of the subtle and not-so-subtle aspects of gender bias in the nation's schools. Because you may find the school environment as comfortable and everyday as a worn shoe, you may miss subtle incidents and the underlying significance of events, making it all too easy to miss much of what you think you see. To become an effective observer, this past conditioning needs to be erased and the realities of school and classroom life re-awakened. Looking for gender bias can be a challenge, but it is one that can be readily overcome. Perhaps you can begin by seeing it more as an opportunity than a challenge. If you observe and record your experiences systematically, then reflect on and interpret what you have seen, you can gain greater insight into how schools promote or inhibit gender equity. So let's begin this last chapter with some practical essential equity questions (EEQs):

- **Essential Equity Question 8.1:** What are some basic considerations in preparing for a classroom observation?
- **Essential Equity Question 8.2:** What techniques can we use to fairly and effectively identify bias in classroom interaction?
- **Essential Equity Question 8.3:** How can we detect and correct curricular bias?

Each Essential Equity Question includes two components: The What We Know section contains a brief overview of the fundamentals of effective observation techniques and of forms of curricular bias. The Interactions offer you the opportunity to implement some of the practical strategies described in this chapter. You will have the opportunity to detect (so that you can eventually correct) gender bias in teacher–student interactions as well as in curricular materials.

ESSENTIAL EQUITY QUESTION 8.1:
WHAT ARE SOME BASIC CONSIDERATIONS IN PREPARING FOR CLASSROOM OBSERVATION?

WHAT WE KNOW

Field experiences and student teaching are integral parts of teacher preparation programs. Both experiences can offer opportunities for you to observe and learn from the successes and limitations of current practitioners as well as to be observed to assess and improve your teaching performance. So before we analyze your teaching practices, let's begin by analyzing the teaching of others. Effective observations and supervision of field placements and student teaching can offer rich insights into the real world of teaching and schools (Bell, 2001). Unfortunately, poorly structured observations can quickly deteriorate into a vacuous waste of time, or worse.

John Dewey, perhaps America's most famous educator, wrote extensively about *reflective thinking,* which he defined as avoiding routine and impulsive behaviors in favor of taking the time to give serious consideration to our actions. According to Dewey, the intelligent person thinks before he or she acts, and action becomes deliberate and intentional (Dewey, 1963; Simpson, Jackson, & Aycock, 2004). If you want to glean knowledge and insight from your teaching experience, your observations must be careful, objective, analytical, and deliberate. The effectiveness of the observations done of your teaching, or the observations you make of others' teaching, should be done with care and consideration. Accomplishing this is the focus of this part of the chapter.

Becoming an Accepted Observer: Do I Fit In?   In many ways, our society consists of a series of minisocieties, each with its values and rules of order (Goodlad, 1984). Schools are examples of such minisocieties, with each level (elementary, middle, secondary, college) having its own unique set of norms. As a visitor, classroom observer, or student teacher, you will be judged on the basis of the school's culture and norms. You may be expected to dress rather formally, to arrive early or notify the school if you will be late, and to conform to the school's rules and regulations.

A principal once told a story of an observer, a visitor to the school culture, who became too comfortable and made too many assumptions. This observer became so involved in a teacher's lesson that he was soon raising his hand, responding to the teacher's questions, inserting personal anecdotes, and monopolizing classroom interaction. By the end of the class, the observer and the teacher were engaged in an animated dialogue, and the students had become passive onlookers. The observer had completely disrupted the classroom activities he was there to study.

So let's assume that you will be observing other teachers to learn more about teaching and, in the process, learn more about equitable teaching. As an observer, you can generally avoid the direct verbal involvement described in the previous anecdote, but another challenge is to avoid even more subtle nonverbal intrusion. What do you do when children engage you in nonverbal conversation consisting only of eye contact and facial expressions? Do you smile back, wink, and establish an unspoken kinship? Or, for fear of disturbing the class routine, do you ignore the students and possibly alienate them?

Although hard-and-fast rules are difficult to come by, it is clear that your presence in someone else's classroom as an observer is not intended either to win friends and influence people or to alienate anyone. You must learn to accept students' and teachers' nonverbal and verbal messages yet avoid prolonging these interactions. Ignoring all eye contact can be just as disruptive as encouraging such contact. With experience, you will be able to accept these subtle forms of communication without amplifying them. In this way, you can demonstrate that, although you are not insensitive to the interest and curiosity of students, your purpose in the school is to observe and collect data, not to alter school life.

Confidentiality of Records.   As you observe and collect data, you must make certain that your actions do not invade the privacy of, or in any other way harm, those you are observing. Most schools require anonymity in observations and confidentiality in the data collected. Individual teachers, students, and others should not risk inconvenience, embarrassment, or harm as a result of your field experience (Sadker & Sadker, 2005). Each school has its own norms and rules regarding what observers can and cannot do. Some require a signed release from school officials or from students (informed consent), whereas others are less formal. You should share your observation plan and data-gathering activities with your instructor to make certain that you are following the appropriate procedures. Your cooperating teacher or the principal in the school where you will be observing may also need to be informed; in some cases, both need to be informed. In cases where permission is not granted, you will need to find another setting. All data that you collect should remain absolutely confidential. The importance of this point cannot be stressed too much. You may wish to use codes for names or numbers for people you describe, and you should never discuss observations with any members of the school community. For example, if you tell teachers some information you have learned about students, you run the risk of losing trust and credibility and possibly harming a member of the school community. Your records should be stored away from the field school, in a location that is both safe and private. In this way, you can ensure the confidentiality of your subjects.

INTERACTION 8.1:
Preparing for an Observation

INTASC Principle 8: Assessment

INTASC Principle 9: Reflection and Responsibility

INTASC Principle 10: Relationships and Partnerships

You have just been asked to observe a colleague's teaching. Create personal guidelines you will follow to respect some of the basic tenets of observations, such as steps you will take to fit in and not disturb the classroom, considerations to ensure the confidentiality of your observations, and any additional concerns that you will address to ensure an effective observation. Take these guidelines with you to school each time you observe as a reminder of what you consider to be an appropriate and respectful code of behavior.

ESSENTIAL EQUITY QUESTION 8.2:
WHAT TECHNIQUES CAN WE USE TO FAIRLY AND EFFECTIVELY IDENTIFY BIAS IN CLASSROOM INTERACTION?

WHAT WE KNOW

This chapter provides you with several observation techniques to collect information. These techniques can open your eyes to the biases that permeate school, a critical step in redressing those problems. The following pages offer several objective approaches to observation, approaches that you can use to analyze your teaching or the teaching of others. You may determine to use only one or two of these methods or all of them. They are here for you to use as you see fit.

Classrooms and schools are complex intellectual, social, personal, and physical environments where the average teacher has hundreds of interactions each day, and each interaction may be filled with different levels and nuances of meaning (Jackson, 1968; Spencer, Porche, & Tolman, 2003). In this multifaceted, fast-paced, confusing culture called school, it is all too easy to miss or misinterpret much of what you think you see. But, if you immerse yourself in this culture, observe and record your experiences systematically, then reflect on and interpret what you have seen, you can gain greater insight into how and why teachers and students behave the way they do. And you will be better equipped to detect the bias so often invisible to the common observer.

Distinguishing Between Description and Interpretation.   Note taking, a technique borrowed from cultural anthropologists, is one of the most commonly used methods for gathering classroom data. When you first begin observing and taking notes, you may find yourself trying to record everything said or done in a classroom. And if you are tape-recording or videotaping your own class, you will find this particularly challenging. You will soon discover that it is impossible to capture accurately so many different stimuli at one time. You will need to narrow your focus and target specific aspects of the environment for your data collection and note-taking activities, whether you are in someone else's class or working through a recording of your own. For example, you may choose to record the gender or racial or ethnic distribution of teacher questions or the way discipline is handled in the class. To select the most important information, you need to go into the environment with a series of focusing questions to guide your observations and help you organize your note taking. It is wise to keep your notes on your laptop or in a loose-leaf notebook. This gives you the advantage of being able to move and shift your notes around into different organizational formats and look for patterns.

The ability to separate fact from opinion in note taking is a crucial skill that can prevent you from jumping to erroneous conclusions. Most of us like to think that seeing is believing, but sometimes believing may be seeing. In other words, each of us brings to any observation a set of biases and perspectives through which events may be distorted. To guard against inaccurate interpretations, make a careful record of what you see. Judgmental comments can also be made, but they should be kept separate from your descriptive observations. Observers can insert interpretations and questions into their records, but they should separate them from their descriptive notes with parentheses.

As you collect data, your information should be recorded in a descriptive rather than a judgmental manner. As a student, your observations about school were probably casual, resulting in the formation of opinions, such as "Teacher A is equitable," "School B is cliquish," or "geometry is hard." These interpretations, although colorful and useful, are personal and may have evoked disagreement from some of your fellow students.

When observing schools, a better approach is to gather descriptive data regarding an aspect of school or classroom life, interpret the data, and, when appropriate, form conclusions and judgments. Rather than saying that the girls are "cliquish" (an interpretation), you might count the gender and racial participation patterns in extracurricular activities, or you might note students' cafeteria seating patterns. All these findings provide objective, descriptive data that confirm or reject your initial impression. Although some of your descriptive data may not be useful, other notes may be crucial to your final interpretations and insights. Don't rely on one visit and then jump to a conclusion about the presence or absence of bias in a classroom. It is best to record several sessions of classroom interaction to obtain an accurate measure of potential bias.

Effective data collection activities ask you to record descriptive details and, after reflection, to interpret the information. The following examples will help you distinguish between description and interpretation:

- *Description:* During a science experiment, Cara and Lance both struggle to adjust their microscopes. The teacher adjusts the microscope for Cara and gives directions to Lance.
- *Interpretation:* The teacher is shortchanging Cara the opportunity to learn this scientific skill and possibly creating a sense of learned helplessness, while empowering Lance to independently learn the skill.

- *Description:* In a ninth-grade physical education course, girls can choose to participate in aerobic dance or volleyball, and boys can choose from weight-lifting or tennis.

- *Interpretation:* Students can legally be separated by gender if the sport involves bodily contact. None of activities offered meets this criterion; consequently, Title IX is violated.

- *Description:* Mr. Miller asks two boys to bring the new social studies texts up from the school office. Sophia calls out asking if she can go, but Mr. Miller explains that the books are too heavy for girls to carry.
- *Interpretation:* Mr. Miller is assigning tasks based on sex-role stereotypes.

- *Description:* Male students of color comprise 70% of students receiving special education services.
- *Interpretation:* Gender and racial bias may result in the overidentification of males of color and the underidentification of females and Whites in special education.

- *Description:* The girls' softball field is pocketed with holes and ruts. The boys' baseball field is neatly groomed.
- *Interpretation:* The girls' field is unsafe, and the disparate conditions indicate a Title IX violation.

- *Description:* Twenty-five out of 27 female students volunteered answers during math class.
- *Interpretation:* The female students are interested in math.

- *Description:* Lining up for recess, students form two lines: one all-girl line and one all-boy line. Ms. Fair announces that there is no reason for two separate lines and asks the students to create one line that includes everyone. After some giggling and hesitation, the students line up single file.
- *Interpretation:* The teacher made a conscious effort to break students' voluntary pattern of gender segregation.

INTERACTION 8.2:
Distinguishing Between Description and Interpretation (Authentic Assessment)

INTASC Principle 6: Communication Skills
INTASC Principle 8: Assessment
INTASC Principle 9: Reflection and Responsibility

To demonstrate that you have this technique down, here is a two part activity:

1. Create your own examples of descriptions and interpretations. Write at least five to become more familiar with the process. Look over your work to ensure that the descriptions and interpretations are correct.

2. Part 2 gives you the opportunity to apply your newly acquired skill in a class-room. Visit a classroom (at any level) and take descriptive notes for at least 10 minutes of the teacher and student behaviors. Then carefully review your notes and circle any adjectives, interpretations, or judgments that are inap-propriate and may have crept into your descriptive notes. Once the notes seem clearly descriptive, you can analyze them and begin to form judgments. Look for descriptive data to support patterns of inequity. Did the teacher praise one group more often or differently than another? Was discipline meted out differently? Did the teacher work more closely with one group than another? The descriptive notes become evidence to be used to form judgments.

WHAT WE KNOW

Data Gathering Using a Seating Chart.   Research on teacher effectiveness emphasizes the importance of active student interaction in promoting learning and positive attitudes toward school (Good & Brophy, 2003; Spencer et al., 2003). Un-fortunately, teachers do not distribute their attention evenly; rather, they ask many questions of some students and few, or none, of others. Recording these patterns on seating charts can reveal a great deal. Teachers may unintentionally direct ques-tions more to children of one gender or race than to those of another. Attention, questions, and praise may be distributed on the basis of which students the teacher likes or where the students happen to be seated in the classroom or which students are disorderly and need to be managed and controlled. One very common form of bias is for teachers to direct most of their questions to the better students because their replies are more likely to be on target and, therefore, satisfying. Both the quan-tity and quality of teacher attention have an impact on student achievement. It is not surprising that students benefit when they receive the teacher's time and talent, and it is important that teachers recognize that each student deserves their time, talent, and attention. So the challenge is to be more equitable and inclusive in these inter-actions (Sadker & Sadker, 1995).

One useful way to capture the distribution of teacher attention is through the use of a class seating chart. Simply diagram where each student is sitting in the class-room. This will allow you to record student–teacher interactions in an objective way. Then, next to each student's seat on the diagram, record the gender, and when possible, race or ethnicity of each student. When you analyze interactions, you can use this demographic data to detect possible patterns of bias. Using a seating chart, let's consider several strategies or approaches that will help you detect gender patterns in teacher–student interactions.

Strategy One: Volunteers and Nonvolunteers.   A useful beginning is to focus on how the teacher interacts with students who volunteer and with those who do not volunteer. Let's define these two types of teacher–student interactions: those that depend on voluntary responses offered by the students and those that are involuntary. Voluntary student responses occur when students raise their hands to respond, call out an answer, or willingly respond to the teacher through any established classroom procedure. Involuntary student responses occur when the teacher requests a response from a student who has not raised a hand, called out an answer, or in any other way indicated an interest in answering.

Each time a teacher elicits a response, record a V or an N for that student directly on the classroom seating chart. V, representing a volunteer, indicates that the teacher is investing time in a student who is volunteering to respond. N, representing a nonvolunteer, indicates that the teacher is intentionally soliciting a response from a nonvolunteering student. (Note: A student calling out or in any other way responding who is not recognized by the teacher does not receive a code. The teacher has ignored this volunteer and not invested any time in this student.)

Now see where your Vs and Ns are. Does the teacher tend to call on volunteering students much of the time? Do nonvolunteers get to participate as well? Does the teacher use a thoughtful practice of balancing this dynamic, calling on different students, even the quiet ones? How many students are neither V nor N but silently sit in the class with little or no teacher attention?

Now you can begin to look at some of these dynamics more closely. Are boys or girls more likely to volunteer? Are there differences in race or ethnicity? Are some students receiving a great deal of attention and others very little? Can you figure out why? The second strategy can give you a bit more insight into these questions.

Strategy Two: Classroom Geography.   Simply examining the pattern of teacher questions directly from the seating chart provides you with an immediate, visual impression of the areas in the classroom that receive a great deal of interaction, as well as the areas that are interaction poor. Some students may be involved in no interaction at all; others may take part in a number of interactions. Some students may only have one or two Ns, whereas others may have a great number of Vs, and gender or race or demographics may have little, if anything, to do with it.

Circle the areas of the classroom that are rich with teacher attention as well as those areas that are interaction poor. Are the rich areas near the teacher? Or are they on a particular side of the room? What you are learning in this strategy is the power of classroom geography. Some teachers tend to have a geographic bias, calling on students in one area of the room and not another. Analyze your findings to see if geography is influencing which students receive rich interactions and which receive few or none.

And while considering geography, take a closer look at where the students are sitting. Is gender determining seating patterns? Are boys and girls sitting in same-sex groups? Did the teacher assign these seats or did the students choose these seats and the teacher permitted gender-segregated sitting to happen? Do the same for race and ethnicity to determine if segregated seating patterns are influencing the classroom climate. Teachers and students need to be made aware of such patterns and learn to desegregate seating to create truly integrated learning communities.

Strategy Three: What do the Numbers Say?   Although educators as a group are firmly committed to educational equity, subtle and often unintentional biases can emerge. Teachers often unknowingly give more attention to students of one gender or one race than to those of another or give different kinds of attention to one group than they give to another. You may be able to detect these subtle biases simply from looking at the data recorded on your seating chart. But sometimes the information is more subtle, or the teacher does not see such a pattern. In such cases, which happen a great deal, an objective and precise system is needed. That's when the coefficient of distribution comes into play. The coefficient of distribution is a simple formula that reports precisely how the teacher is investing attention in different groups. Let's walk through this approach together.

First, identify the expected number of interactions or questions (i.e., a fair share) for each group. This can be done with race or ethnicity or economic class, but for now, let's focus on gender. If, for instance, a class consists of 40% female students, then a fair share would mean that, over time, females receive approximately 40% of the teacher's questions. If females receive less than 40%, they are not getting their fair share. For the second step, determine the actual number of interactions that each group receives. Finally, compare the figures and see if there is a gap in how the teacher is distributing attention. This gap is measured by the coefficient of distribution. And it is pretty easy to figure out.

Let's create a class to practice. You visit a class with 25 students, 15 girls and 10 boys. So a fair distribution of teacher attention should approximate this percentage of students in the class, in this case, girls consist of 67%, or two thirds, of the students in the class, and boys, one third. Over time, you would expect the teacher to ask questions and interact with students in roughly this proportion. You visit the class and note that the teacher has asked about 60 questions in a 35-minute session. But as you count who receives these questions, you discover that the girls received on average 45 questions a session, whereas the boys averaged only 15 questions a session. This means that the boys are receiving 15 out of 60 questions, or 25%. But the boys are 33% of the students, so they are receiving 8% fewer questions than expected. The girls, on the other hand, are receiving 45 out of 60 questions, or 75% of all of the questions. But the girls are 67% of the students, so they are getting 8% more questions than expected. Although the teacher might believe he or she is equitable, your numbers are telling you something different. There is, in fact, gender bias in this class, a somewhat unusual gender bias in that it is favoring the girls, but it is gender bias nonetheless.

To share this information with the teacher, you decide to use the coefficient of distribution, an objective approach that will enable the teacher to measure the degree of inequity in the class. Here is how it works: The coefficient of distribution is computed by adding how far each group is from a fair or equitable distribution. In this case, add the 8% more attention the girls receive to the 8% less attention the boys receive and the coefficient of distribution is 0.16 . There is a 16% gap in distribution that the teacher needs to bridge if fair interaction is to be achieved.

The power of the coefficient is that it is not a judgment or an opinion; it is a precise number that can be objectively obtained, and teachers can readily see the gap. You will find the coefficient a useful tool. The lower the coefficient, the closer to equity the teacher is. In this case, 0.16 suggests that the teacher has some work to do to achieve a more equitable classroom environment. By the way, a zero coefficient means that equity in distribution has been achieved.

Strategy Four: Questioning Level.   John Dewey was one of many noted educators who believed that questioning is central, not only to education, but to the process of thinking itself. Unfortunately, research indicates that most teachers do not use effective questioning techniques (Dewey, 1933; Altermatt, Jovanovic, & Perry, 1998). Not only is the distribution of questions often inequitable, but also, teachers rarely use challenging classroom questions. Instead, they tend to rely on lower order, or memory, questions.

Lower order questions are those that deal with the memorization and recall of factual information. The student is not required to manipulate information. There is nothing inherently wrong with asking memory questions or prompts, such as "When did the American Revolution begin?" or "Identify one poem written by Robert Frost." However, a heavy reliance on such questions reduces opportunities for students to develop higher order thinking.

Conversely, higher order questions are those that require students to apply, analyze, synthesize, or evaluate information. They encourage students to think creatively. When a teacher asks, "What is your opinion of this poem by Robert Frost, and what evidence can you cite to support your opinion?" that teacher is asking a higher order question. Only 10% of teacher questions fall into this category, so they become precious indeed. Research suggests that these relatively rare but important higher order questions may be more often asked of White, male students, which is another cause for concern (Sadker & Sadker, 2005).

Let's take a moment to distinguish between lower order (memory) questions and higher order (thought) questions and then sort out a strategy to see how these questions are distributed in the class. Here are a few examples of lower order questions:

- Who founded abstract art?
- Name three Romantic authors.
- Whose signatures appear on the Declaration of Independence?
- In what year did women win the right to vote?
- Who wrote your text?

Here are a few examples of higher order questions:

- What conclusions can you reach concerning the images Shakespeare uses to portray death?

- What forces motivated Romantic authors?
- Why did no females or African Americans sign the Declaration of Independence?
- What does this poem mean to you?
- What would you say in a letter to the president of the United States?

To analyze these types of questions, we return to our useful seating chart. Simply identify the level of questions asked of each student and enter that on the seating chart. When a lower order question is asked, record an *L* on your seating chart for the student receiving the question. When a higher order question is asked, record an *H* on the seating chart. You will find that most teachers ask a preponderance of lower order questions, but distribution of these questions can vary greatly. You may detect a bias in this distribution, a bias by gender, ethnicity, race, and other factors.

You might want to consider some of the following questions in your analysis:

- How many questions were asked? What was the average number of questions per minute (total questions divided by minutes observed)?
- What was the ratio of lower to higher order questions?
- What is the ratio of girls to boys in the class?
- What is the racial and ethnic ratio of the class?
- Using a coefficient of distribution, how were the higher and lower order questions distributed in this class? Were they equitable or is there a gender gap? Or a race gap? Or some other gap?
- Is there geographic bias (i.e., were there areas of class that received a greater number of higher order questions)?

INTERACTION 8.3:
Identifying Bias in Classroom Interactions (Authentic Assessment)

INTASC Principle 7: Instructional Planning Skills

INTASC Principle 8: Assessment

INTASC Principle 9: Reflection and Responsibility

INTASC Principle 10: Relationships and Partnerships

This is your opportunity to use your new data-gathering skills in actual classroom settings. Although you probably can observe and record data in a college classroom pretty easily, it would also be useful to visit a classroom on the grade level or in the subject area that you are interested in teaching. Observing in this setting may offer you the most useful insights. Then, to assess the teacher's equitable instructional skills (as well as your observational skills), try the following steps:

1. Draw a seating chart of the room. If you know the students' names, write them in. If not, assign a number to each student. Also record the gender, race, and ethnicity of the students whenever possible.
2. Record each question the teacher asked as either higher order or lower order and identify the student receiving the question. Ask yourself: Are there any patterns? Are the questions going to one group more than another? Or to one area of the room? What else can you detect?
3. In the same class, continue your observations on a second seating chart by recording which students are volunteering and which are not. Is there a relationship between your two seating charts? Can you offer a descriptive statement about which students get attention and which do not and relate that to seating patterns, volunteerism, or group affiliation?
4. Now add up all your interactions—that is, every time a student received a contact by the teacher—and record it on the seating chart.
5. Determine the coefficient of distribution for the class.
6. Pull all your findings together and write several descriptive sentences that sum up your findings. Now write a few sentences based on your findings that might help the teacher create a more equitable classroom dynamic— or congratulate the teacher for creating an equitable dynamic. One more sentence: describe what you learned from this experience.
7. By this time, you are probably thinking, "I have now carefully collected and analyzed teaching in other classrooms and now I am ready! I would like someone to observe and give me this objective and valuable feedback in my own teaching." The good news is that this is now a real possibility. Feel free to share this chapter and these skills with a colleague, another student teacher, a university supervisor, or a cooperating teacher. Ask them to observe your teaching using these techniques and share their findings with you. At this point, you truly understand the power of systematic classroom observations and are ready to learn and grow in your own teaching.

ESSENTIAL EQUITY QUESTION 8.3:
HOW CAN WE DETECT AND CORRECT CURRICULAR BIAS?

WHAT WE KNOW

In this text, you have learned about biases that emerge in instructional materials. Several of the chapters reported on the findings of researchers who detected several forms of bias in the curriculum (Zittleman & Sadker, 2002). Looking around the classroom at the displays, or reading through the textbooks, or even going online to review Internet resources gives you the opportunity to assess how gender (or ethnicity, race, etc.) are being presented. Do stereotypes exist? Is one group invisible?

Research suggests that gender bias continues to permeate school life (Sadker & Sadker, 2005; Zittleman & Sadker, 2002).

At this point, let's put these curricular detecting skills to practice. But before we begin, here is a refresher on the seven types of bias for you to use as you examine texts, wall displays, and other curricular resources:

1. *Invisibility:* Certain groups have been underrepresented or ignored in education. When women and people of color are missing from displays and materials, the implication is that these groups are of less value and importance in our society. Do the classroom displays include women of achievement? Do curricular materials accurately mirror the nation's people?

2. *Stereotyping:* By assigning traditional and rigid roles or attributes to a group, the diversity, abilities, and potential of that group are limited. Too many people stereotype males as all sharing one set of characteristics and females sharing a completely different set. Adults may reward males for active, assertive, curious behavior, but reward females for appreciative, dependable, and considerate behavior. When models, pictures, and other displays reinforce these stereotyped expectations, children receive more messages of appropriate behavior, and many young people limit their careers and capabilities to fit these stereotyped roles.

3. *Imbalance/Selectivity:* The media and text materials have perpetuated bias by presenting only one interpretation of an issue, situation, or group of people. As a result, millions of learners have been given a limited point of view concerning the contributions, struggles, and participation of certain peoples in our society.

4. *Unreality:* Materials, media, and books have frequently presented an unrealistic portrayal of U.S. history and contemporary life by glossing over discussions of discrimination and abuse. But by ignoring past or current realities, even unpleasant ones, students are denied the information needed to recognize, understand, and perhaps someday conquer the problems that plague society.

5. *Fragmentation/Isolation:* By separating issues related to people of color and women from the main body of schooling, curricular materials have implied that these issues are less important than and not a part of the cultural mainstream. By arbitrarily separating males and females into a separate bulletin board or distinct sections of the text, the curriculum promotes fragmentation and isolation of the sexes and diverse ethnic groups. Purposeless fragmentation serves as a divisive influence and suggests that these groups are little more than a sideshow to the nation's history and progress.

6. *Linguistic bias:* Materials can reflect the discriminatory nature of the dominant language by using only masculine terms and pronouns, such as *forefathers* and the generic *he*. Occupations labeled with *man*, such as *cameraman*, deny the legitimacy of women working in these fields. What subtle and not-so-subtle linguistic bias can be found in the classroom?

7. *Cosmetic bias*: Textbook publishers are aware that educators and reform movements are demanding better, fairer, and more comprehensive materials in education. To rewrite text requires thorough research and infusion. Occasionally, publishers and authors minimize the process by creating an illusion of equity. Two common shortcuts are pictures of nontraditional people prominently displayed or special sections or displays that discuss yet segregate women and other groups. Is there real equity in these materials or is it more an illusion?

INTERACTION 8.4:
Identifying Bias in Classroom Interactions (Authentic Assessment)

INTASC Principle 8: Assessment

INTASC Principle 9: Reflection and Responsibility

These concepts can be helpful in countering bias in books, from preschool through high school. Here are a few activities to help you do just that:

1. Look through your textbooks and see if you can identify each of these seven forms of bias.
2. Now, suggest ways to remove the bias and create more equitable textbooks.
3. Extend this activity by teaching these forms of bias to your students and asking them to identify them in their own texts and suggest revisions. This will teach them to be more critical and aware of the limits of their own instructional materials.
4. These forms of bias emerge in magazines, television programming, and on the Internet. Ask your students to find them there and bring examples to class.
5. How do these seven forms emerge in instructional interactions? Give an example of each. We will start you off with two examples: Teachers may stereotype when they ask males to help with physical classroom tasks or, perhaps, they fragment their instruction by studying women only during Women's History Month. What other biased instructional interaction have you encountered?

These seven forms of bias offer a useful conceptual handle for analyzing classroom materials for gender and other forms of bias. In fact, all of the strategies in this chapter are designed to be practical tools in your teaching. These skills, insights, and approaches can help new and experienced teachers implement fair interactions and equal educational opportunities for all students. It is the hope of the authors and editors of this book that you will find these skills a rich resource in unlocking the futures of all your students.

RESOURCES

Books

Frank, C. (2000). *Ethnographic eyes: A teacher's guide to classroom observation.* Portsmouth, NH: Heinemann. *Ethnography* derives its meaning from the Greek *ethnos*, nation or people, and *graphy*, or writing. Literally, ethnography is writing about people. Ethnographic research uses observational strategies to describe classroom dynamics. *Ethnographic Eyes* reveals interview techniques, case studies, and methods for observing, analyzing, and recording observational data in an effort to help teachers see classroom practices and patterns.

Reed, A., & Bergemann, V. E. (2005). *A guide to observation, participation, and reflection in the classroom* (5th ed.). New York: McGraw-Hill. This hands-on guide to classroom observations is specifically designed for use by teacher education students prior to their student teaching. The workbook provides detailed guides for observing the dynamics of the classroom and then reflecting on the experience. It also includes more than 50 practical blank forms that cover all aspects of observation, participation, and reflection, from the structured observation of a lesson to a checklist for determining teaching styles to reflections on small-group teaching.

Sadker, M., & Sadker, D. (2006). Questioning skills. In J. Cooper (Ed.), *Classroom teaching skills* (8th ed., pp. 104–150). Boston: Houghton Mifflin. Probably no teaching behavior has been studied as much as questioning. This is not surprising, because most educators agree that questioning strategies and techniques are key tools in a teacher's repertoire of interactive teaching skills. This chapter provides opportunities to classify and construct questions according to the six levels of Bloom's taxonomy; to explore related areas of wait time, probing, scaffolding, and feedback that can enhance questioning skills; and to explore how the growing diversity and multicultural nature of America's students affect classroom interactions.

Internet Resources

ADL Curriculum Connections: Anti-Bias Lesson Plans and Resources for K–12 Educators: http://www.adl.org/education/curriculum_connections/: *Curriculum Connections* is a collection of original lesson plans and resources that help K–12 educators integrate multicultural, antibias, and social justice themes into their curricula.

A Questioning Toolkit: http://www.fno.org/nov97/toolkit.html: The *Educational Technology Journal* integrates philosophy and pragmatism to assist teachers in developing effective questioning techniques that involve all students.

REFERENCES

Altermatt, E., Jovanovic, J., & Perry, M. (1998). Bias or responsivity? Sex and achieve-ment-level effects on teachers' classroom questioning practices. *Journal of Educational Psychology, 90,* 516–527.

Babad, E. (1998). Preferential affect: The crux of the teacher expectancy issue. In J. Brophy (Ed.), *Advances in research on reaching: Expectations in the classroom* (pp. 183–214). Greenwich, CT: JAI Press.

Bell, M. (2001). Supported reflective practice: A programme of peer observation and feed-back for academic teaching development. *International Journal for Academic Development, 6*(1), 29–39.

Dewey, J. (1933). *How we think.* Boston, MA: D. C. Heath.

Dewey, J. (1963). *Experience and education.* NY: Macmillan.

Good, T., & Brophy, J. (2003). *Looking in classrooms* (9th ed.). New York: Longman.

Goodlad, J. (1984). *A place called school.* New York: McGraw-Hill.

Jackson, P. (1968). *Life in classrooms.* New York: Holt, Rinehart & Winston.

Sadker, M., & Sadker, D. (1995). *Failing at fairness: How America's schools cheat girls.* New York: Touchstone.

Sadker, M., & Sadker, D. (2005). *Teachers, schools and society.* New York: McGraw-Hill.

Simpson, D., Jackson, M., & Aycock, J. (2004). *John Dewey and the art of teaching: Toward reflective and imaginative practice.* Thousand Oaks, CA: Sage.

Spencer, R., Porche, M., & Tolman, D. (2003). We've come a long way—maybe. New challenges for gender equity education. *Teachers College Record, 105*(9), 1774–1807.

Zittleman, K., & Sadker, D. (2002). Teacher education and gender equity: The unfinished revolution. *Educational Leadership, 60*(4), 59–62.

Appendix: Key Concepts

INTASC Principles

	1. Subject Matter Knowledge	2. Human Development and Learning	3. Diversity in Learning	4. Variety of Instructional Strategies	5. Motivation and Management	6. Communication Skills	7. Instructional Planning Skills	8. Assessment	9. Reflection and Responsibility	10. Relationships and Partnerships
CHAPTER 1: Strong Women Teachers: Their Struggles and Strategies for Gender Equity	Interaction 1.8	Interaction 1.6	Interaction 1.4		Interaction 1.7	Interactions 1.1, 1.4, 1.7		Interactions 1.1, 1.2, 1.3, 1.8	Interactions 1.2, 1.9	Interactions 1.3, 1.9
CHAPTER 2: Gender Differences in Cognitive Ability, Attitudes and Behavior	Interaction 2.5	Interactions 2.1, 2.2, 2.3, 2.6, 2.7, 2.8, 2.9	Interaction 2.1		Interactions 2.6, 2.7				Interaction 2.4, 2.5, 2.10	
CHAPTER 3: Teachers, Students, and Title Ix: A Promise for Fairness									Interactions 3.1, 3.2, 3.3	Interaction 3.3
CHAPTER 4: Citizenship Education for the 21st Century: Gender Equity and Social Studies	Interactions 4.4, 4.5, 4.6, 4.8, 4.9, 4.11, 4.25, 4.26	Interaction 4.2	Interaction 4.3, 4.26	Interactions 4.1, 4.7, 4.12 – 4.24		Interaction 4.10		Interaction 4.26	Interaction 4.26	

Chapter									
Chapter 5 Literacy With a Critical Lens: A Gender Inclusive Approach to English/ Language Arts Methods	Interactions 5.1, 5.3, 5.12	Interactions 5.2, 5.5, 5.9, 5.10	Interactions 5.4, 5.6, 5.7, 5.12, 5.13, 5.14	Interactions 5.8, 5.11		Interaction 5.2	Interactions 5.15, 5.16, 5.17		
Chapter 6 Gender Inclusive Approach to Science Teacher Education			Interactions 6.1, 6.3, 6.5	Interaction 6.2, 6.4	Interaction 6.6				
Chapter 7 Gender Inclusive Approach to Math Teacher Education		Interactions 7.1, 7.2	Interactions 7.3, 7.4						
Chapter 8 Practical Strategies for Detecting Gender Bias in Your Classroom					Interaction 8.2	Interaction 8.3	Interactions 8.1, 8.2, 8.3, 8.4	Interactions 8.1, 8.2, 8.3, 8.4	Interactions 8.1, 8.3

Contributors

Karen N. Bell is the Associate Dean of the School of Education and Associate Professor of Elementary Education at the State University of New York, New Paltz. She teaches undergraduate and graduate courses in mathematics, science, and technology methods of instruction and is particularly interested in multi-sensory learning experiences.

Shirley P. Brown taught for over 25 years in the School District of Philadelphia and served as the administrator of a program for pregnant and parenting teens. She continues to teach occasional education courses at the University of Pennsylvania. In addition to being one of the authors of *Gender in Urban Education* and a Program Associate at a national professional development organization, she has contributed chapters and journal articles to a variety of publications.

Kimberly Wright Cassidy is Associate Professor and Chair of the Department of Psychology at Bryn Mawr College. She teaches courses in cognitive, developmental, and educational psychology. Her research interests include gender stereotypes and the theory of mind development.

Margaret Smith Crocco is Professor and Program Coordinator for Social Studies Education at Teachers College, Columbia University. She teaches master's and doctoral level courses in the history of social studies, teacher education, and research in social studies education. She also offers a course called "Women of the World: Issues in Teaching," which is open to students from across Teachers College, and has written widely on issues of gender and social studies.

Janice Koch is Professor of Science Education for the Department of Curriculum and Teaching at Hofstra University, Long Island, New York. She teaches courses in elementary and middle school science methods, gender issues in the classroom and techniques of classroom research. She is the Director of IDEAS—the Institute for the Development of Education in the Advanced Sciences at Hofstra University. This outreach institute fosters the public understanding of science as well as furthering development in science and technology.

Andrea S. Libresco is special assistant professor in the Department of Curriculum and Teaching at Hofstra University, where she teaches social studies methods to pre-service and in-service teachers at the graduate and undergraduate levels. She was named Distinguished Teacher of the Year in 2005. Her positions in the public schools have included lead teacher for elementary social studies, social studies chair at a 7-12 school, and secondary social studies teacher for 13 years. She has written on a variety of topics including citizenship, current events, gender and social studies, and the effects of testing on social studies instruction.

Theresa McCormick is Professor Emeritus, Iowa State University. Her books and articles focus on multicultural and gender studies in teacher education. Other areas of her work include peace activism, women's and girls' education, feminist pedagogy, and international studies.

Karen Norwood earned an EdD in mathematics education from Temple University in 1988. She is Associate Professor of Mathematics Education at North Carolina State University and President of the Benjamin Benneker Association, Inc. She is the author of several articles, textbooks, chapters in books, and other curriculum materials. Her research area is the effect of the use of a multiple representation approach to teaching the function concept on a student's understanding of functions.

Paula Alida Roy has worked as a teacher at both high school and college levels; at Westfield High School as chairperson of the Department of English responsible for the training and supervision of many teachers; and as an educational consultant who developed and delivered workshops and seminars on teaching strategies, curriculum development, gender equity, diversity, student centered learning, and writing process. Ms. Roy is also a writer, whose articles and chapters have been published in journals such as *Women's Studies Quarterly* and such books as *Overcoming Heterosexism and Homophobia,* edited by Sears and Williams; and *Women in Literature: Reading through the Lens of Gender,* edited by Fisher and Silber. Her poems have appeared in several journals; and her chapbook, *The Gradual Day,* was published in 2004. Ms. Roy is currently living and writing in the Adirondack mountains of New York State.

David M. Sadker is a professor at American University and co-author of several books, including *Teachers, Schools and Society* (McGraw-Hill, 2007) and *Failing at Fairness* (Touchstone, 1995). His articles have appeared in numerous professional journals and his work has been recognized by the American Educational Research Association and the American Association of University Women. His research and teaching interests focus on educational equity, teacher education, and spirituality in education. He holds two honorary doctorates.

Ellen S. Silber is Professor of French at Marymount College of Fordham University, Tarrytown, NY, where she also chairs Women's Studies and is the Director of the Marymount Institute for the Education of Women and Girls. She edited *Critical Issues in Foreign Language Instruction* (1991) and coedited *Analyzing the Different Voice: Feminist Psychological Theory and Literary Texts* (1998) and *Women in Literature: Reading Through the Lens of Gender* (2003) with Jerilyn Fisher. She was an associate editor of the *Women's Studies Quarterly: Keeping Gender on the Chalkboard* (2001). Silber is especially interested in gender equity in education and received a grant from the Ford Foundation to work with the team of authors that produced this volume. She is currently the director of Mentoring Latinas, a project in which Hispanic female college students mentor their middle school counterparts.

Karen Zittleman is an adjunct professor at American University and coauthor of both the brief edition (2007) and the 8th edition (2008) of *Teachers, Schools, and Society.* Her articles have appeared in the *Journal of Teacher Education, Educational Leadership, Phi Delta Kappan, Principal* and other professional journals. Her research and teaching interests focus on educational equity, foundations of education, teacher preparation, and spirituality in education.

Author Index

Subject Index